THE MOSQUES OF COLONIAL SOUTH ASIA

Islamic South Asia Series

Series Editor: Ruby Lal, Emory University

Advisory Board

Iftikhar Dadi, Cornell University
Stephen F. Dale, Ohio State University
Rukhsana David, Kinnaird College for Women
Michael Fisher, Oberlin College
Marcus Fraser, Fitzwilliam Museum
Ebba Koch, University of Vienna
David Lewis, London School of Economics
Francis Robinson, Royal Holloway, University of London
Ron Sela, Indiana University Bloomington
Willem van Schendel, University of Amsterdam

Titles

Sexual and Gender Diversity in the Muslim World: History, Law and Vernacular Knowledge, Vanja Hamzic
The Architecture of a Deccan Sultanate: Courtly Practice and Royal Authority in Late Medieval India, Pushkar Sohoni
Sufi Shrines and the Pakistani State: The End of Religious Pluralism, Umber Bin Ibad
The Hindu Sufis of South Asia: Partition, Shrine Culture and the Sindhis in India, Michel Boivin
Islamic Sermons and Public Piety in Bangladesh: The Poetics of Popular Preaching, Max Stille
The Mosques of Colonial South Asia: A Social and Legal History of Muslim Worship, Sana Haroon

THE MOSQUES OF COLONIAL SOUTH ASIA

A Social and Legal History of Muslim Worship

Sana Haroon

I.B. TAURIS
LONDON • NEW YORK • OXFORD • NEW DELHI • SYDNEY

I.B. TAURIS
Bloomsbury Publishing Plc
50 Bedford Square, London, WC1B 3DP, UK
1385 Broadway, New York, NY 10018, USA
29 Earlsfort Terrace, Dublin 2, Ireland

BLOOMSBURY, I.B. TAURIS and the I.B. Tauris logo are trademarks of Bloomsbury Publishing Plc

First published in Great Britain 2021
This paperback edition published 2023

Copyright © Sana Haroon, 2021

Sana Haroon has asserted her right under the Copyright, Designs and Patents Act, 1988, to be identified as Author of this work.

For legal purposes the Acknowledgments on p. ix constitute an extension of this copyright page.

Series design by Adriana Brioso
Cover image: Friday prayers at Feroz Shah Kotla Mosque in New Delhi, India.
(© All Rights Reserved/Getty Images)

All rights reserved. No part of this publication may be reproduced or transmitted in any form or by any means, electronic or mechanical, including photocopying, recording, or any information storage or retrieval system, without prior permission in writing from the publishers.

Bloomsbury Publishing Plc does not have any control over, or responsibility for, any third-party websites referred to or in this book. All internet addresses given in this book were correct at the time of going to press. The author and publisher regret any inconvenience caused if addresses have changed or sites have ceased to exist, but can accept no responsibility for any such changes.

A catalogue record for this book is available from the British Library.

A catalog record for this book is available from the Library of Congress.

ISBN: HB: 978-0-7556-3444-6
PB: 978-0-7556-4300-4
ePDF: 978-0-7556-3445-3
eBook: 978-0-7556-3446-0

Series: Library of Islamic South Asia

Typeset by Deanta Global Publishing Services, Chennai, India

To find out more about our authors and books visit www.bloomsbury.com and sign up for our newsletters.

For Raza and Rafay

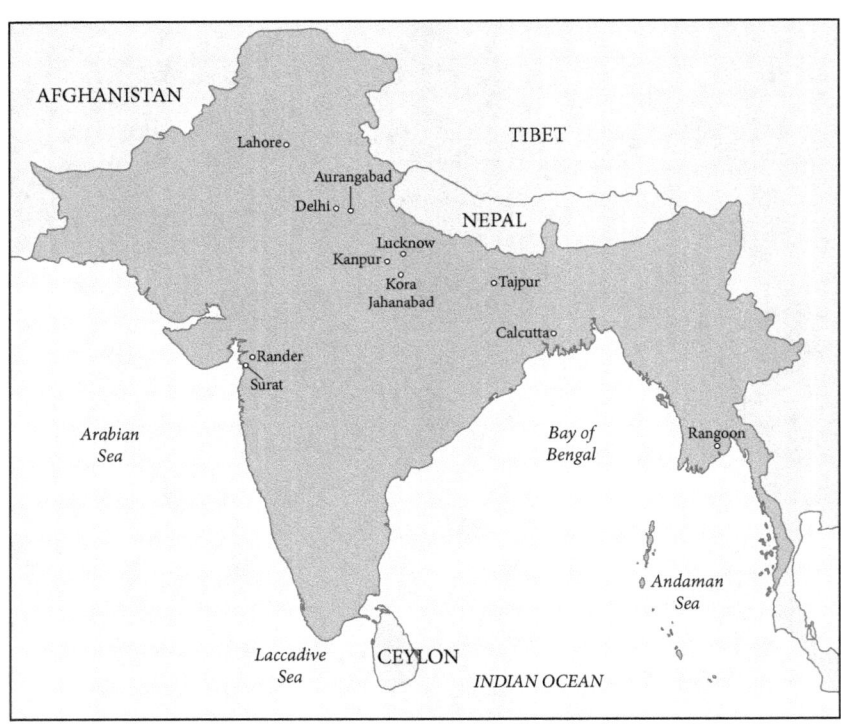

Figure 1 Map of colonial South Asia.

CONTENTS

List of Figures	viii
Acknowledgments	ix
Note on Transliteration	x

INTRODUCTION — 1

Chapter 1
TAJPUR, BIHAR, 1891: LEADERSHIP IN CONGREGATIONAL PRAYER — 27

Chapter 2
RANGOON, 1916: MUSLIM DIVERSITY AND CUSTODIAL CONTROL OF INSTRUCTION IN THE MOSQUE — 47

Chapter 3
AURANGABAD AND KANPUR UP, 1924: THE MAGISTRATE'S CONTROL OF THE MOSQUE PERIMETER — 71

Chapter 4
LAHORE, 1940: GOVERNMENT CONTROL OVER THE LAND RECORD — 107

Chapter 5
KORA JAHANABAD, UP, 1947: MUSLIM ASSOCIATIONS WIN BACK CONTROL OVER MOSQUES — 135

Afterword	155
Glossary	159
Notes	162
Bibliography	215
Index	229

FIGURES

1. Map of colonial South Asia — vi
2. Center segment key of the map of Delhi published in Dihlavi's *Vaqi'at* (1919) — 75
3. Design for a temple or mosque (1915) — 76
4. The Kanpur mosque July 1913 — 81
5. Residences around the Rangoon Friday mosque — 93
6. Police lines around the Rangoon Friday mosque in 1893 — 94
7. The Shahidganj Mosque *Masjid Shahidganj Masjid Shah Chiragh* (1936) — 108
8. Extract from Record of Rights 1868 — 115
9. Plan of Gurdwara Shahid Ganj Bhai Taru Singh 1927 — 118
10. Plan of mosque and other buildings at Shahidganj 1929 — 119

ACKNOWLEDGMENTS

My biggest debt is to my colleagues and friends at UMass Boston. Rajini Srikanth, Elora Chowdhury, Terry Kawashima, Ben Johnson, Ayesha Irani, Ruth Miller, Maria Brincker, Pratima Prasad, and Mohinish Shukla, who enrich my intellectual life in so many ways. Shilpi Suneja brought her boundless energy and creativity to our class and to this project. The Dean's Research Fund enabled my travel to Yangon in the summer of 2016 and a pre-tenure research intensive semester enabled me to produce the first draft of this book. The untiring Healey Library interlibrary loan staff located elusive nineteenth- and twentieth-century printed texts for me. Other colleagues, Avril Powell, Sarah Ansari, Sara Suleri, Sunil Sharma, Peter Robb, Christophe Jaffrelot, Ron Sela, Brannon Ingram, Sherali Tareen, Usha Sanyal, and Nile Green, offered valuable feedback at critical junctures. The *Indian Economic and Social History Review* provided crucial feedback and published an early version of my work on the Lahore Shahidganj. Jon Sims at the British Library enabled my access to and understanding of the records of the Judicial Committee of the Privy Council. I started this project as a Malathy Singh Fellow at Yale University's South Asian Studies Council in 2011–12. As I tried to imagine a unifying history of South Asian Muslim society, I found inspiration in early conversations with K. Sivaramakrishnan (Shivi), Abbas Amanat, and Juned Shaikh. Finally, at I. B. Tauris, I had the pleasure to work with Sophie Rudland who saw the potential in this project early on, and with Yasmin Garcha who steered me through the editorial process. An anonymous reader provided critical feedback at the final stages of review.

Amena Saiyid, Saira Awan, Abid Imam, Sacha Uljon, Misbah Naqvi, Nadia Majeed, Obaid Ilyas, Subuhi Asheer, Mustafa Menai, Samia Rehman, Nida and Adnaan Tapal, Salman and Catherine Ahmed, Saba Shaikh, Sehr Ahmed, Bina Shamim, Junaid Shameem, Shaheen and Sultan Ahmed, Faisal Haq, Adeel Rizki, and Saba Haroon have stayed close through it all. My father Mohammed Haroon, my sisters Aassia Haq and Nida Rizki, my brother Saad Haroon, the beautiful little people Zoya and Adam Haq, Zidane and Emre Rizki, and Zayn Haroon kept me going when we lost the most important person to us all and through the difficult years that followed. I look forward to putting them behind us and looking ahead to happier things. Raza and Rafay came all the way with me on this journey: to New Haven, to Boston, to Lahore, and back again. I owe everything to them.

NOTE ON TRANSLITERATION

I have transliterated Urdu, Persian, and Arabic words for readability and consistency. I have followed the rules laid out in the Library of Congress romanization tables with some changes. All diacritical marks have been omitted. With the exception of a few words, notably *'ulama* and *buzurgan*, plural forms are indicated by adding an *s* to the word in singular, as in *fatwas* rather than *fatawa*. In the case of some Arabic words adopted into Urdu, I have used the standard Arabic transliteration, as with shari'a and hadith. I have relied as far as possible on translations of South Asian vernacular terms, liberally substituting English translations current in the time and relating to the events described here, such as custodian and mosque. I have not italicized words and terms which have already been normalized in scholarly writing on South Asia or should be, such as 'ulama and patwari.

INTRODUCTION

Rangoon's Mogul Street and 29th Street were filled with shops and residences belonging to Muslims as well as Buddhists, Parsis, Jews, Christians, and Hindus. The cool interior of a Friday mosque drew Muslims to offer their five obligatory daily prayers and special Friday, festival, and funeral prayers through the period of British rule. Islamic values appeared to catalyze in pious congregation and observances within its walls.

On the Eid of the cow sacrifice in 1893 thousands prayed in congregation at the mosque.[1] As they flowed out, they clashed with Hindus who held the cow to be sacred.[2] It was a period of heightened interreligious tension in colonial South Asia; in Bengal and the United Provinces (UP), Muslims ranged in defense of mosques defiled by pigs' blood and corpses. In Rangoon the newspapers reported that the riots continued for three days and culminated in a mob gathering outside the courts.[3] The appearance of radical collectivity engendered in the mosque is deceiving. Management schemes for the mosque, records of the colonial government, and writings of leading members of community come together in long histories of the Rangoon Friday Mosque and others like it. Mosques did not foster consensus among worshippers; they were sites of social control.

The Rangoon mosque congregation was deeply divided along ethnic and class lines. Firm and powerful custodians and prayer leaders of the mosque disciplined worshippers within and retreated behind windows high above the rioting crowds when the conflict began. The city magistrate cordoned the streets and deployed mounted police to control egress from the mosque. In the years that followed the riot, officers of the mosque tightened their controls over this building and district officers issued binding decisions to Muslims claiming rights in other mosques. The courts shrugged off collective Muslim demands for rights in mosques, lacking the capacity to engage with their religious philosophy, and the mosque was gradually consigned to the control of petty officers over the course of colonial rule.

This is not a history of colonial law; that story has emerged in a rich and important body of work which I will discuss further along in this introduction. This book presents a history of the South Asian mosque and Muslim worship as subjects of the law through stories of successive judicial authorizations of forms of control in the mosque. Documentation of endowment and land use and testimonies about the lives of worshippers contained in the legal archive, together with vernacular sources and references to mosques which emerge in political archives, constitute rich veins of evidence of social transformation.

This story of the colonial authorization of control in the mosque begins in the middle of the nineteenth century in Bihar, in a mosque of the small town of Tajpur as Hanafi worshippers, remembering piety as an element of subjecthood to Mughal imperial state, objected to the prayer leader's ritual preferences. The story then moves to Rangoon, the new colonial city marking the eastern most extent of the empire and the Friday mosque in the commercial district where ethnically diverse Muslims disputed the control of the custodians of their mosque. Colonial cities were developing rapidly and were highly regulated; by the early 1900s, densely populated streets abutted the mosque and two disputes over the boundaries of mosques in the United Provinces were adjudicated by district officers whose authority over the mosque perimeter was, in turn, challenged by Muslims. At heterodox religious sites in Lahore and the UP, Muslim worshippers challenged the revenue department officers who assigned rights in land.

Each of these mosques was subject to the legal regime which emerged in colonial India. Each story of contest for control in a mosque presents the textures and contours of life in and around these mosques of colonial South Asia, demonstrating the sheer diversity of colonial Muslim society. Each of these disputes elicited a precedent setting judgment of the Judicial Committee of the Privy Council, the final colonial court of appeals, that authorized the discretionary control of an officer over the mosque.

Chapter 1 brings the role of prayer leaders who gave the five times daily call to prayer and organized the Friday sermons to light. Unlike the 'ulama who have been extensively studied by historians and Islamic studies scholars, particularly Muhammad Qasim Zaman,[4] these prayer leaders are not well understood as historical actors in South Asia. Their leadership of Muslim congregations was not defined as an authoritative practice under Islamic law. In 1891, colonial courts authorized these prayer leaders to establish the ritual observance for congregational worship in mosques without reference to general Muslim expectations.

This study also brings to light the role of South Asian mosque custodians (*mutawallis*), invested with control over mosque finances in Islamic practice. As "trustees of endowments" under colonial law, they chose styles of instruction and other non-obligatory ritual for the mosques under their charge, but were not accountable to their own congregations for their choices. Highlighting the influence and control of custodians in mosques, Chapter 2 complements and modifies Gregory Kozlowski's conclusions about Muslim religious benefactors and their endowments.[5]

District magistrates (known as collectors in Bengal and deputy commissioners in the Punjab) controlled religious expression on streets, and by extension controlled the perimeters of mosques. These officers used discretion rather than drawing on law and policy to resolve disputes relating to devotional performances and claims at the junction of the street and the mosque, and delimited and policed this liminal space.

Chapter 4 turns to the role of officers of the Board of Revenue who were the final arbiters of land rights in endowments. These officers drew on laws relating to property to resolve interreligious disputes and competing heritage claims. And in Chapter 5 we attend to the moment at which Muslim "experts" were authorized to express and assert collective Muslim interests in mosques. Together these officers, of the state, of the mosque and of the community, controlled worshippers in and around the mosque.

Far from being a space of participation within which shared values and interests could catalyze, the mosque was a place of ascendancy of control of a variety of officials, each authorized by the state to evaluate and manage social uses of the mosque according to his own discretion. They relieved the state of the burden of religious reasoning, controlling what is assumed to have been a freely accessible public arena. A vast Muslim body politic, unmoored by the end of Islamic rule and the overturning of Islamic jurisprudence, might have come together in mosques. But worshippers were gradually enclaved and disciplined by the judgements of the Judicial Committee of the Privy Council (JCPC).

The Histories Which Reveal the Mosque

This history of the South Asian mosque draws on a large body of research on colonial law, religious endowments, culture, politics, religious publics, and the state. This body of work situates the mosque as an urban architectural form, as a symbol inspiring Muslim feeling, as the product of global religious firms, and as an instrument for the creation of perpetuities. This body of work has produced methods and theory for the study of Muslim collectivity. And it has highlighted the centrality of religion in politics.

Anglo-Muhammadan law was a select body of law which guided colonial jurists in their treatment of Muslim disputes related strictly to personal matters, primarily marriage and inheritance.[6] In consultation with the 'ulama, colonial jurists applied their readings of Islamic doctrine to such family affairs. Matters which were not strictly intra-Muslim matters were dealt with under the Indian Penal Code and the Code of Civil Procedure. Certain fundamental principles for mosque use were derived from shari'a and governed jurists' treatment of intra-Muslim disputes. Among these were the principles that bequests of land and moneys for mosques could not be taken back by benefactors (*banis*), Shi'as and Sunnis must have separate mosques, and that no Muslim could be refused the right to worship in a mosque. Other principles which could be derived from shari'a were troubling for jurists because of their implications for state policy, among them the idea that a mosque could never be demolished.[7]

Julia Stephens's recent work periodizes the introduction of English law in India and highlights the underlying attitudes of administrators and jurists toward Christian beliefs and English law as fundamentally rational and their treatment of Islam as profoundly irrational. Stephens mines the archive of the Judicial Committee of the Privy Council for the decisions of colonial judges to demonstrate a pattern of shallow readings of Islamic law.[8] These decisions were the equivalent of state-sanction and a deviation from regional norms of state neutrality and not in keeping with the fluidity and dynamism in Islamic legal and philosophical thought, particularly as exemplified in Hanafi scholarship and by the Deoband school. Decisions of the colonial courts produced new forms of Muslim patriarchy, encouraged breakaway sects and fed interreligious conflict. Stephens highlights the moral culpability of the colonial state for the development of intolerance and hierarchy in Muslim society owing to its failure to engage in a meaningful way with the legal discourses and ideas prevailing in India. This powerful reading of colonial legal treatment of Islamic subjects establishes the limited and inadequate nature of the jurisprudence which is the inheritance of the postcolonial states of India, Pakistan, and Bangladesh.

Religion was not relegated to the private realm by colonial state in South Asia. South Asian colonial secularism was a political doctrine and an ontology riddled with contradictions and hypocrisies. Humeira Iqtidar has argued that the political purpose of secularism is itself poorly understood and undertheorized,[9] and Cassie Adcock tells us that the Indian nationalist philosophy of tolerance, inspired by colonial secularism, was a thinly disguised restriction on Hindu proselytizing.[10] Nandini Chatterjee, whose professional efforts to increase scholarly access to the archives of the Judicial Committee of the Privy Council brought my attention to the records of mosque disputes, has proposed a basis for understanding colonial secularism as a policy of government neutrality toward Indian religions and the consequent "privatization of religion."[11] The regulatory apparatus which emerged in mosques under colonial laws was intended to confine religion to a private realm of practice. It disciplined members of Muslim society whose political identities were derived from their religious associations. Although philosophies which found their inspiration in non-Western ideas were critiqued with a secularist lens, religion was not really excised from statecraft during the colonial period.

Jurists upheld the primacy of religious customs in personal law but did not engage with religious reason as a source of rights. Teena Purohit describes histories of two suits which originated in the Khoja Gujarati community and the judgments which derived a history of conversion, syncretism, and legitimacy in the faith from a reading of sacred poetry. This narrative of conversion was appropriated into community history, producing the Khoja Shi'a Ismaili identity and the authority of the Aga Khan over it. Purohit offers an additional close reading of the Hindu cosmology in the sacred Khoja texts to demonstrate alternatives to the simple conversion narrative and Islamic genealogy preferred by colonial jurists.[12] Jurists attended to these texts insofar that they produced religious genealogies and qualified claims to the community's trust property.[13]

Certain domains of community life were expressed in and shaped by legal culture, as Mitra Sharafi shows us in her lively account of *Law and Identity in Colonial South Asia*. She chooses her analytical framework to highlight the "legalistic and litigious" qualities of Parsi life in colonial India and demonstrates how community evolves through the law-related activities of a vast variety of participants.[14] Sharafi, more than any other historian, has demonstrated the possibilities of using the legal archive to write social history. In addition to offering technical advice on locating and referencing legal sources, she provides a clear account of the nature and hierarchies of different courts in the colonial legal world, establishes whose voices are contained in their archives, and then methodically extracts and organizes the evidence related to intra-community disputes preserved in this archive to demonstrate the workings of intimate marital relations, the establishment of an orthodoxy, and the development of a racialized identity among the Parsis of colonial India. Disputes over Parsi trusts demonstrated that the territorial unity of colonial trust law was most significant for the ways in which it served as a fertile ground for debates over specific ritual procedures, and for their impact on Parsi religion itself.

A large body of Indian case law is being systematically mined by the legal historians of South Asia. My choice to work with a legal archive, that of the Judicial Committee of the Privy Council, is based in the great amount of work which has been done on these archives, and the demonstration of its uses. This is not a choice made lightly and the JCPC was no simple agent of the colonial judicial system. Rohit De tells us that the authority and jurisdiction of this "peripatetic court," while providing an umbrella of imperial justice, was deeply contested, and he questions its neutrality. De sees the JCPC as an actor which both allied with the colonial executive and was invested in the institutional integrity of the judiciary. Other colonial courts, from district level to the high courts, worked in myriad ways alongside the colonial executive. The judiciary was not a constant and independent pivot of colonial rule that produced its own logic. But the JCPC did produce important rulings which shaped the institutions of India, from family to corporation to administrative division.

Studies of colonial trust law in general and waqf in particular provide an indispensable foundation for understanding the legal framework which governed mosques. A body of work on colonial trust law has outlined the legal conditions which governed religious endowments in South Asia. Ritu Birla takes up the complex overlays of private and public categories of trusts, marking the introduction of statutes that clearly designated trusts as private, and those which included them with charities in the realm of the public. She periodizes the development of case law and the development of statutes relating to temple endowments between 1863 and 1920. Birla's work is most significant for this study in the manner in which it provides a roadmap of the transformation of indigenous benefaction and property as political and legal conditions changed, from those of precolonial sovereign authority to those of colonial regulation of the economy. Her work provides much of the narrative for the transformation of colonial law pertaining to public trusts which I set out later in this introduction.

In a creative and original intervention into the social history of mosques, Nile Green's *Terrains of Exchange* gives us two stories of establishment of mosques by global religious firms. Sadiq Khan's Ahmadiyya initiative in Michigan in 1921 and the Kobe Muslim society's mosque established in 1935 "planted Islam" in new terrains. Merchant capital and enterprise transmitted the Islamic form of the mosque as well as religious ideas, strategies and texts, beyond India.[15]

Gregory Kozlowski's work on *Muslim Endowments and Society in British India* remains the defining study of waqf in colonial India. Kozlowski's conclusions derive from his method; he aggregates the beneficiaries of Muslim endowments in the UP, Bengal, Madras, dismissing the legally encoded distinctions between public endowments, those which served members of the public, and private waqfs, those expressly created to maintain future generations of family members. He looks at the growth of powerful and wealthy shrine keepers, and the benefit to family enabled by private waqfs, and concludes that Muslim endowment in South Asia was primary instrumentalist and designed to protect capital for personal and familial benefit, what he calls conjoined spiritual and temporal interest which bolstered claims to superior status. At the end, Kozlowski offers a theory of a "particularist style in Islam" which deviated from theoretical, truer, universal expressions of Muslim faith. He tells us that this particularist Islam was expressed in acts of benefaction reinforcing claims of superior status. In endowing a mosque, a patron

> reached out to touch the lives of other believers. Such a grant provided not only a place of prayer, but paid the salary of the man who led the prayers, the man who recited the holy Quran and taught it to the children. It even provided a small sum for the man who kept the mosque clean and watched over the worshippers' shows. A mosque might also be a local welfare establishment, a place where food and alms were given to the poor.[16]

Muslim Endowments successfully indicates the extent of capital which was protected by Islamic trusts; Kozlowski guesses "several tens of thousands" of trusts were established during the British period, and confirms that there were a total of 100,000 in India at the time that his book was published, in 1985.[17] But Kozlowski extrapolates his findings to suggest that waqf law was purposefully exploited by Muslims to place their property beyond the reach of capital and creditors, and to thereby contest the vagaries of the colonial property regime. Kozlowski generalizes his findings relating to private waqfs and does not sufficiently account for legal provisions which limited benefactors' rights in mosques, classed as public waqfs, and accorded Muslim worshippers rights in these same mosques. Many millions of worshippers are presented as entrapped by the influence of wealthy landowners and their progeny in a "social grid" which is solely structured by the rights of the endower over capital held in trust. It is likely that the value of lands and buildings endowed to mosques paled in comparison to the value of agricultural lands, houses, and rental properties tied up in private family waqfs, but that unequal monetary value should not eclipse the significance of interests in, worship in and access to mosques and other public waqfs for Muslim society. In short, Kozlowski's important observations of social hierarchies that were reinforced by the structure of the waqf are too reductive. It was not just the influence of the endowers over appreciative Muslim beneficiaries that created the grid of social relations around the waqf, but a more complex interplay of law, administration, and social expectations.

Since the first publication of *Muslim Endowments and Society in British India*, a freely accessible space for collective organization has itself come to be seen as a source of social change. *The Mosques of Colonial South Asia* is informed by a body of work that identifies the spatial and discursive qualities of the colonial public and offers frameworks and possibilities for understanding Muslim social organization. The public sphere is, in principle, any assembly of private citizens in which all participants have an equal opportunity to convince each other. It is a space where ideas are presented on their own merit and where there is no authority other than that of the public sphere itself. Douglas Haynes has, notably, followed Kozlowski's understanding of Muslim giving and cautioned against treating the mosque as an unconditional public space, arguing that the mosque as a recipient of Muslim charitable giving was a site of "rhetorical and ritual efforts in organizing local Muslims," and a site of violence and conflict with police and other state authorities.[18] For J. Barton Scott and Brannon Ingram and participants in the 2015 conversation as to "What is the Public?," the public appears to be nebulous; it is a zone of debate which takes shape in print, or more recently in new media, though its existence within the built environment is less certain.[19] While the ambivalence described by Scott and Ingram is widely shared, scholars of politics and society in South Asia have generally agreed that the mosque is a space of unfettered access and Muslim organizational freedom.

Sandria Freitag, most notably among scholars of the public in South Asia, originally conceived a spatially defined public, "the city's streets and lanes, or within its mosques and eidgahs" which served as "spaces of cooperation,"[20] in which symbols of Prophet, Quran, and mosque were shared among Muslims who might disagree on more substantive issues. Freitag's 2015 essay "Aspects of the Public," taking account of the expanded scholarly terrain in which the idea of the public has relevance, cautions that temples, shrines, and other sites within the urban built environment may be better understood as places of the ascendancy and production of authority.[21]

For Dale Eickleman and Armando Salvatore, the public sphere of distinctively Muslim societies is the place where debates take place over the definition of the common good. A contemporary Islamic public "encompasses the publishing business (magazines, books, audiocassettes and their networks of distribution), reading groups, relief associations, solidarity networks and political movements, and—of particularly significance—the mosque and the collective Friday prayer and sermon."[22] William Glover, an urban historian who follows these approaches to the public in South Asia, suggests that the municipal authorities of colonial Punjab introduced concepts of public space, accessible to all of the town's residents and none in particular, and these came to permeate understandings of traditional spaces of the city, in particular bazaars and mosques. Julia Stephens, while qualifying our understandings of colonial legal reasoning relating to Islam, treats the Tajpur mosque as a "Muslim public space." The congregation, she says, was a "particularly democratic form of participating in religious debate that could potentially involve every Muslim, regardless of position or level of education."²³

The Mosques of Colonial South Asia closes the gap between Kozlowski's conclusion, that the act of endowment of a mosque was an expression and assertion of social influence, and those of scholars of the colonial public who see the mosque as a space of unrestricted and egalitarian social participation. Attending to the efforts of Muslims to claim public freedoms in and rights over mosques, and to the limits to social freedoms and rights imposed by statute and colonial jurisprudence, the mosque appears as a space of ascendancy of unexpected forms of authority and control which checked and disciplined Muslim society.

Several scholars have taken up the subject of Muslim participation in mosque defense movements in colonial South Asia with a focus on the symbolic significance of mosques for Muslims at the time of such mobilizations, and the manner in which these movements shaped emerging Muslim public identities. In these frameworks, Muslim actions relating to mosques are the catalyzation of a Muslim public. Sandria Freitag understands mosque agitations in the United Provinces in the early twentieth century to be led by commercial men, Congressites, Khilafatists, and labor unions, who leveraged religious symbols and "mutual jealousies."²⁴ Francis Robinson describes mosque defense as reactive: "every mosque, every graveyard as the scene of a bitter battle; howls of execration were raised when buildings demolished and graveyards levelled." These, he says, were instrumentalist efforts to mobilize Muslims; the Kanpur mosque affair was only the result of the journalist Mahomed Ali's search "for agitational issues."²⁵ These studies frame the symbolic importance of mosques in inspiring public Muslim organization, but do not capture the longevity, the range, and the legal context for efforts to introduce mosques as a public priority.

Postcolonial state and communal interest in religious buildings has been explored by Gregory Kozlowski in his essay "Community Building and Community Control of Muslim Endowments," an effort to highlight that new systems of communal oversight of waqfs emerged in independent Pakistan and India.²⁶ Hilal Ahmed's work *Muslim Political Discourse in Postcolonial India* examines the legal status of the Sunni Auqaf Board and the Jama Masjid Trust in the management of the Friday mosque of Delhi and the discourse which monumentalizes mosques in India.²⁷ Jamal Malik's "Waqf in Pakistan" describes the Waqf Act of 1960 as a nationalization of waqf property by Ayub Khan's administration.²⁸ These developments all had their roots in legislation created in the colonial period, discussed in Chapter 5 of this book.

The Mosques of Colonial South Asia effectively broadens our understanding of religious authority[29] in South Asia by identifying previously unrecognized patterns of control over the ubiquitous mosques of South Asia. Muhammad Qasim Zaman has cautioned against simplistic understandings of religious authority and sets out a thorough and nuanced account of aspects of South Asian Islamic intellectual history, discouraging casual reference to the authority of the 'ulama. This authority was not appropriated by reform-minded individuals, he argues. It was produced through argumentation, caution, and instruction communicated through the 'ulama's writing and publishing. Zaman has classified the "overarching and overlapping themes" which have shaped internal debates among the 'ulama in the twentieth century, demonstrating that these debates respond to technological, social, and even economic change. Zaman's careful crafting of the nature and the limits of the 'ulama's authority suggests that there is a danger of attributing too much of the history of Muslim religious organization in the colonial period to the influence of parochial leaders where other figures were also able to lead and direct collectively organized Muslims.

While fundamentally related to and reliant on studies and theories of Indian secularism, colonial jurisprudence, Muslim communalism, and authority, this study breaks new ground by attending directly to the rich and nuanced history of Muslim worship in South Asian mosques under colonial law. This social history describes the imperatives and ideals which fueled Muslim worshippers and their encounters with the laws which limited them.

The Stories That Follow

Each chapter of this book attends to the history of a mosque of colonial South Asia, a social movement for reimagining general Muslim rights in that mosque, and the establishing of process which consigned some aspect of mosque use to the paternalistic control of an officer of the state or community. The records of the Judicial Committee of the Privy Council, an increasingly popular resource, center this study. My attention to these records is complemented by an equal attention to vernacular Urdu accounts of mosque worship and expectations relating to the specific sites attended to here, and close attention to colonial administration.

My interest in the JCPC case files crystalized in 2014 during my search for a statement of Sikh charitable grants compiled by the colonial administration of Lahore. The 1849 document appeared in a handlist of the Punjab Archive in Lahore but had been removed from the bundle in which it was contained and then misplaced. Later that year I discovered that the document had been submitted as evidence in the Shahidganj suit and was preserved intact in the JCPC case file related to this case. I began to engage more purposefully with the legal archive constituted by JCPC cases pertaining to South Asian mosques and discovered that the documentation captured the richness of debates, governance, and everyday practices in these important institutions. When studied together with administrative reports and vernacular texts, the JCPC mosque dispute case files reveal the legal and administrative practices and social expectations which influenced worship in South Asian mosques.

In the story told in Chapter 1 the reformist Ahl-i Hadith, reviled by the Hanafi religious establishment and the state, took over management of the Tajpur mosque of Bihar and were challenged by other mosque worshippers for their unusual ritual preferences. The Ahl-i Hadith sought legal clarification on how to derive normative principles for worship in the mosque; they won the judgment that prayer leaders were not bound by popular preference, only by reference to the Quran and hadith. The judgment disregarded the authority of the ʻulama in defining religious normativity and consigned the prayer hall to the control of the prayer leader. Chapter 2 presents the story of a Friday mosque in the new port city of Rangoon at the turn of the twentieth century. Motivated by a desire to influence management of the mosque school, the ethnically diverse Muslim worshippers at the mosque argued creatively that members of the congregation should participate democratically in management. The 1916 judgment of the JCPC conferred the mosque, and all instruction that took place within it, to the paternalistic control of its custodians.

Chapter 3 describes the social interest in the liminal space of the mosque perimeter through which sound transgressed into the mosque and worshippers entered and existed. This space of pious self-conduct was also a part of the street and under the charge of local and provincial governments which developed, straightened, and regulated the use of roads in the interests of public health and the efficient movement of human and automobile traffic through the city. These overlapping interests provoked political and legal mobilization by Muslims in Kanpur when a corner of a mosque was demolished to make way for a new road in 1913, and by Shiʻas demanding unmitigated rights of religious procession in Aurangabad UP in 1916. In 1924 the Judicial Committee of the Privy Council established the only social right on the street to be the right of individual passage and that the magistrate must regulate and police every expression of devotionalism on the street, and by extension at the vulnerable mosque perimeter.

Chapter 4 explores the final and binding conclusion of the Sikh and Muslim contest over the Mosque known as Shahidganj, an eighteenth-century mosque which had come under the control of a Sikh priest (*mahant*) in the nineteenth century. Sikh "adverse possession" of the mosque was authorized through official documentation of the occupation of the site more than twelve years earlier. Muslims asserted that this law was based in the treatment of land as property and denied its relevance to the mosque, presenting doctrinally and legally derived ideas that the land pertaining to a mosque was God's land and could never be alienated. The 1940 judgment established the petty officer of the Revenue Department, who documented occupation of the endowment, as the final arbiter of its fate.

Public interest in contested religious sites continued to grow and in the United Provinces Shi'a organizations initiated law suits to take over management of a mosque and imambargah (a building for collective Shi'a ritual commemoration), managed by the Hindu descendants of the original Muslim endower. The judgment in this final case in July 1947, weeks before decolonization and partition of South Asia, recognized the regulatory oversight of a provincial committee over all Muslim endowments, accepted the recommendation of this committee to remove the Hindu custodian, and gave instructions for the appointment of a new custodian. Chapter 5 leads us to a final and pivotal success at the very moment of decolonization, the admission of the testimony of Muslim experts by courts seeking to characterize a disputed endowment estate as a mosque, and the authorization of such officers to serve on provincial waqf regulation committees. A long era of Muslim efforts to reclaim collective rights in mosques produced new norms for mosques which were the administrative inheritance of the nation states of India, Pakistan, and Bangladesh.

State Regulation of Mosques from Punjab to Rangoon in the Eighteenth and Nineteenth Centuries

Rulers of north Indian states maintained official responsibility for mosques and worship in them through the late eighteenth and early nineteenth century. State administrators in the Punjab, the northern Indian plains, Bengal, and Burma oversaw endowment and patronage of mosques through grant of revenue remissions on mosque lands and the authorization of official land grants for artisans and custodians of mosques. They constructed mosques and authorized special grants for expansion or renovation. They financed management and ensured public access to mosques and trained and appointed officers of law who would resolve disputes relating to access, entry, and ritual preference. Political and administrative strategies for mosque finance and management varied across this region but the notion that state was responsible for enabling Muslim devotion prevailed. Patrons and worshippers understood mosques to be public spaces subject to both state oversight and social consensus over preferences for ritual practices.

Agricultural lands provided funds for the maintenance of mosques and salaries for staff and generous incomes for custodians. In comparison to their predecessors, Mughal emperors preferred to bestow grants on individuals rather than providing direct support to religious institutions.[30] These imperial title holders in turn were the primary benefactors of mosques, among them Wazir Khan of Lahore and Mahabat Khan in Peshawar.[31] Deeds of grant of land and title (*sanads*) and other official orders issued by the Mughal state establish that, as in other parts of India, substantial land grants to nobles provided for the expenses of mosques, both the upkeep of the buildings and the expenses of their staff, across Bihar during the Mughal period. A grant of approximately 1 acre of land (three *bighas*)[32] was given in a perpetual and hereditary grant (*madad-i mash*) to the muezzin of the Friday mosque of Arrah in 1648.[33] Over 3 acres of cultivable land were granted rent free in the name of Shah Muhammad Kabir and his sons for meeting the expenses of a mosque and a Sufi khanqah, in 1596.[34] A grant of a village of Bishenpur in Bengal was "exempt from payment of revenue and [the] produce applied to the support of religious mendicants and students and to the repair of mosques and other edifices" in the reign of Aurangzeb in 1679.[35] The incomes from these estates were mostly utilized for the upkeep of mosques: the costs of maintenance and repairs for the shrine and mosque of Muhammad Rooposh in Rajshahi district far exceeded the annual revenues of the associated land grant.[36]

Land endowments provided stipends for mosque custodians, many of them women,[37] none of whom had any particular religious qualifications, and provided for maintenance of mosque buildings. Revenues from these lands were managed by custodians who deducted their stipends and then reinvested the revenues in the mosque waqf, enhancing the built environment of the settled locale for social benefit. Custodians also oversaw agricultural and other revenue generating activities on endowment lands, made financial provisions for aesthetics and repair of mosques, hired and managed mosque staff including the muezzin, caretakers, and cleaners, and made arrangements for the expansion and enhancement of facilities where they were insufficient to serve the needs of the congregation. These arrangements served the civic needs of local community and did not rely on contributions from members of the congregation.

The mosque of Tajpur, Bihar, which is the subject of Chapter 1, was one of at least three religious sites in that town. An eidgah (pavilion for the biannual eid congregation) had been "built by Mughal emperors."[38] The karbala (a site used during the annual Muharram rituals) was a meadow with a pond.[39] The mosque was a "Mughal waqf from ancient times"[40] consigned to the custodianship of the local Mughal law officer or qazi who managed its finances. The Tajpur mosque included a space for worship, a well, some pastureland, and a guesthouse and was frequented by the local tailors. A prayer leader of the Tajpur mosque, hired in 1867, had been charged with giving the five-time daily call to prayer and convening the congregation as well as cleaning, maintaining, and managing access to the mosque and associated buildings and land. The income from one village provided funds, disbursed by the custodian, to meet the religious devotional and civic needs of the community. The custodian dispensed Mowla Baksh's pay, provided the funds for maintenance and management of the mosque and its attached infrastructure, and worked with Mowla Baksh to determine the times at which prayers would be offered and other matters relating to public access to the mosque.[41]

Worshippers at mosques like those in Tajpur demonstrated a number of expectations for the management of the mosque as imperially endowed civic infrastructure. They expressed belief in community rights to the use of guesthouses,[42] and stated expectations that tanks, wells, and fountains would be well maintained.[43] The qazi mediated disputes relating to mosques through interpretation and application of Hanafi legal precepts of awqaf,[44] in order to see that they served the civic needs of imperial subjects. He acted as a bridge between "shari'a and the exigencies of administration" and worked closely with the district administrator, the nazim, in his capacity as an imperial official.[45] The qazi provided oversight over the manner in which the infrastructure of the mosque served local settled community, mediating the wishes and intent of the mosque benefactor with a view of the exigencies of civic life. The qazi was empowered to question and scrutinize the sale of any mosque asset by its custodians with reference to the needs and requirements of the people of the neighborhood.[46] Vernacular Urdu commentaries on Islamic law unambiguously forbade the sale of any of the mosque belongings, from the rushes on the floor, green cuttings from trees, the rubble left over after renovations, or houses and shops that belonged to the mosque, without the approval of the qazi. In Bengal, a scholar published an Urdu text on the rules governing mosque endowment.[47] This pamphlet asserted the utility of the religious endowment accrued to the people of the neighborhood, and it was for this reason that the qazi, a legal officer of state, must maintain strict oversight over financial management of mosque properties and moneys.

Sikh rule ended Muslim imperial and elite patronage in much of the Punjab. In addition to transforming economic relations and government in Punjab and Kashmir and initiating a new era of Punjabi literary and cultural growth, Sikh rule led to the occupation and restructuring of Mughal-period urban settlements. In Lahore many of the Mughal period palaces and neighborhoods which had grown up within and outside the city walls were dismantled or desecrated,[48] including the mansion (*haveli*) and neighborhood (*muhalla*) of Zain Khan, a governor of the much reviled Afghan emperor Ahmad Shah Abdali. Buildings in the neighborhoods of the Khojas, the Qasaban, and Mughalpura outside the walled city were also demolished. This radical restructuring was read by a variety of colonial era historians as having been motivated by political and religious animosity.[49] Within the city the Chinyanwali Masjid was stripped of its marble. Masjid Mai Lado, outside the walled city, was occupied by a Sadhu, and it was alleged that a mosque site at a bazaar outside Delhi Gate was taken over and converted into a Sikh holy site. The Badshahi Masjid, Masjid Bazaar-i Tibbi, and Masjid Masti Dawazah were taken over and used as arsenals and the custodian of the imperial Friday mosque was sent away from Lahore and placated with a high-level post at the court in Kashmir.[50] An Akali Sardar whose mansion adjoined the Sunehri Mosque complained to the court that the noise of the azan could be heard in his gurdwara, violating the sanctity of the Guru Granth Sahib which he had placed there. Ranjeet Singh allowed the Akalis to take over the mosque and its attached commercial properties. These anecdotal accounts suggest that the Sikh state's civic priorities were derived from religious ontologies that privileged Sikh notions of sanctity and public priority over Muslims ones.

Sikh rule in the Punjab did not entirely disrupt Mughal patronage practices which had shaped the built environment. When Muslims of the Sunehri Bazaar neighborhood, represented by two 'faqirs of renown', asked Maharaja Ranjeet Singh to reconsider, the mosque was returned to the care of its custodian.[51] Individuals instead of statesmen initiated a new period of mosque building in the Punjab. Some of them built mosques near their homes in the southern and the eastern part of the walled city. A mosque was built by a dancing girl who was Ranjeet Singh's lover, in the bazaar Papar Mandi in the south of the city in 1224/1809. The mosque was entrusted to two "maulvis" (men with some Islamic scholarly credentials) who set up a school in the mosque and offered classes for the local children—both Hindu and Muslim. This came to be one of the best-known schools in Sikh Lahore.[52] A Muslim statesman built two mosques—one using the title given to him by the maharaja, Masjid Nur Iman Wala, and another at Kashmir Bazaar near his own house. Nur Muhammad Iman Wala invited a popular Maulvi to take up residence in this mosque, and gave up his own house for the maulvi's residence. It was said that thousands came to hear the sermon at this mosque every Friday.[53] A wealthy Muslim man who conducted trade between India and Europe built a mosque on his street in the neighborhood Chahal Bibiyan, also near the southern Mochi Darwaza, in 1829.[54] In 1257/1841 a mosque was built at Mochi Darwaza by Bukan Khan, the superintendent of Ranjeet Singh's stables, to replace an older mosque in disrepair.[55] During the 1780–1850 period, Sikh notables also made generous contributions to shrines in Dera Ismail Khan and in Kashmir, and it was said that the shrine of Data Sahib in Lahore was primarily maintained through donations from the Sikh court.[56] New mosques, built by new patrons connected to the Sikh court (the Lahore Darbar), continued to provide civic amenities in their neighborhoods, sustaining and reinforcing the significance of mosques in the everyday lives of Muslims.

New rulers in the north Indian plains perpetuated cultures of mosque patronage there during the eighteenth century after the invasions of Nadir Shah and Ahmad Shah Abdali and the Maratha expansion eroded Mughal control over these territories. Political projects and building projects attracted settlers, scholars, poets, Sufis, and 'ulama to new states as worshippers in and architects of new mosques.[57]

In the state of Rohilkhand, the Pashtun-lineage ruler Hafiz Rahmat Khan chose the city of Bareilly as his capital. He built a mausoleum for the founder of the Rohilkhand state at Anwala, and at Badayun he built a mosque and located his father's grave in its courtyard. Hafiz Rahmat Khan's family and allies made their own contributions to the built environment. His sister built a mosque at Bareilly known as Bibiji ki Masjid, and in Besoli, his ally Nawab Dunday Khan built a fort, a mosque, and a bathhouse (hamam).[58] Hafiz Rahmat Khan's building projects were motivated partly by an effort to employ migrants to his lands, a concern exemplified particularly when a famine hit Rajasthan in 1762 and large numbers of people from surrounding areas moved into Rohilkhand. Hafiz Rahmat Khan designated the walled city of Pilibhit as a new settlement for migrants and commissioned the building of a palace with an inner and an outer court, a fort, and a bridge. In 1767, he commissioned a Friday mosque to be built in imitation of the imperial mosque of Delhi. Hafiz Rahmat insisted that the architects build over a marsh that would otherwise cut the masjid off from the palace and the courts. This was done at great expense and the mosque was completed in 1781 at a total cost of more than three lakh rupees.[59] His insistence demonstrates his sense of the significance of the mosque as a link between the court and the newly settled population. Farrukhabad, an Afghan polity allied with Rohilkhand, was consolidated in this period. The ruler founded a capital city, Mau Rashidabad, and granted revenue estates to his allies.[60]

"Some hundreds of families lived along the roadside from the fort to Mau Gate. They were people of all castes who had followed the [Nawab Ahmad Khan 1750-1771] from Delhi in a year of famine. . . . They had acquired their name [Khopiwalas] from the rough earthen huts which they built to live in." Ahmad Khan built a mosque at the Mau Serai adjoining the tombs of his ancestors, and a neighborhood of rough dwellings grew up behind it.[61] The mosque and tombs anchored new settlement.

The Shi'a nawabs of Awadh were the most glamorous patrons of the built environment in nineteenth-century north India. In the capital city of Lucknow, private bastions of wealth and privilege, "splendid, fairylike and luxurious" residences, surrounded the mosques, imambargahs, and palaces.[62] The Nawab Asaf ud Daula constructed a monumental imambargah complex here in the late eighteenth century, a public site of ritual mourning.[63] The complex included a Friday mosque and the construction of the site coincided with efforts to institutionalize congregational Friday prayer, not commonly observed by the Twelver Shi'as of Awadh before that time. The Nawab bestowed expensive *taziyas* (small replicas of tombs) on the imambargah, drawing Shi'a ritual mourners to pay their respects at the site. Asaf ud Daula also constructed the forecourt of the imambargah around the administrative offices of the state. The imambargah and mosque together projected the political autonomy and authority of the Nawab, served as a site of state diplomacy and adjudication of justice, and shaped a Shi'a body politic.

Alongside the rulers of north Indian states, British administrators in East India Company territories adopted Mughal religious patronage practices as an aspect of their own statecraft, extending financial support and regulation to religious institutions. Government regulations paved the way for colonial officials to intervene in the management of a public religious site to guarantee its "good management."[64] In a number of instances of colonial annexation of territories, the new colonial administration provided financial support for mosques as part of a strategy of conciliation. In Delhi in 1809, shortly after a colonial residency was established there but before its direct annexation, the residents of the old city wrote to the resident to request that the well of the Friday mosque should be repaired.[65] Delegates from the city of Pilibhit were sent to meet the superintendent of the Western Provinces while he was on a tour of these recently conquered territories and complained about the disassembling of city infrastructure and auctioning of the materials of the city walls, bridge, and inn by the local collector.[66] Conceiving that this would be "highly gratifying to the Inhabitants of Delhi, particularly to the Mohummedans,"[67] repairs were commissioned there under a prestigious French architect in 1811,[68] and again in 1834 and in 1851.[69] The superintendent recommended that the tomb of the vanquished Hafiz Rahmat Khan and adjoining mosque and caretaker's house at Pilibhit should be repaired at government expense of 5,396 rupees in order to elicit the 'gratitude and respect' of the city's inhabitants.[70] In the town of Bareilly in 1826, Muslim residents asked for financial support for the repair of and construction of a covering for a pavilion used for the biannual Eid congregational prayer;[71] a sum of 2,400 rupees was allocated.[72] The Friday mosque of Allahabad, which had served as the governor's residence for the early colonial administration, was renovated at the cost of 4,000 rupees and reopened for Muslim congregational worship. Monetary support for religious sites placated and elicited the gratitude of newly incorporated colonial subjects. The British saw themselves as "dynastic heirs to the Mughal and Sikh Kingdoms" and believed that the conservation of the built environment would gratify their new subjects.[73] These strategies of management of the built environment produced a sense of imperial continuity and dispelled anxieties about the legitimacy of rule.[74]

East India Company administrators in Delhi paid pensions to religious leaders directly out of the treasury as well as assigning revenues from villages for the support of both Muslim and Hindu shrines. These payments totaled almost 80,000 rupees in 1857.[75] There is evidence that early colonial administrators sanctioned grants of otherwise undeveloped and non-proprietary land to elites to build mosques. In 1831 an application was put forward by Bannu Begum, the widow of the Mughal scion Mirza Sikander Shikoh, for a grant of a 2,000-yard plot of land valued at 4,000 rupees in the neighborhood of the Turkman Gate in Delhi on which she wished to build a mosque and serai (resthouse). Great "inconveniences [were] experienced by weary travelers coming in by the Tookman and Ajmer Gates of the city from which the serais are a great distance," she wrote. Begum Bannu added that "the late Fuzoolah Khan Bangash and others" had been granted small plots of land for similar purposes. An official note in the margins of the application affirmed this policy line, adding that an acre and a half of waste land was granted rent free to a "rich native of Ajmere for the purpose of forming a garden and maintaining a Brahmin to entertain travelers."[76]

After the British occupation of Rangoon in 1852[77] a number of the valuable plots in the new city, designed for 36,000 inhabitants, were granted to religious establishments,[78] among them a synagogue, a convent, a Roman Catholic church, an Armenian chapel, a Chinese temple and a separate Macao Chinese temple, a Parsi Fire Temple,[79] a Brahmin temple, and a Shi'a mosque. In 1862 the patrons of a mosque together successfully petitioned the government for an additional grant of land for the mosque and received two lots, one adjoining the mosque and the other behind it. This sort of land grant was unusual by 1860, but so was the creation of a new city; religious conciliation was a strategy in an experiment in civil and social engineering. This mosque, the subject of Chapter 2, was imagined to be a charitable trust and intended to serve all Muslims of Rangoon under the watchful eye of the state.

> His Majesty's Government in India doth grant Moolla Ibrahim, Goolam Moiuddin Moolla and Cassim Ahzim for ever all that parcel of land . . . measuring 115 feet in length and 100 feet in breadth . . . for the intent and purposes hereinafter mentioned; that is to say:
>
> Upon Trust to build and maintain upon the said parcel of land a mosque of place of worship for and to the free use of all persons professing the Sunni sect of the Mahomedan religion.
>
> Provided always that the same [trustees] . . . or any future Trustee to be appointed in their or either of their steads, shall happen to die or shall refuse or shall become incapable to act in the aforesaid trust, it shall be lawful for the Deputy Commissioner of Rangoon for the time being from time to time nominate substitutes and appoint any other person or persons to become a trustee or trustees . . .
>
> Provided also that if a good and substantial mosque is not erected on the said parcel of land within one year from this date or if the said parcel of land is at any time put any use or purpose other than that for which the trust aforesaid provides, it shall be lawful for the Deputy Commissioner for Rangoon . . . to revoke this grant.[80]

Indian rulers and elites and colonial officials treated, funded, and regulated mosques as important civic spaces into the middle of the nineteenth century. Scholars fostered dialogue and civic debate about the uses of mosque land and properties, and state-appointed officers of courts across north India served as the final authority in disputes relating to mosques. Regulation of mosques during this period, spanning the dissolution of Mughal authority and the rise of colonial power, can be broadly understood to be state endorsement of the principle of elite patronage of these institutions, critically reinforced by state oversight and underwriting of the civic functions that mosques served. State patronage and regulation of mosques shaped these as public arenas[81] that served as spaces of civic organization while also reinforcing the legitimacy of the rulers.

The Colonial State's Disavowal of Responsibility for Religious Institutions

After the East India Company's annexation of territories and gradual consolidation of control in northeast and then north India, between 1781 and 1802, elaborate registers of revenue-free lands were compiled by the administration. Around Chittagong in eastern Bengal, Mughal rulers had given large tracts of jungle land in grant as endowments for rural mosques.[82] Income from 118,149 acres, over 1,171 villages of "lakhiraj"[83] land was given over to religious and cultural institutions in Bihar's Darbhanga Collectorate alone.[84] The Company assessed the uses of the incomes of these lakhiraj estates against European preferences for charity that benefitted the old, the infirm, the widow, and the orphan, and determined that land grants to custodians of religious institutions should be resumed.[85] Over the next fifty years, the local collector's office identified "improper" or "unfeasible" claims of rent-free tenure and resumed lakhiraj land,[86] a process that was completed in the Darbhanga district in 1850.[87] While mosques and temples themselves were not touched in this process, the grants of land that had been given in perpetuity to mosques and were free of tax, lands that had provided funds for repairs, maintenance, renovations and day-to-day running, were taken back by the state.

A process enabling the government to "divest itself of the management of religious endowments" unfolded at the same time.[88] The Religious Endowments Act, which started out as the Bengal and Madras Native Religious Endowments Act No. XX of 1863 before it was extended in other parts of administered India, was conceived for the "expediency of relieving Boards of Revenue etc. in Bengal and Madras from management etc. of religious endowments."[89] The statute differentiated public infrastructure such as bridges, rest houses, and government buildings from mosques and Hindu temples, retaining the former under superintendence of government officers, and releasing religious establishments to the charge of their own custodians. Any dispute over appointment of a custodian or the property pertaining to the religious establishment was to be decided by the civil court. In cases where the government had become the only recognized authority in a religious establishment, like at the wealthy imambargah at Hooghly where the "unworthy" hereditary custodian had been removed to enable better uses of the endowment's enormous wealth, the government appointed committees of coreligionists to take over management.[90]

The office of the qazi was abolished in 1864 and the functions of this state-appointed Muslim law officer were now fulfilled by colonial courts and administrators.[91] The Kazi Act of 1880 reduced the role of qazi to that of a marriage registrar, and did not account for the ways in which the precolonial state had provided a legal framework for resolution of disputes over social and cultural transactions through the office of the qazi.[92] Mid-nineteenth-century British domestic politicians and bureaucrats were disapproving of involvement in non-Christian charitable institutions and warned against regulating these endowments in the public interest.[93] The colonial state rejected all Indian religious ontological underpinnings for law or policy, and instead accorded narrow forms of control over mosques to officers of the mosque trust, the executive, and later the legislature. The state was relieved of responsibilities for financial support to mosques, for incubating consensus over ritual practice in mosques, and for assessing religious rights in public spaces.

The resumption of such grants impoverished religious establishments. In Tajpur, Bihar, the revenue village of Chuck Adawlat was resumed and no longer supported the costs of the mosque.[94] Heightened colonial anxieties about Indian political loyalties after mobilizations and attacks on East India Company interests in 1857 sparked a review of payments to religious institutions. In the Punjab, the chief commissioner cancelled grants of land and title on the grounds that many recipients of grants had been disloyal to the colonial government.[95] The administration at Delhi contemplated blowing up the imperial mosque in an act of political vengeance.[96] In Rangoon, the district government reviewed the land grant of 1862 and found that the land had not been used for the mosque building itself. Moolla Hashim had used this land and other donations to build eight shops with frontages on Dalhousie Street, residential quarters for the mosque's muezzin, a room which could be rented out at nominal rates to travelers, and a building to serve as a school and extra prayer space for large religious congregations.[97] Incomes from the commercial and residential rental properties provided funds for the day-to-day running of the mosque but the land grant was cancelled on the grounds that "this first class lot was put to uses other than what the Government contemplated for it."[98]

Certain civic function of mosques, including maintenance of water sources, lighting, charity for orphans, instruction for the young, and the aesthetic development of the built environment, were taken over by the state. District boards and municipalities began to take responsibility for the supply of water to towns and cities in Bengal and Bihar from as early as 1887. They constructed and maintained waterworks where this was financially feasible, and took responsibility for any tanks, streams, watercourses, springs, and wells that were not claimed as private property.[99] Civic development was dramatically expanded, regularized, and rationalized under dedicated public institutions.

Colonial resumption policies effectively ended the Mughal-era revenue remissions on agricultural lands in favor of religious establishments, drastically reducing the income stream, and conditions of management. Other forms of elite patronage of the built environment continued in a dynamic relationship with the colonial state and its articulated objectives for the development of the built environment. In Bengal, zamindars built river embankments in active conversation with district administrators. In Bombay, they built and maintained water tanks.

A Private Act of Religious or Charitable Benefit

Administrators, merchants, and other elites had produced the sovereignties of precolonial states and the early colonial state through "socially beneficial gifts"[100] and involvement in the affairs of temples and mosques. Having divested the state of all responsibility for religious establishments in 1863 but cognizant that they were not private property, colonial administrators had to produce laws to differentiate religious establishments from both private and public property. Between 1870 and 1930, as they framed regulations to govern capital and the market, they simultaneously created laws treating land and buildings of mosques and other places of worship as privately owned assets committed to trust to serve a religious cause in perpetuity.[101] Social claims on that infrastructure ceased to be regulated and mediated by officers of the state acting ex-officio. The legal structure of the English trust which defined objectives and beneficiaries, endowed properties, and the uses of these properties was superimposed on mosques and became the only source of the rights of worshippers.

Two subsequent pieces of legislation emerged. The Charitable Endowments Act of 1890 required that every religious site had to be shown to serve either public or private worship. The Religious and Charitable Endowments Act of 1920 sanctioned Muslim (and Hindu, Parsi, and Sikh) worshippers' demands that custodians of religious establishments prepare annual financial accounts. Colonial treatment of mosque endowments was inspired by the history of treatment of religious and charitable endowments under English law. The English model had emerged to check alienations of land to the use of families and religious houses that could be used to defraud creditors and which restricted the action of market forces on land.[102] The alienation of land in perpetuity for religious objectives was admitted on the principle that this benefitted large sections of the public, and these perpetuities came to be subject to "intensive" bureaucratic supervision of a Charity Commissioner during the nineteenth century.[103] The creation of private Muslim family trusts in India was bitterly opposed by the colonial state well into the twentieth century which anticipated fraud and circumvention of the market.[104] However, this history should not be conflated with the colonial treatment of mosques;[105] English laws of trust were introduced and adapted to accommodate the prevailing alienation of land to mosques and to temples as the creation of perpetuities for charitable or religious public purposes. The simple act of dedication of land and buildings for the purpose of Muslim worship was deemed a legal creation of a public trust and allowed retroactive recasting of all mosques in British Indian territory as trusts and governable under English trust law. Creation of laws of trust governing mosques allowed the civil courts to hear and resolve disputes relating to mosques, like the one in Tajpur.

English trust law provided for three parties in a trust: the benefactor or grantor, the trust manager, and the beneficiary. The trust manager (or trustee) had to be designated to sufficiently account for the separation of the grantor/benefactor's interests from the objectives of the endowment. The work of the trustee was to ensure that the benefit of the trust was received by the beneficiary. The law did not provide for a dynamic relationship between grantor, manager and public beneficiary; grantors made reference to broadly subscribed civic and religious discourses to justify the alienation of lands in public trusts, and unless grantors made explicit arrangements for the involvement of beneficiaries in decision making for the trust, trust managers did as they saw fit to fulfill the objectives for the trust set out by the grantor. Colonial laws of trusts supported a number of cases for government resumption of land grants to mosques across India over the course of the nineteenth century leading up to the Tajpur case of 1891; these cases demonstrate a gradual alignment of the idea of the mosque waqf and the framework of the English trust.

Worshippers were designated as beneficiaries of the mosque trust and custodians were designated the managers. A case was brought by the residents of a neighborhood in Banaras in 1877 against the custodians of a mosque for repurposing two rooms attached to the mosque. The right of the worshippers to sue as beneficiaries of a trust was upheld and the decision disallowed the custodians' use of mosque resources in a manner that did not provide for Muslim worship.[106] In 1892, a petition brought by a "habitual worshipper at a certain Muhammadan mosque" against a trespasser Ram Chand who took over this land was admitted, significantly revising the decision of a divisional judge who had earlier dismissed his suit on the grounds that worshippers "were not competent to maintain it."[107] Mortgages and sales of mosque land were also determined to be unacceptable. In Bombay in 1899 the children of a custodian who had sold the land attached to a mosque successfully brought a suit against the purchaser of the land despite their silence at the time of the sale.[108] Muslims exercised the rights granted to them under colonial trust law and regularly initiated litigation in defense of mosque land and buildings.

Until 1920 the right of worshippers to bring suits against custodians of endowment properties was derived from Section 539 of the Civil Procedure Code of 1882, later replaced by section 92 of the Civil Procedure Code of 1908 which enabled any two persons with an interest in the trust to challenge the trustees. Yet securing this right to litigate was so complicated as to have made these laws ineffective. The Advocate General had to give permission for the suit to be filed and petitioners had to establish that the religious site was indeed a trust before the latter could proceed to assert their expectations as worshippers.

In South Asia, the exact correlation of religious endowment and charitable benefits that justified the creation of perpetuities under English trust law[109] remained undefined in the various statutes that addressed charity, non-profit oriented enterprise and philanthropy. Public interests were only vaguely alluded to in the Registration of Societies Act of 1860, the Religious Endowments Act of 1863, and the Indian Income Tax Act of 1886.[110] The use of the term "public" to refer to mosques is, therefore, misleading; where endowments had been regulated as by qazis by the Mughal state, and where the public trust was subject to state regulation in England, the ways in which mosque trusts served their "public" objectives were not regulated at all. Identification of mosques as public trusts was validated by evidence that these buildings and lands did not serve the uses of named, private individuals and they did not serve immoral or illegal objectives. The 1891 Tajpur judgment established that mosque benefactors could set out the terms, manner, and means by which the custodians of a mosque fulfilled the purpose of the mosque.

Under laws of trust, the social and political significance of mosques as public waqfs contrasted sharply with endowments deemed to be private waqfs. All waqfs were created in perpetuity and all waqfs were exempt from revenue demands, but their impact on society was entirely different. By definition, the land, buildings, and incomes of mosques could not serve the private or personal interests of the benefactor or the custodian, though no doubt some benefits accrued indirectly to them. The beneficiaries of these public trusts were anonymous members of a general Muslim public. Buildings, lands, and incomes associated with a mosque endowment served those unnamed worshippers and all administrators and jurists were highly attentive to this principle. Private waqfs, on the other hand, were land and buildings committed in trust in perpetuity to serve named beneficiaries, usually descendants within a family line or else in the case of a shrine, descendants in a spiritual teacher-to-student line. In other words, private waqfs were created to explicitly benefit closely interrelated individuals. Ameer Ali, who wrote strongly in defense of the legality of private waqfs in Islamic law, and Muhammad Ali Jinnah, who passed the Muslim Private Waqf Validating Bill in 1913, openly testified that the purpose of private waqfs was to protect the wealth and preeminence of elite Muslims who benefitted society through their leadership or other exemplary behaviors.[111] Private waqfs served private legacies, and while it would be very useful to understand how Muslim religious observances at private waqfs shaped Muslim consensus and collectivity, that is not a topic of study in this book.

Mosques were financially supported and regulated by precolonial states and early colonial statesmen through the early nineteenth century, the period directly preceding the Tajpur mosque case. The colonial state gradually dismantled this financial and regulatory apparatus and in its place assembled a legal framework that treated mosques as charitable trusts which provided facilities for worship. Wary colonial government officials distanced themselves from mosque affairs but tightened their control over other civic infrastructure. Mosques now served a diffuse cross section of Muslim society under the control of their custodians. By the time of the Tajpur mosque litigation these principles of control were mostly established and in the years that followed Muslims across north India organized challenge and response. The stories of these contests follow, demonstrating what was at stake for Muslim worshippers, and the extent to which trust law enabled the control of petty officers over the mosque.

Chapter 1

TAJPUR, BIHAR, 1891

LEADERSHIP IN CONGREGATIONAL PRAYER

Introduction

Hafiz Mowla Baksh, the muezzin of the Tajpur mosque in Bihar, preferred to vocalize the word "*amin*" and raise his hands up to his ears when pronouncing the greatness of God, when standing before the congregation in worship. Persianized dress, conduct, and tastes derived from a Mughal courtly culture still dominated life in this part of India, but a new society was emerging. From the late eighteenth century, the East India Company had worked to create a legal framework for resolution of civil disputes and to secure the revenues of the valuable estates, large and small, as the sovereign power of the Mughal Empire and the authority of its officials and deputies waned. Agriculturalists saw increases in efficiency of irrigation and cultivation through the 1870s as the population increased dramatically.[1] Merchants took on grand and public philanthropic projects and developed close relationships with the old military-bureaucratic nobility.[2] The officers of the massive estate of the Darbhanga Raj collected over 3 million rupees in rents just a few miles to the east.[3]

Omed Ali and the other challengers of Mowla Baksh were weavers and their profession itself was deeply connected to the burgeoning colonial economy. To the southwest, master carpet weavers fulfilled an almost unlimited demand for cheap floor coverings as well as producing exquisitely dyed and woven floor coverings on commission[4] while Omed Ali and others produced fine tapestries under the supervision of their master tailor. While in many ways connected to a new colonial economy and society, Omed Ali and other worshippers' understanding of Islamic normativity was a carryover from the late Mughal period. They described the significance of imperial patronage and the mosque infrastructure for civic life in their quarter of this town some forty-five miles from the city of Patna in Bihar, a predominantly agricultural region. Precolonial elites had built mosques and undertook a variety of other public works in Bihar from the sixteenth century onward. These projects had been both displays of political authority and acts of public welfare.[5]

Omed Ali and some members of the congregation objected to Mowla Baksh raising his hands to his ears in prayer, considering this to be a violation of prevailing norms. They began boycotting the prayer led by Mowla Baksh and convening their own congregation in the same mosque behind an imam of their own choosing. Mowla Baksh's legal battle, supported by the custodians of the mosque and wealthy and influential north Indians identifying as Islamic reformist Ahl-i Hadith, outlasted his own lifetime. Omed Ali's appeal for official admonishment of Mowla Baksh was rooted in memories of Mughal statecraft, support for and regulation for mosques, but the economy and political order which had knitted together an Islamic narrative and normativity had long been erased. The consequences of such change in the mosque did not become clear to Omed Ali and others until the conclusion of their suit in 1891: colonial law, which recognized and enforced the public right to worship, would not engage with or enforce Muslims' expectations about the exact cadence of ritual, even if they were presented as norms of Muslim worship and the prevailing opinions of a Muslim public.

When confronted with the Tajpur mosque suit, the JCPC was unwilling to mediate the complex disagreement over ritual authenticity despite Omed Ali's assertion that the innovation in prayer was profoundly offensive to those who observed the Hanafi norms which prevailed during the Mughal period. The Judicial Committee of the Privy Council ruled that an Ahl-i Hadith prayer leader was free to vocalize the *amin* and equally, a Hanafi prayer leader could prefer the silent observance. Colonial jurists were committed to a secularism whose rationalism and logic were informed by English law, religion, and culture and ignored demonstrated authoritative practices and reasoning embedded in the Islamic legal tradition.[6] This ruling against conformity in worship undermined the widely subscribed and long established authority of the Hanafi 'ulama,[7] and removed congregational ritual from the concerns and oversight of a Muslim body politic. Granted the right to refuse the recommendations of the Hanafi 'ulama and the expectations of a general Muslim public in his ritual preferences, the prayer leader's role crystalized in a new and hitherto unknown form of religious control within the mosque.[8]

State Authorization of Congregational Prayer in Mughal India

The denizens of mid-nineteenth-century Tajpur had inherited the culture of mosque worship prevalent in the late Mughal state. The emperor's prerogative to convene the Friday congregation and maintain oversight over neighborhood mosques oriented religious practice around the doctrinal preferences of the state and conformity in ritual preference. The imams, muezzins, and custodians of mosques had no authority to set out ritual priorities for a mosque.

An ideal implicit in Mughal imperial administration was that the Friday congregation could only convene at the imperial mosque of a city whose boundaries were demarcated by a qazi, a legal officer of the king, and where a delegate of the king's authority, had been appointed. An imam, a term which referred to an authority in religious interpretation, gave the Friday sermon.[9] The imam of a Friday mosque had to be authorized by the king or his delegate, and he could only give the call to congregation for the Friday prayer in the presence of the king or his delegate. If the king or his representative was not present, no Friday prayers could be offered.[10] A jurist of the emperor Jahangir's era rationalized this control over the mosque, asserting that it was critical that the king, among other things, use his power to integrate the "community of the leader of humanity, the Prophet Muhammad,"[11] and Jahangir himself noted that the Shi'as and Sunnis of his realm met together in prayer unlike the Muslims of Safavid and Ottoman lands.[12]

The five daily prayers could be offered at any neighborhood mosque. Congregations were within their rights to replace a prayer leader (imam) who was preferred by a minority with another more acceptable to the majority.[13] However the king had the right to override popular consensus with regards to the appointment of a prayer leader in any mosque. Emperor Aurangzeb exercised this prerogative in Gujarat where he appointed a religious officer who was charged with "installing an orthodox imam and an orthodox prayer leader in the mosques erected by the Isma'ili sect."[14] A prayer leader, therefore, nominally recognized and upheld the doctrinal preferences of the Mughal state. The shoe seller's riot at the Friday mosque of Delhi in 1729 was put down through a violent enforcement of the state's overarching authority over the congregation.[15] Abishek Kaicker tells us that an "urban body politic" coalesced around religious symbols and affiliations as well as an expectation of justice for a murdered kinsman, but the mosque was not a freely accessible arena.[16] Participants in a congregation observed normative political and religious strictures and the Delhi shoe sellers were quickly reminded of the state's expectations of their self-conduct in the mosque.

The Mughal Emperor Aurangzeb (1658–1707), the patron of the comprehensive review of Hanafi law *Fatawa Alamgiriyya*, designated this school of Islamic jurisprudence as the primary source of religious reason for the qazis and other law officers of his realm. Chroniclers of his time believed that he both sought to implement Hanafi laws in the courts and to encourage the people to "live according to the shariʻa."[17] The *Fatawa Alamgiriyya* included detailed instructions on the act of calling the faithful to prayer (*azan*) and the act of convening the congregation (*aqamat*).[18] The reciter of the call to prayer, the muezzin, had no discretion over timing, bodily comportment or vocalization in prayer; his was a perfunctory role. He called the *azan* by determining the level of the sun against the horizon according to prescribed method,[19] his recitation of the *azan* had to be uninterrupted and loud enough to be heard by more than one person, and he was expected to recite the *azan* with the pauses, repetitions, and emphases described in the important Hanafi text, the *Hedaya*.[20] A deviation from these norms such as elongating the pronunciation of *Allah-hu Akbar* at its beginning was described as heresy in one Hanafi text, the *Fatawa* noted. Elongating the pronunciation of *Allah-hu Akbar* at its end was described as embarrassing immoderation.[21] If a muezzin's recitation was not adequately loud or was interrupted, another could give the *azan*, starting over, assuming his role.[22]

Prayer leaders were authorized by their appointers to convene the prayer, and efforts by members of a congregation to convene for prayer in mosques outside of their scheduled appearances were frowned upon, although not forbidden under Hanafi law. In the absence of an appointed muezzin or an imam, different groups among the people of the mosque could legitimately convene separate and independent congregations for prayer.[23] Although authorized to lead the congregation in prayer and not expect dissent, the prayer leader's intonation was regulated by defined Hanafi precepts. An imam was expected to intone certain phrases loudly, notably the call of Allahu Akbar (*takbir*), in order that the congregation meditate on this pronouncement and experience spiritual awareness. Other words were to be recited silently, among them, the *amin* (amen).[24]

In Tajpur, the local qazi had overseen the financial affairs and management of the small imperially endowed mosque. He appointed the muezzin to "call and lead the congregation" and to keep the mosque well lit and clean and to take care of any guests visiting the attached guesthouse. The qazi gave orders regarding the mosque and was within his rights to make enquiries as to whether the muezzin was fulfilling his responsibilities as expected, and to dismiss the muezzin if he did not do so. While the official post of qazi and with it the Mughal oversight over mosques were abolished in 1864, the people of Tajpur asked the qazi, Ramizuddin, to continue overseeing the mosque affairs. Qazi Ramizuddin hired Haji Mowla Baksh as a servant of the mosque, subject to his authority and his orders, in 1867.[25]

Prayer leadership in Mughal India, and at the Tajpur mosque in 1867, was not an authoritative act imbued with discretionary power. Rather it was a perfunctory act scripted through reference to the same Hanafi sources which shaped public discourse and had directed the actions of Mughal state officials. The Mughal state had authorized references to Hanafi scholars and Hanafi law across the region and public observance of Hanafi ritual and congregation behind the emperor or one of his delegates at Friday prayer was an act of political fealty.

The 'Ulama and the Ahl-i Hadith

The Ahl-i Hadith were self-identifying Muslims who believed that all Muslims should read the Quran and hadith themselves and should derive their everyday observances from a real understanding of divinity and individualism and the example of the Prophet Muhammad as described in these texts.[26] Ahl-i Hadith writers and preachers disputed the authority of the Hanafi 'ulama to set out principles of interpretation of Islamic law and personal conduct and engaged in public sparring with Hanafis. This conflict has been exhaustively studied and there is little new information that this section will add to general understandings of nineteenth-century Muslim reformism and revivalism. However, because the tensions between the Hanafis and Ahl-i Hadith fueled tensions in the Tajpur mosque which in turn invited colonial adjudication, I recount them here.

'Ulama trained in Hanafi jurisprudence had held positions at the Mughal court from the earliest times. The early colonial establishment of Bengal, engaged in the "reinvention" of Mughal government, appointed scholars trained in Hanafi law as Indian law officers overseen by Company officials.[27] These officers engaged principles of Islamic law to adjudicate disputes within a framework of colonial justice.[28] Scholars trained in Hanafi law and the textual tradition also engaged with the colonial project from the late eighteenth century, participating in the codification of Anglo-Muhammadan law and translating key texts including the *Fatawa Alamgiriyya* and *Hedaya*.[29] Among them were the 'ulama of the Rampur and those of the Calcutta Madrassa founded by Warren Hastings in 1780 to train Muslims in Persian, Arabic, and Islamic law and prepare them to participate in the East India Company administration.[30] Up until 1857, the Rampur madrassa served the Rampur state, and its scholars engaged deeply with the Islamic textual tradition. Both madrassas' graduates were employed as public officials, as teachers in private madrassas,[31] and as qazis, occupying the position of legal officers in the courts, advisors, and marriage registrars and fulfilling colonial ambitions for the governance of social life in India through enforcement of a codified legal system.[32]

The business of knowledge production and training at the two madrassas continued to serve statecraft, broadly defined.[33]

Hanafi scholars involved in the compilation of the *Fatawa* had come to social prominence; Shah Wali Ullah Dehlavi indicated that participation in the Hanafi jurisprudential tradition increased his family's closeness to the Mughal court and others were awarded land grants or advanced administrative posts.[34] Hanafi scholars produced important commentaries on religious pluralism,[35] inheritance,[36] and bodily and psychological[37] conditions. One graduate of a Hanafi madrassa who at first taught in a school, went on to find employment in the offices of a Mughal princess, then became a guardian of the treasury at Delhi and finally became imperial legal secretary before he died in 1747. The practice of religious inquiry brought imperial recognition and meritocratic promotion from "insignificance to comfortable prominence."[38] Instruction in Hanafi texts was also part of the curriculum *Dars-i Nizami* which was taught at the Madrassa Rahimiyya in Delhi and Firangi Mahal in Lucknow. Hanafi law deeply influenced Persianate intellectual discourse and participation during the late Mughal period and was brought to life in the judgments of the jurists,[39] orienting any legal representations and decisions.

The 'ulama published translations of major works and refutations of Ahl-i Hadith ideas as their conflicts with the reformist grew in tenor and visibility.[40] Graduates of madrassas with a more mystical bent took Hanafi precepts to a wider public.[41] A Sufi of the Delhi region called Shah Ramzan Rohtaki who had given up his hereditary seat at his shrine and received training in Hanafi ideas under Shah Abdul Aziz, the son of Shah Wali Ullah, became an itinerant reformist preacher in the late eighteenth century. He told his followers that if an elder was to offer them learning, they should listen and should not abandon the rigor of formal learning, that they should distinguish the fakir who "errs on a point of shari'a" and should "keep their religion uncompromised."[42] This mystic presented respect for Hanafi scholarly opinion as a principle of piety.

Engagement with Hanafi discourse had long been a facet of imperial subjecthood which simultaneously enabled legal agency. Perspectives on religion presented by Hanafi-trained 'ulama in their capacities as jurists, teachers, landowners, administrators, or mystics had been authorized by the state; adherence to their dogma was, by extension, an act of political loyalty. Engagement with this intellectual and legal culture was deeply empowering as well; under legal procedure introduced by the *Fatawa Alamgiriyya* in the eighteenth century, opinions of muftis which were derived from Hanafi precept could overrule the pronouncements of qazis.[43] Adherence to Hanafi Islam in matters of worship as well as law and justice invoked a contract between imperial state and society.

Ahl-i Hadith were those who accepted the teachings of Shah Ismail of Delhi by rejecting unthinking deference to the Sunni jurisprudential tradition and scholarly authority in favor of personal readings and understanding of the Quran and hadith.⁴⁴ Ironically, the Ahl-i Hadith religious position had its origins in the teachings of Shah Wali Ullah and Shaikh Ahmad Sirhindi. Sikander Bhopali, an influential nineteenth-century Ahl-i Hadith, asserted that personal readings of translations of the Quran and hadith, and a small number of legal-philosophical texts, among them the *Mishkat Sharif* of Abd Allah Tabrizi, helped the pious to understand and reach conclusions about Islamic law, faith, and practice and to circumvent their reliance on scholarly interpretation.

A large number of scholars (including myself) have historicized the Ahl-i Hadith interventions. The earliest British observers termed them Wahhabi conspirators, inspired by visits to Mecca and led by Sayyid Ahmad of Rai Bareily to lead an anti-Sikh jihad. Barbara Metcalf considers them the intellectual descendants of Shah Wali Ullah, counterparts in this sense, to the Deobandis. Religious reformist impulses drove a number of teaching and learning movements across colonial north India in the nineteenth century but few, if any, provoked the ire of the colonial state in the manner that the Ahl-i Hadith did. Sayyid Ahmad's jihad produced suspicion and hostility among European statesmen who believed that hostile anti-colonial sentiments motivated this "Wahhabi" conspiracy. The Hanafi 'ulama accused Sayyid Ahmad, Shah Ismail, and their supporters of misleading common people into making financial contributions in their support.⁴⁵

The Ahl-i Hadith embraced print technologies and gained visibility and influence through strongly argued, concise, widely circulated pamphlets, newspapers, and magazines written in the vernacular⁴⁵ and the formation of lecture or discussion groups. In Bihar, Abdul Aziz Rahimabadi returned from his study in Delhi where he had been tutored in Ahl-i Hadith ideas, and began a program of inviting people to join the preaching mission of the Ahl-i Hadith (*dawat-i tabligh*), and inviting them to initiate others in this manner of religious practice.⁴⁷ Unlike instruction in Hanafi jurisprudence, fully internalized by only a very few highly tutored scholars and jurists, Ahl-i Hadith teachings were intended to be widely received, to influence daily religious practice, and to be communicated from person to person. Ahmedullah, one of the prominent Ahl-i Hadith of Bihar who would become a primary supporter of the Ahl-i Hadith position in the Tajpur mosque case, offered a concise statement on what it meant to be part of this movement: "a worker for the cause has got books."⁴⁸

Ahl-i Hadith ritual choices produced a personal, sensory experience of and response to worship and reinforced the autonomy of worshippers in the mosque.⁴⁹ They vocalized the pronouncement of *amin* and the remembrance of God during prayer and raised their hands to their ears in a gesture of humility. In doing so, the Ahl-i Hadith broke from the silent offerings of prayer preferred by the Hanafi 'ulama, while asserting their practice to others within the congregation. This practice drew on Ahl-i Hadith pedagogy that was articulated more fully in the *Sirat-i Mustaqim*, the work of Muhammad Ismail translated by Sikander Bhopali. Muhammad Ismail asserted that the oral recitation of the Quran and the recitation of God's name were cornerstones of Islamic practice alongside jihad, charitable giving, and pilgrimage,⁵⁰ as both increased a love and awareness of God.⁵¹ He also asked that men acknowledge the Ahl-i Hadith as their guides or leaders because, like the companions of the Prophet Muhammad, they were enablers of a justice and politics embedded in awareness of the religion.⁵²

The devotional performance preferred by the Ahl-i Hadith increased the influence and significance of the devotee.⁵³ It did not preclude the emergence or development of disciplinary aural cultures, or the reconstitution of unified legal and political authority within the tradition, but at the point at which the Ahl-i Hadith came into conflict with the Hanafis in Tajpur, they directly rejected mosque practice as a Hanafi performance of subjecthood in favor of a personal and a sensory worship that, in turn, unified the congregation. The Ahl-i Hadith "movement" was, in this case, a pattern of use of a devotional method in the mosque and not a deliberate or rationalized endorsement of a new legal school of religious interpretation; in their time, the Ahl-i Hadith were only one such group shaping a self-affirming model of devotion.

In 1849, Hanafi scholars of the Calcutta Madrassa wrote and circulated a pamphlet criticizing the Ahl-i Hadith for having created a "fifth," Wahhabi, school alongside the four main schools of Sunni jurisprudence.⁵⁴ The authors condemned the Ahl-i Hadith for creating public turmoil (*fasad*) in the bazaars of Calcutta, for being ignorant (*jahil*), and for misleading people through intervention "in mosques, among Muslims observant of the namaz (prayer)"⁵⁵ in Lucknow and the Carnatic.⁵⁶ The pamphlet reproduced an 1845 newspaper article published by Maulvi Hakim Ahmad Hussain in the *Akhbar-i 'Ainah-yi Giti Numa*, in which he described the Ahl-i Hadith beliefs as innovation (*bid'at*), clearly forbidden in all schools of fiqh, as renunciation of the faith (*shirk*), and as the devil's work (*shaitani*).⁵⁷ The pamphlet indicated four points of Ahl-i Hadith divergence from Hanafi norms for ritual practices, three of which related to ritual practice in congregational prayer: the Ahl-i Hadith prescribed a different length of nightly recitation of the Quran and prayer in the month of Ramadan than that recommended in Hanafi practice; they gave vernacular translations of the Quran into the hands of people and declared the commentaries of the scholars of Islam as *bid'at*; they bound their hands just below the navel during prayer, right hand over left;[58] they loudly recited the *amin* during the prayer.[59] Of these ritual preferences, the Hanafi's considered the last to be the most egregious owing to the blatant disregard for the stipulation, "the *amin* (amen) and *tasbihin* (invocation of God's name during prayer) should not be loudly intoned," taken from the Hanafi text *Bahar al-Raiq* and encoded in the *Fatawa Alamgiriyya*. The *Fatawa* recommended that if someone was to intone these words loudly, they should carry out 100 repentant prostrations.[60]

To the Hanafi 'ulama, the Ahl-i Hadith appeared deliberately incendiary; the 'ulama of Calcutta,[61] Delhi,[62] Madras,[63] and Mecca[64] issued condemnations of their ritual preferences, of the public spectacles which they made of themselves, and of ways in which they undermined the values and beliefs of a wider community of Sunni believers.[65] Other Hanafi scholars presented the accusation that maulvis from Delhi arriving at mosques in villages and small towns were using water to wash for prayer which had been polluted by animals fallen in, an illustration of Ahl-i Hadith disregard for principles of purity that was repeated in multiple Hanafi pamphlets and discourses at the time. Such remarks were presented by Hanafis as counsel to a Muslim public, encouraging identification with Hanafi principles of bodily comportment.[66]

Antagonism towards the colonial administration and the Hanafi religious establishment fueled Ahl-i Hadith efforts to achieve a landmark judgment in the Tajpur mosque case in 1891. The Ahl-i Hadith had committed to a course of legal activism in defense of vocal devotionalism in congregational prayer across the region. In at least two other cases brought to colonial courts in the late nineteenth century, Ahl-i Hadith worshippers asserted the permissibility of their ritual preferences in Sunni, presumably Hanafi, mosques. In Maddanpura, Banaras, in 1884, three men joined the congregation and recited the *amin* loudly. A relative of the mosque's founder brought an accusation to the magistrate and the instigator of this intervention was tried under criminal law, at first sentenced to rigorous imprisonment for having "insulted the religion of the Hanafi Muslims," and then released on appeal as it was argued that the case should have rightly been tried under civil law. Justice Mahmud, son of Sayyid Ahmad Khan, composed the final ruling in the Maddanpura matter based on a reading of Islamic sources and strongly defending his correctness in engaging this jurisprudential tradition in his deliberations. Mahmud concluded that while there were hadith that told that the Prophet Muhammad had recommended that the *amin* be uttered in a low voice and Hanafis preferred these traditions, Muslims of the Shafi school did not concur. More importantly he argued that a mosque, being God's land, was open to all Muslims and a majority could not deprive a minority of a "right of worship" through accusations that their intonations constituted a criminal disturbance.[67]

In Jalalipura, Banaras, in 1889 the custodian and patron of that mosque had sought to bar the Ahl-i Hadith from entry,[68] but Justice Mahmud once again ruled in this case that the mosques must be open to all and "cannot be dedicated or appropriated exclusively to any particular school or sect of Sunni Muhammadans. Members of the Wahhabi sect are Muhammadans and as such entitled to perform their devotions in a mosque."[69] Ahl-i Hadith were successfully engaging colonial law to elicit broad legal and social recognition of their legitimacy despite the fact that they were a "minority" and at odds with the Islamic normativity articulated and defended by the Hanafi 'ulama. Their established network of financiers and advisors became involved in the affairs of the Tajpur mosque.

The Tajpur Mosque Dispute

Many of the worshippers at the mosque of Tajpur believed that prayer leaders should fulfill public expectations which were, in turn, shaped by the principles of Islamic normativity established during the Mughal period. In the absence of a state which would enforce Hanafi doctrinal precedent and emboldened by the suspicions of the 'ulama and British officials toward the reformist Ahl-i Hadith, Omed Ali and others refused to pray in the congregation convened by Mowla Baksh. Omed Ali gave a separate call to prayer and the Hanafis prayed in congregation behind him, acting on their conviction that members of the congregation should worship as they expected to. The Ahl-i Hadith took the matter to the court.

Omed Ali and others, the Hanafi defendants in the Tajpur case, were supported by Muhammad Yahya, Omed Ali's employer and also a lawyer with connections to the court of the district magistrate.[70] Muhammad Yahya scripted a response: as the law then stood, the courts in fact had no jurisdiction in the matter as "the determination of religious matters is opposed to public policy." But he, in fact, sought a ruling on what constituted normative Islamic values. Opponents of the Ahl-i Hadith in Maddanpura and in Banaras invoked criminal law to describe the reformists as disruptive and to bar them from the congregation. The Hanafis of Tajpur denied the authority of Mowla Baksh over the congregation while defending that of the prayer leader and the silent Hanafi congregation in the other cases. Their attention was not on the mosque but on a debate in which even colonial officers took righteous positions: what constituted Islamic normativity and deviance. Their case set up the legal, doctrinal, and historic reasons why their expectations for the appropriate form of congregational prayer in the Tajpur mosque should prevail.

This site was a Mughal waqf, argued the Hanafis, and therefore worship must conform to the Hanafi "creed" as Mughal emperors who endorsed Islamic law and scholarship had made the endowment and it had been entrusted to the qazi's office in this religious spirit. The expectations of Hanafi practice upheld by the congregation, argued Omed Ali and others, were derived from the original vision for the mosque which they remembered, naming the authorized custodians of the Mughal period, recalling also those involved in construction and renovation projects. These same observant Muslims were "dissatisfied with" Mowla Baksh and the custodians and "do not wish that they should have a hand in its management."[71]

Omed Ali approached the magistrate in 1882 and asked that the magistrate carry out an enquiry and investigation into the religious dispute. The magistrate agreed with Omed Ali's allegation that Mowla Baksh's actions were "illegal" and "should not be performed in the presence of orthodox Sunnis" and passed an order directing Mowla Baksh not to loudly intone words of the prayer "before the Muslims of the Hanafi persuasion" in the mosque at Tajpur.[72] He was in accord with Omed Ali that Hanafi practices were normative religious behaviors, an impression which originated in his social and political understanding of northeast Indian community as this British administrator professed he was "not at all acquainted with the Mohammedan religion."[73] When Mowla Baksh continued to vocalize the *amin*, the magistrate took the only action he was authorized to: he sent in the police on the charge that Mowla Baksh had disrupted the public order by vocalizing the *amin* and antagonizing the Hanafis and then picking up a stick to beat Omed Ali and other worshippers who congregated in silent and peaceful prayer outside the mosque.[74]

The weakest of Omed Ali's arguments and the most critical was that the creed of Hanafism should be differentiated from Wahhabism, the "heterodox" and "interreligious creed" of the qazi's sons who had inherited the custodianship of the mosque. He argued that "conversion" from Hanafism to Wahhabism violated the terms of custodianship under Anglo-Muhammadan law, that earlier management of the waqf had provided for Mowla Baksh as a muezzin and an imam, roles ordained in the Hanafi text and without equivalent in the Ahl-i Hadith discourse and therefore Mowla Baksh had effectively eliminated his own role at the mosque. While these views were passionately articulated by Omed Ali and others who refused Mowla Baksh's leadership, their lawyer could not back up the accusation of deviancy through reference to Islamic legal texts which expressly forbade the vocal *amin*.

In response, Mowla Baksha and the two custodians together filed a suit for a legal declaration that they alone had the rights to "deliver the Friday oration and perform the daily prayers in the mosque," in spite of the disagreement of members of the congregation with their preferred choice of ritual,[75] and any interference with these rights was mischief, defamation, ridicule, and trouble. The suit brought forward by Mowla Baksh and the custodians was supported by Ahmedullah, a local zamindar and an early adherent to Ahl-i Hadith practice who identified as Sunni of the "Ahl-i Hadith" preference and paid the 200 rupee cost of the first suit and appeal on behalf of the custodians and prayer leader.[76] The total costs incurred in the Indian courts totaled over 500 rupees, and the cost of the appeal in the Privy Council totaled almost 250 pounds sterling. The costliest part of the case was summoning witnesses who could dispute the administration's belief about the deviancy of Ahl-i Hadith practice; over half the total costs were incurred summoning witnesses.[77]

The Ahl-i Hadith of Tajpur confronted their challengers by describing a present which had broken from the politics and patronage systems of the past. Every witness testified that there were no longer any incomes from waqf land to speak of. A financial crisis faced the mosque after the confiscation of waqf lands and so the pastureland was given over to Mowla Baksh[78] to supplement a salary of 2 rupees and 8 annas[79] that was paid by Fazal Karim out of his personal income.[80] Mowla Baksh testified that he did not receive any supplemental allowance for travelers visiting the mosque.[81] One defendant gave testimony that "so long as Kazi Ramizuddin was alive the attached inn (*musafirkhana*) was in existence," but he had not "seen" the inn in five or six years.[82] Sheikh Ahmedullah had contributed a great deal of personal funds for the renovation of the mosque in the 1870s.[83] Abdul Wahhab, the Munsiff of Tajpur who provided crucial testimony in the case, had himself advanced the money for the renovation of the mosque in the 1870s.[84] Other residents of Tajpur were asked to commit funds or "subscriptions" to the mosque funds in any amount that they could afford and had done so at the time of the renovation of the mosque.[85] This financial restructuring of the mosque had ensured its survival. This philanthropy is notable; unlike the imperial and elite waqfs that created surplus funds for mosques by creating revenue remissions on agricultural land, mosque subscriptions or donations were funded by individuals using their personal income; the very structure of patronage had changed and a contemporary form of giving eclipsed the founding bequests of the past. References to Mughal-era patronage seemed dated and irrelevant.

As the case progressed through the courts, the Ahl-i Hadith criticized the state for its involvement in the Tajpur matter. Drawing on Justice Mahmud's language in his judgment in *Ramzan v. the Queen Empress*, the Ahl-i Hadith labeled the first magistrate's order banning Mowla Baksh from his vocalizations during prayer as harassment and an "unauthorized interference with their religious rights."[86] Their lawyer also presented an 1876 judgment of the judicial commissioner of the Punjab that stated that a local magistrate had not been empowered to order the Wahhabis of a village to convene their congregation in a mosque and pray thirty minutes after the Sunnis.[87] The magistrates in both cases had invoked a section of the criminal procedure code which allowed them to temporarily stay religious and cultural activities that provoked social tensions. We learn in Chapter 3 that the courts recognized the rights of magistrates to invoke section 144 of the criminal procedure code to control the perimeter of the mosque but colonial jurists described the magistrate's arrangements for prayer in the interior of the mosque as unwarranted interference in religious matters which were to be derived from the Quran and hadith. Omed Ali and others had not demonstrated any commendable variety of loyalty to the state, the Ahl-i Hadith argued. Rather, they had revealed a corrupted and rotting vein of the colonial administrative system: those officers who sought to assume authority in native religious affairs.

Ahl-i Hadith facility with text, language, translation, and notions of authority enabled them to produce an insurmountable defense of their style of worship. Mowla Baksh and the custodians of the mosque produced a single fatwa signed by some prominent 'ulama of Delhi which set out that while Hanafi scholars may have discouraged the loudly intoned *amin* or the remembrance of God, they did not prohibit these practices, and differences between the great *mujtahids* of the four Sunni schools were minor and unremarkable. These same differences were being exploited, they said, by those promoting fractious politics.

> And whereas at Delhi and other cities, often ignorant men having raised meaningless contentions on minor religious doctrines have published notifications and pamphlets of various kinds, and on many occasions such notifications and pamphlets have been seen by us. Although in our own way we wanted to put a stop to and suppress the same, yet the foolish people did not desist, and in minor matters carried contention to Court. Each party in their speeches and writings began to denounce

their opponents as reprobates excluded from the Sunnat Jamat (members of the Sunni community) and allowed mischief and perverseness to go on increasing among ourselves. The mischief which came into existence at this place caused contentions and disputes to be spread among the Moslems of other towns and hamlets and criminal cases were instituted. . . . Inasmuch as when the noble companions of the Prophet and the great mujtahids often differed from one another in minor religious doctrines, but not withstanding the existence of this difference, they did not bear any ill feeling towards one another. One did not consider the other as excluded from the Sunnat Jamat . . . . The questions in which differences exist are the following: impurity of water, speaking aloud of the word amen at the time of saying prayers, raising up of hands at the time of saying prayers, and raising up of the forefinger. Other acts in which differences exits, are considered by some people as prohibited and by some as permissive [sic]. In short, the bounds of moderation have been exceeded. One party must not revile and disdain the other party's mode of saying prayers. The saying of prayers by one party behind the other party is allowable, provided the act does not in any way tend to any evil purpose.[88]

They asked, therefore, for the courts to recognize that, under Islamic law, "Mussalmans in general have no right of any kind beyond attending the masjid at the time of prayer and saying such prayers under the leadership of its imam and going away," and to do otherwise was contrary to "Mahomedan Law."[89]

While the expectations of Omed Ali and others related to the use of mosque infrastructure and social rights of access to this important civic space, the dispute was reduced to one over ritual authenticity and argued on that basis. The Ahl-i Hadith presented Mowla Baksh's vocalizations as permissible, asserted his right to convene the congregation and lead prayer in the Tajpur mosque as singular and inviolable, denied general social rights of access to the mosque for any purpose other than participating in the congregation led by Mowla Baksh, and cast Omed Ali and others as disrupters of community peace. The unity of the congregation in the mosque was presented as the alternative to the unity of the Muslim public outside the mosque, and the more effective means of maintaining peaceful interrelations between Muslims.

The Disengagement of the Colonial State with the Congregation

The Ahl-i Hadith had been under the scrutiny of the state and the Hanafi establishment on the principle that their organization, utterances, and motives should be related to and examined in relation to public imperatives. In 1882, the mosque was a space of surveillance and state intervention and the first two judgments in the Tajpur mosque case asserted the deviancy and incendiary nature of Ahl-i Hadith practice, but admission of the Ahl-i Hadith appeal to the Privy Council[90] recalibrated the relationship between law and administrative policy. In the absence of a qazi whose "moral probity and knowledge of local arrangements could translate precept into practice"[91] the Tajpur mosque case provided an opportunity to examine and limit the extent of the courts' involvement in the interpretations of doctrine, establishing the principle of colonial secularism while acknowledging the complex interplay of religion in the everyday lives of Indians.

The case originated in the newly constituted court of the munsif of Muzaffarpur. This lowest order of civil court in northeast India ruled against the plaintiffs in 1883 on the grounds that "the mosque was of the nature of an endowed public property. . . . The court, it seems, is not empowered to compel the defendants to adopt certain forms of religions which are against their principles and contrary to their faith." The munsif believed that Muslims could pray how and when they chose in that space and so long as they did not commit any criminal nuisance or offense in the mosque, "they could not be prohibited from having an access" to the mosque. Moreover, this jurist felt the courts had no role at all in mediating contests over rights in the mosque and these should be resolved naturally.[92]

The case had originated in the court of another jurist, Nurul Hassan, who was very sympathetic to the Ahl-i Hadith case for a legal declaration of the rights of the imam and custodian in the mosque. However the Ahl-i Hadith asked for the case to be moved from Nur Ahmed's court in order that he could appear as a witness for them.[93] Rather than seeking sympathizers, the Ahl-i Hadith were involved in a negotiation of the very substance of the law. The subsequent appeal by the Ahl-i Hadith challenged, among other things, the reduction of the rights of the custodian and imam to playing a service role in the mosque. "The custodian of a mosque," the plaintiffs said, "is a real managing proprietor and the mosque is solely under his charge, and the imam and muezzin of the mosque is the assistant and under the custodian."[94]

The first appeal court found that there were precedents for treating places of worship as trusts, an evolution of colonial law that has been charted by Ritu Birla. The laws governing the custody of places of worship were first articulated in 1863. The Indian Trust Act of 1882 sought to eliminate any personal or private benefit that accrued from the use of and management of places of religious worship, and further defined a collective benefit from the act of endowment; this legal process ascribed equal rights over and interests in religious buildings to those who could be associated with the faith.[95] Under these laws, Hindu temples were identified as tax-free trusts or perpetuities under the proposal that each was "serving a public purpose of a religious or charitable nature." In the case of Hindu personal law regarding temples, the Hindu deity was the beneficiary of the trust and Hindu worshippers of the deity moved the courts to defend the deity's rights;[96] in the case of mosques, Muslim worshippers were the beneficiaries of the trust and moved the courts in defense of their own rights of worship in mosques. "A suit related to noise (of the vocal *amin*)... is tenable in a civil court," argued the judge in the Tajpur case in 1884, and "a suit in which the right to an office is contested is a civil suit."[97]

A third judgment in 1884 offered an involved juridical argument based in a Hanafi precept that the custodian and imam must indeed fulfill the expectations of the congregation.

> The duties of [Mowla Baksh] being the imam and muezzin of a mosque, his principal duties are to give *azans* and to lead the prayers in it, and such being his duties, all worshippers are to pray behind him; and if a portion of the worshippers or followers believe that their imam has changed his faith and that his prayers are not being made in accordance with the principles and doctrines of their faith, the prayers of those worshippers would necessarily be incorrect. That this is the opinion of all the learned doctors of the Mahomedan religion, has been satisfactorily established by almost all the authoritative books of the Hanifi mazhab.[98]

The first and third judgments, delivered by members of the colonial district administration, were reinforced by the polemical position that the custodians and Mowla Baksh were Ahl-i Hadith and therefore "dissenters from the Hanafi practice (*madhab*)," while Omed Ali and others were "Hanafites and followers of the orthodox faith of Islam, and for whose prayer the mosque in question seems to be original erected, have rather preferential and more superior claims to... pray in the mosque."[99] Both of these judgments grappled with the notion of what a mosque was in relation to other spaces and territories subject to colonial jurisprudence. The first judgment treated it as an unproblematically public space while the third was inspired by Hanafi jurisprudence to invoke a role for the government in defending the righteousness of the individual worshipper.

The judge who issued the prevailing judgment also assessed the prevailing civic functions of mosques and offered a crucial clarification. While "the mosque is dedicated to the public... [the custodians and imam] have, I think, a right to prevent it being used for any other purpose.... The mosque, unlike a public road, is not to every intent and purpose a public place."[100] Road building, construction, and management preoccupied district governments and the Public Works Department across the region and enhanced the significance of this metaphor for the infrastructure that could be claimed in use by all, and the uses of which were the concern of the state.

The prevailing judgment also used sectarian categories as a means to orient and reconcile diverse uses and objectives for the mosque. The Ahl-i Hadith vocalization in worship was, he said, admitted by Shafis, and

> in all Mahomedan countries like Turkey, Egypt, Arabia itself, Hanafis and Shafis go to the same mosque, and form members of the same congregation. And whilst the Hanafis say the word "amen" in a low voice, the Shafis pronounce it aloud, and that in the greatest mosque, viz., the Kaaba itself, the followers of all four imams are at full liberty to pray according to their own tenets.[101]

Anecdotal references to the monumental mosques of the Islamic empires elicited an ideal of worship associated with normative Sunni or Shi'a doctrinal approaches. It followed that any Sunni religious practice should be sanctioned in a Sunni mosque, and any Shi'a religious practice in a Shi'a mosque.

Despite making reference to religious and cultural precepts and admitting a religious dispute for adjudication by the courts, colonial jurists asserted that they had a secular outlook in all legal matters. The Tajpur mosque case offers a unique opportunity to understand this paradox of colonial law. A judge of an appellate court asserted that the dispute between the two groups at the Tajpur mosque was not of a civil nature, purely a religious one.[102] A few months later an appellate court delivered a verdict on the incompatibility of Hanafi and Ahl-i Hadith practice using a device from the Islamic juridical tradition to assess whether the Ahl-i Hadith subscribed to the juridical traditions of the Hanafi 'ulama in matters of *ijma'* or consensus and ascertained that they must be considered to have deviated in their practices. These judgments highlighted the lacuna in colonial civil procedures: where the lower courts had been compelled to admit mediation of the dispute, the judges were not empowered or able to rule on the derivation of religious practices or the correctness of religious predisposition.

The evaluative procedures followed by the courts in the Tajpur case demonstrated the difficulties of examining and judging normativity according to religious doctrine. No evidence of normative Hanafi doctrinal principles was presented in the first suit; the munsif of Muzaffarpur received and evaluated evidence of prevailing ritual practices based on oral testimonies of Omed Ali and others who identified as "Hanafi" to establish a pattern of customary practice in the Tajpur mosque. The courts did not judge the correctness or incorrectness of those majority practices according to Islamic law but rather through a casual enumeration of social consensus regarding mosque use. These proceedings demonstrate how judges in the lower courts evaluated religion as a social preference and steered clear of engaging with the reasoning at its core, a strategy which was the colonial state's legal secularism at work.[103]

The treatment of two different pieces of evidence in the 1886 judgment of the district judge of Muzaffarpur demonstrates how the problem of religious reasoning and legal process was resolved. The fatwa by thirty-six 'ulama of Delhi signed in the presence of the commissioner of Delhi[104] included excerpts from the reformist text *Hujatullah al-Baligha* and the *Fatawa Alamgiriyya* and provided evidence of established Hanafi practices of management of the mosque including the following quote: "even if the imam be a *fasik* (reprobate), still it is necessary that the Friday prayers be said under his leadership."[105] Maulvi Nurul Hasan, the munsif of Tajpur, also testified and was classed as "the best witness in this case owing to his position and learning in religious matters which entitle him to the greatest credit."[106] While self-identifying as a Hanafi, learned and able to discuss texts, Nurul Hasan testified that he saw nothing wrong with praying behind an Ahl-i Hadith in the mosque and had often done so.[107] It was, finally, not text but this socially respectable interlocutor who had personally mediated the established doctrines of the faith with the exigencies of religious change in the Tajpur mosque who swayed the court. This evidence compelled the court to admit that Ahl-i Hadith practices were not at odds with other Hanafi practices and constituted a general category of Sunni worship which was permissible in a Sunni mosque because they were subscribed to by a learned, socially responsible gentleman.[108] The courts adjudicated disputes between people but did not admit ideals and philosophies from Indian religions. Nurul Amin modeled an ideal pious citizen for the courts, and the judges held that if Ahl-i Hadith practice did not offend him, it should not offend anyone.

The judgment delivered by the Judicial Committee of the Privy Council in 1891 enabled the state to distance itself from engaging with the inevitable future disputes over religious authenticity which would occur in mosques across South Asia. The judgment stated that the prayer leader was free from "his predecessor's practice," and from the obligation to follow all four Sunni schools of law as "no imam can follow all four in everything." It freed the imam or muezzin of the mosque to introduce "variations" in "gesture, intonation or otherwise" that were not explicitly forbidden in Sunni law. Julia Stephens's recent work on colonial governance of Islam attends to the logic employed by the author of the JCPC judgment, Arthur Hobhouse, who was prone to unsettling religious authorities in the colonies. His judgment rejected the social principle of *taqlid* (following established authority in religious practice).[109] Hobhouse "not only ruled against *taqlid*, he refused to even acknowledge the possibility of an argument in its favor."[110] Stephens establishes the implications of this decision for colonial jurisprudence in general: colonial law categorically rejected reason derived from Islamic authorities. The decision had an equally profound impact on everyday Islam: the prayer congregation was consigned to the authority of the prayer leader, a hitherto powerless and insignificant servant of the mosque. The colonial mediation of the Ahl-i Hadith case for legitimation of control over the Tajpur mosque, itself a result of reformist transformations of Islam, produced even greater freedoms of religious leadership in the mosque. Now the colonial establishment, beginning with the magistrate's office, needed to intervene only when broad sect-based laws of worship were violated.

Conclusion

The case put together by Muhammad Yahya to defend Omed Ali and others' expectations of prayer in the mosque fell apart almost immediately. "Against all this evidence of learned and devout Mahomedans and of the actual practice of Mahomedan worshippers," the JCPC said in reference to the Ahl-i Hadith position, "what is there on the other side? The evidence is an absolute blank. No book, no opinion, no practice of any community of worshippers is cited."[111] Within two years, eight of the defendants standing with Omed Ali withdrew their assertions that the Ahl-i Hadith style of prayer was an unacceptable deviation. They were unable to establish that their expectations for the mosque and the legitimacy of their separate congregational prayer had any foundation in classical Islamic legal tradition or the practice of Anglo-Muhammadan law and became uncertain of this position.[112]

The Hanafi case had not been inspired so much by Islamic law as it had originated in precolonial and early colonial statecraft in which the mosque was regulated as civic infrastructure and legal officers of the state attended to the expectations of a Muslim public. The legal procedures in the Tajpur mosque case allowed jurists to ignore the authoritative reasoning of the Hanafi 'ulama and unburden themselves of responsibility for adjudicating future disputes in mosques, the goal of colonial secularism. This had its profound consequences for the state. The Judicial Committee of the Privy Council reflected that the mosque was not a public place in the manner that a road was. It neither fell to the state to oversee its use, nor was it appropriate for a general Muslim population to assume general rights and interests in it. Under a disinterested state, the only right remaining to the general Muslim public was that of attending the mosque for the purpose of worship and the performance of the congregational prayer was consigned to the control of the prayer leader. This was the first of several judgments committing aspects of mosque use to the charge of officers who could resolve disputes among Muslims and model preferences for them using their own discretion and reasoning. Transferring an important role of the precolonial state to everyday religious functionaries in neighborhood mosques, this decision authorized prayer leaders to impose their ritual preferences in the mosque to produce unity and peace within the congregation.

Chapter 2

RANGOON, 1916

Muslim Diversity and Custodial Control of Instruction in the Mosque

Introduction

Moolla Hashim was a trader from Rander in the western Indian trading city of Surat. He moved to Rangoon shortly after the colonial conquest of the delta region in 1852 and built a timber mosque on a corner plot on Mogul Street, an intersection which would become the heart of the city. This became the popular Rangoon Friday Mosque which drew the Muslims who migrated to Rangoon as a major port of colonial India. Other Indian laborers, professionals, and capitalists followed; they purchased property, set up rice mills and timber companies, and offered financial services, stimulating trade and commerce. A large number of places of worship were built by migrant Hindus, Muslims, and Parsis who shaped the emerging built environment to serve their communities. Multiple mosques were established alongside the Rangoon Friday Mosque, each serving a community of Muslims of common regional origin or ideological leaning. A variety of instructional priorities influenced the choice of religious celebration, sermon, and schooling at each of these establishments.

In 1908 a dispute arose within the Rangoon Friday Mosque congregation over the election of new custodians: some socially powerful members of the community, inspired by the ideal of democratic Muslim organization, challenged the hereditary rights of Randeris who had been authorized by the founder of the mosque to manage the mosque. In response the custodians provided evidence of sizable personal contributions for the mosque by its founding Randeri trustees and denied the principle of a parity of Muslim rights over and ties to this iconic institution. The suit escalated to a final appeal hearing by the Judicial Committee of the Privy Council. The legal proceedings led to a 1916 judgment that authorized custodial control without reference to the congregation's preferences in the mosque.

The fact that custodians exercised social influence from their positions in mosques has been established generally by Gregory Kozlowksi in his seminal work on *Muslim Endowments and Society in British India*. In this chapter I work from Kozlowski's conclusions to evaluate the impact of the legal principle of custodial control in the mosque. Custodians of the Rangoon Friday Mosque sanctioned the mosque school curriculum and the appointment of the preacher who delivered Friday sermons, controlling discourse and the communication of ideas in this space. The JCPC judgment reaffirmed that they could exercise this control without referring to the preferences or expectations of their diverse congregation. This was the social influence that mosque custodians exercised, and it in principle prohibited the sort of public debate and dialog in the mosque which has been presupposed in a large body of scholarly work.[1]

The Mosque Trusts of Rangoon and their Custodians

By the late nineteenth century state and Muslim society understood mosques to be established through an act of endowment,[2] governed in perpetuity according to the preference of the founder and managed day to day by a mosque trustee, referred to as custodian of the trust. The mosque trustee took the name of "custodian" from English law and the title "*mutawalli*" from an Islamic legal and religious tradition. Terms of appointment of the custodian were set out by, or interpreted from, the declaration of the endowment. Custodianship of an endowment was usually hereditary or passed to a successor by the incumbent without reference to the community of worshippers at the mosque. This norm was mutually constituted by mosque benefactors and the framework of colonial law which did not require congregations' authorization of custodians as managers of mosque assets and activities.

A mosque custodian managed and accounted for the income from mosque assets and made investments for the trust. He appointed the prayer leader and staff for cleaning and maintenance, planned for renovation and expansion of the premises, distributed charity, and gave approval for other activities in the mosque. These other activities could include instruction for children, extraordinary prayers services for a death on an important calendar date such as the Prophet's birth anniversary. Colonial Burma's many mosques, established during the nineteenth and early twentieth century in close proximity to one another, offer a unique opportunity for comparison of and focus on programs of activities in mosques, migrant Indians' deep concern with the nature of this programming, and the manner in which congregations' rights were constrained by the rights of the mosque custodian in the mosque.

It is important here to recollect that trusts were, in principle, financial instruments which safeguarded private capital. Trustees or operators of a trust have fiduciary responsibilities to beneficiaries which are governed by the terms on which the trust is created. Trusts were widely used in Burma in the late nineteenth century by many of the same wealthy entrepreneurs who endowed the mosques of Rangoon. Moolla Hashim, the benefactor who endowed the Rangoon Friday Mosque, also entrusted a small portion of his considerable wealth for his second wife. His shrewd use of the instrument of waqf supported his family's "transition into a new economic, social and political situation," like that of propertied Muslims across north India.[3]

> I direct my said executors and trustees to hold ten shares of the Soortee Barra Bazaar Company, Limited, upon trust, to pay the dividends and income to my second wife Hassan Boo ... during her lifetime and on her decease [sic] to transfer the said shares to my sixth son.[4]

The financial instrument of the trust protected a portion of Moolla Hashim's capital, in this case ten shares worth about Rs 5,000 at the time, from immediate distribution among inheritors and made it possible for Moolla Hashim to provide for his second wife in a different manner than what was dictated by Islamic inheritance laws. The named managers of the trust, Moolla Hashim's three oldest sons, were directed to fulfill his wishes to provide the income from the ten shares to his second wife for her lifetime. Details of the bequest were undoubtedly communicated to Hassan Boo as well.

Mosque custodians took on these same fiduciary responsibilities and obligations with regards to the mosque trust, managing mosque assets and infrastructure for the purpose of preserving the building as a place of worship, and thereby serving worshippers as beneficiaries of the trust. The Islamic concept of waqf, the parceling of private land and properties to finance a religious objective, was understood by colonial legislators to correspond to the instrument of the trust. We may recall that in the precolonial context, the creation of a waqf by elites was not necessarily a private act as we cannot draw a clear distinction between private and public roles of landowners, minor notables, and wealthy merchants who were allies of the state. However the act of endowing a religious activity, shrine or mosque, became classified as an act of a private individual, drawing on private resources, to benefit the public in the same manner that Moolla Hashim's small bequest of ten shares benefitted Hasan Boo. A trustee with fiduciary responsibilities also had to be appointed to this "public" trust to fulfill its objectives, to define the interests of public beneficiaries and determine the activities of the trust which would fulfill those interests.

Moolla Hashim's waqfs provide us important examples of the public trust as corollary to the private trust: he left money to several preexisting religious trusts in Surat, Moulmein, and Rangoon, cities he called his own by birth, residence, and business interest respectively, indicating the specific purposes for which he wished the capital to be put to work. He set up endowments benefitting six madrassas:

> To the Trustees of the Surat Madrassa of Surat six shares of the Rangoon iron Bazaar Company Ltd., upon trust that the income and dividends thereof shall from time to time be expended by them on the education of Mahomedan children.... [T]o the Trustees of the of the Variao Wali [Madrassa] at Rander twelve and a half shares of the Soortee Bara Bazaar Company Limited, upon trust that the income and dividends thereof shall from time to time be expended by them for the education of Mahomedan children.... To transfer to the Trustees of the Sunni Bhona Jama'at Panchayat of Rander my plank house and premises at Opho Dinewunkwin Moulmein upon trust that one-half of the net rents and income shall be expended by them for the benefit of four madrassas at Rander and the other half for the maintenance and funeral expended of travelers who happen to be there and die there.

He created charitable funds for the poor:

> To the Trustees of the Kushatee Jumat at Randeer forty shares of the Naya Bustee Bazaar of Moulmein upon trust that the income and dividends thereof shall from time to time be expended by them in distributing among the paupers of that place annually ... to the Trustees of the Sunni Chona Panchayat of Rander eighty shares of the Naya Bustee Bazaar of Moulmein upon trust that the income and dividends thereof shall from time to time be expended by them in distributing among paupers of that place annually.

And he gave funds to support religious activities of other Muslims:

> To the Trustees of Moolla Cassim's Mosque at Kaladan in Moulmein my pucca house and premises built on first class lot No. 2051 and adjoining the said Mosque and the other half for the maintenance and funeral expenses of travelers who happen to be there and die there.... [T]o the Trustees of the Sunni Bhona Jama'at Panchayat of Rangoon my pucca house in Barr Street in Rangoon ... that the net rent and incomes thereof

shall from time to time be expended by them for the following objects and purposes: To pay the sum of ten rupees to each pilgrim who may desire to go to Mecca from Rangoon, Rander and Moulein. . . . To pay towards the repair and lighting of all the mosques at Rangoon Rander and Moulmein. . . . To pay for the performance of [milads] at Rander Rangoon and Moulmein. . . . To pay towards the breaking of fast in the Ramzan holiday at Rangoon, Rander and Moulmein. . . . To purchase a house at Mecca for the lodging of [hajis]. . . . I also direct my said executors and Trustees to hold ten shares of the Soortee Barra Bazaar Company Limited, upon trust to expend the dividends and profits . . . in annual religious ceremonies after the custom of our faith for my benefit.[5]

Trustees of existing institutions named in Moolla Hashim's waqfs were charged with deploying the income from the entrusted capital for defined purposes: education, paying for expenses of paupers or travelers, funding pilgrimages to Mecca, lighting of all mosques across Rangoon, and ritual congregational activities in Ramadan, on the anniversary of the Prophet's birth and in Moolla Hashim's own memory. The work of the trustees was governed by the brief dedications alone and the public beneficiaries, many of them guest workers who travelled to Burma in the rice growing season or for trade, were unknown and unknowing of the bequests made in their names until the trustees planned and scheduled and advertised the activities which fulfilled Moolla Hashim's general instructions.

The Urdu vernacular term for the custodian, *mutawalli*, was taken from works on Islamic law that described the *mutawalli* as appointed manager and guardian of the mosque. Under colonial law, the custodian's responsibilities in the mosque were reinterpreted as a custodianship of assets and fiduciary responsibility to beneficiaries. Custodian/*mutawallis* were not required to refer to public expectations for that trust although these were widely debated in literature, works or Islamic law, and popular discourse, a topic I will explore further in Chapter 3. Custodian/*mutawallis* were only required to make reference to broad parameters set out by the endower a premise which gave them expansive and largely arbitrary control over trust, that is, over the mosque itself. As we know from Tajpur, custodians were required to observe the bounds of normative Islamic practice but retained discretionary control over a variety of other activities. These other activities could be minor rituals in prayer, as in Tajpur, and they could be any of a number of non-obligatory activities that took place in mosques.

A large number of mosques were established around the dense urban space of colonial Rangoon, and their custodians made arrangements for a variety of activities for the communities they served. Three men associated with the Cholia community privately purchased land and built a wooden building in a street north of Dalhousie for prayer on this land around 1856. The land was registered as a waqf in 1869 through a deed of conveyance to two named individuals as custodians of the mosque. The endowers of the mosque relied, at the time, on an instrument of transfer of title, but explained their intent in a deed of waqf (*waqfnamah*).[6] The mosque land was expanded by additional purchases of plots in 1858, 1879, and 1882 and a *pucca* brick-and-mortar prayer building and nine shops with frontages onto Dalhousie Street were erected. In 1899, a scheme for management of the mosque was filed and five trustees were appointed. They solicited donations and refurbished, expanded, and rebuilt the mosque several times in later years, enhancing the mosque endowment and its incomes. They operated a madrassa on the mosque premises from 1924 to 1928 and hired a renown Armenian architect to redesign the mosque in the 1930s. In later years the buildings adjoining the main prayer hall were used as wedding halls and could be rented out by members of the community.[7] A mosque was endowed by the ethnically Variao-Gujarati Cassim Moosajee Gunda in 1903 and came to be known as an Ahl-i Hadith mosque of 25th Street.[8] While most Rangoon mosques, like the Friday and Cholia mosques, were endowed for the purpose of serving ethnic communities, a few, like the 25th Street mosque, promoted ideological and ritual approaches in Islam. The custodians of this mosque regularly invited reformist Ahl-i Hadith religious scholars from India to deliver the Friday sermon and drew an audience from across Rangoon.[9]

In 1852, the colonial establishment gave the Shi'as of Rangoon a plot for the construction of the "Mogul mosque," one of a number of free grants of land accorded for places of worship.[10] Other allotments "free from taxation and from purchase price" were also given to the American Baptist Mission, the Armenian Church, a Hindu temple, and a Chinese temple. Construction of a wooden building on the site was completed by 1854. In 1918, the Shi'a mosque was built anew in stone structure and included several shops. This construction was financed entirely through undocumented private donations. Two revenue properties were donated to the mosque in 1922 and 1930 and given out on rent to provide an income stream for the mosque.[11] A Shi'a Mogul Mosque Management Scheme was registered in 1910 articulating a vision for the mosque: to integrate Rangoon's Shi'as and connect them more directly and visibly to Persian culture. The Shi'as were influenced by the establishment of the Young Men's Persian Association, later renamed the Persian Association, in 1909.[12] Eight custodians who were named to the Shi'a Mogul mosque in 1910 were made responsible for communication with all the Shi'as of Rangoon to ascertain their collective will in matters of appointing new trustees and appointing a prayer leader (*pesh namaz*).¹³ These trustees and the democratic structure of "consultation" with the Shi'a community showed it was possible to knit worshippers into the system for mosque management.

The Rangoon Friday Mosque, a few blocks from the bazaar and north of the river docks, was the most spectacular mosque of late-nineteenth-century Rangoon and the subject of the pivotal 1916 decision. It had been endowed by Moolla Hashim during his own lifetime and was known both as the Surati Sunni Mosque of Rangoon and as the Friday Mosque. The original wooden structure erected in the 1850s was expanded and rebuilt in later years through a number of gifts including a 40 by 60-foot plot of land given over to the mosque by Cassim Ajim Dooply in 1860,¹⁴ and two plots of land given in grant by the commissioner's office, for "the purpose of Sunni Muslim worship," in 1862. Moolla Hashim added shops, residential quarters for the prayer leader (the Randeris preferred the idea of a *khatib*, a full time employee who was charged with giving the Friday sermon as well as leading the daily prayers), a room which could be rented out to travelers, and a building to serve as a school and extra prayer space for large religious congregations.

Where all private lots in Rangoon's town center were 100 by 60 feet, and most buildings were divided into apartments occupying a single floor, the mosque occupied most of a city block and was three stories high. Glossy teak floors reflected the lights from the Belgian glass chandeliers, and the expansiveness of the main prayer hall was accentuated by the height of the roof and the thickness of the walls that kept the building cool. The Friday mosque offered some relief from the cramped urban living conditions that new migrants to the city faced. Men washed away the dirt from the overcrowded city in a pool of water and watched colorful fish flit just under the surface as they washed their hands, arms, and faces in ritual ablution. Eid prayers were an opportunity for gathering of Muslims from around the city and drew worshippers who offered daily and Friday prayers in local mosques.¹⁵ The mosque was expanded and rebuilt in brick and stone in 1882 and then renovated again during the twentieth century at which time a magnificent pulpit arrived from India, its two symmetrical halves carved out of matching solid blocks of translucent marble. Mosque properties, including a four-story building adjacent to the main building and six shops which lined the back wall,¹⁶ brought in rents that in turn supported the maintenance and periodic renovation of the mosque and paid the salary of the mosque *khatib* and other mosque staff.

The mosques of Rangoon were established and governed with reference to the structure of the trust while also serving Muslims in a variety of ways beyond simply providing arrangements for the obligatory prayer. The structure of the trust locked mosque lands, properties, and incomes into the service of subsections of Muslim society—neighborhoods, ethnic groups, and ideological communities. Mosque programming in each of these institutions served a benefactor's priorities for Muslim society.

Kozlowksi has argued that Muslims used waqfs to safeguard private wealth and paid out large stipends to their families from waqf incomes, providing for them in perpetuity as well as benefitting from the social preeminence that came with creating monumental endowments.[17] Records of financial planning for the many mosques and madrassas of Rangoon, including the charities created by Moolla Hashim, do not provide evidence of such financial benefit to patrons' families. These records do, however, support Kowlowski's observation that endowments increased the social preeminence of custodians, many of whom may well have been related to the benefactors of mosques, by putting them in control of the resources of the mosque. Resources were devoted to arrangements for the obligatory prayer, funereal rites, pilgrimage, schooling, and extraordinary religious observances. These religious endowments enabled worship, congregation and moral advancement and provided everyday spaces of rest and respite. Under colonial law, mosque custodians were powerful agents of Islam.

Diversity and Disagreement

The custodians of the Rangoon Friday Mosque did not seek to fulfill either the state or the Muslim public's expectations for the mosque. They did not follow the early colonial administration's recommendation to build an addition to the mosque on land allocated in a government grant. Instead they mimicked a common north Indian strategy of mosque development and built shops on this land to create a source of income for the mosque, incurring the administration's disapproval. The commissioner's office once again accused the mosque custodians of being shrewd and calculating when the riot outside the mosque in 1893 brought the city to a standstill and the district magistrate blamed the mosque custodians for not having done more to prevent the violence.[18]

Unlike the custodians of the Shi'a Mogul Mosque, the committee and custodians of the Rangoon Friday Mosque did not seek or derive legitimacy from the broader patterns of public organization and identification that were emerging across the city and the region. Nor did they seek to unite and lead the ethically and economically diverse Muslim traders, money lenders, industrialists, laborers, and plantation workers who had immigrated to this delta region from as far west as Afghanistan and as near as eastern Bengal. They managed the mosque through strategies of community fund raising, social organization, and legal creativity which were unlike those at the Tajpur mosque or any of the other mosques which you will learn about in later chapters in this book, which were in turn unlike each other. Like all participants in all mosque affairs across South Asia, custodians, benefactors, worshippers, and observers had disagreements about priorities for this mosque. These differences catalyzed into a major legal suit for control over the Rangoon Friday Mosque in 1908.

Bequests of land and contributions of cash for the Rangoon Friday Mosque endowment had produced a unique management structure for the mosque and edged the city administration out of mosque affairs while also making it clear that nobody was intended to personally control or benefit from management of these assets. Five Randeris together contributed 2,000 rupees to purchase the grant lots outright and registered the land as "solely dedicated for the purpose of divine worship" in the "Sunni Friday mosque," and stipulated that "no one could lay exclusive claim to the liberties, privileges, easements, profits, emoluments, hereditaments [of the] said pieces and parcels of land."[19] After Moolla Hashim's death a committee of Randeri Suratis was charged with appointing custodians for the mosque trust.[20] The committee was identified in the documents of endowment of the Rangoon Friday Mosque and had also been named in Moolla Hashim's will, a close group of socially prominent and wealthy Randeri Suratis, all of whom were heavily invested in shared trade and business interests.[21] The committee had called a meeting in 1869 to discuss the financial affairs of the mosque. The meeting was held in another Randeri Surati's home, a place where business affairs were also often discussed.[22] These community notables appointed custodians for the mosque in 1879, 1894, and 1907. Moolla Hashim modeled a practice of giving into the hands of the committee of notables for the mosque; the notables appointed custodians. The complex relationship between the mosque and the ethnically defined merchant migrant community in Rangoon was mediated by recognizable benefactors and custodians.

Like all patterns of Muslim religious participation, there were exceptions to the Randeri Surati predominance in mosque affairs and therein lay the origins of the dispute related to this mosque. Because the mosque had received many contributions of land, objects, and cash over a number of years, the very question of who the original endower was whose will would govern the management of the trust could not be easily answered and a variety of people expressed their expectations for its governance. The 1869 meeting was attended by non-Randeris as well.[23] Collectively, these non-Randeris contributed something over Rs 3,000 into the hands of a leading non-Randeri businessman who turned the money over to the custodians. The Randeri Suratis contributed the largest amount of funds, over a thousand rupees each. The predominance of Randeri contributions appeared to stem from a coercive relationship between the custodial board and other Randeri families. When one Randeri Surati paid only Rs 1,500 of the Rs 3,000 he had promised, complaining that there had been too much pressure to pledge his contribution, the committee voted that he should be cast out of the community, rescinding this decision only when the remaining Rs 1,500 were paid on his behalf by a close relative.[24] Women were notably absent from meetings; men gave their assent to nominations by contributing their signatures on lists that were circulated.[25] In 1908, the registration of the dispute over the management of the Rangoon Friday Mosque produced a more complete definition of the custodians' nomination committee as constituted by "members of the [Gujarati trader] community, residents in the town of Rangoon who originally came from Rander . . . and the descendants of such persons."[26]

Control over all properties of the mosque, twenty houses, a four-story building adjoining the mosque, an attached madrassa, and the six shops at the front and back of the mosque was vested in the custodians. They received rents from the various properties belonging to the trust, received all offerings, subscriptions, and donations made to the mosque, and kept accounts in the Gujarati language. They were to make all arrangements for the repair of the mosque and buildings concerned with it, erect new buildings as they thought necessary, and maintain direct control and management of all trust property matters connected with it.[27] The "matters connected" with the mosque endowment included the arrangements for the mosque school, and ritual practices conducted at the mosque. Ethnically restricted custodial control was justified by the Randeri trustees on the premise that it was "contrary to the principles of Mahomedan law that the management and control of a mosque should be vested in or exercised by so vague and unascertainable a body as the entire Sunni community of Rangoon."[28]

The structure of the trust conferred managerial authority over the mosque to custodians, the manner of whose appointment was determined in the mosque's founding documentation. The example of the Shi'a Mogul Mosque demonstrated that it was not necessary that custodians should be appointed without reference to the congregation and the terms of endowment could enable community participation and oversight over custodians. But mosque management was in principle limited by the ideas, visions, and language scripted by founding benefactor(s). In turn mosque custodians, their authority in the mosque sanctioned by the structure of the trust, their status elevated by the religious nature of the trust, were paternalistic figures and served congregations in purposeful ascendancy. Custodians controlled mosques in this way across north India, in all territories governed under colonial law as well as in the Rangoon Friday Mosque at the turn of the twentieth century.

Visions of Egalitarianism in Mosque Management

This hierarchical structure of mosque management came under direct challenge at the Rangoon Friday Mosque in 1908. Mosque congregations were comprised by a diverse group of immigrant laborers, traders, and moneylenders. These ethnically and professionally diverse Muslims could pray in the mosque at the times for prayer arranged by the custodians. The custodians "in no way fettered or controlled the right of every [Muslim] to worship in the said mosque or had imposed any other condition repugnant to [Muslim] religious tenets."[29] But the custodians and the committee which appointed them jealously guarded their own rights over mosque management. Although all Muslims were in agreement that the five obligatory prayers should be offered in the mosque, there were points of religious difference informed by ethnicity, class, and occupation which related to other ritual matters and activities which took place in the mosque, most importantly, children's education and religious instruction.[30] Late-nineteenth-century Rangoon Muslims were deeply interested in democratizing movements and organizations and took inspiration from these movements to reconsider their participation in mosque affairs.

Near the end of the nineteenth century, Muslims made up 18 percent of the population of Rangoon, a little over 43,000 people.[31] The Randeris were traders and had investments in property and industry in Rangoon as well. Memon and Variao Suratis had migrated in the 1860s and 1870s as traders of piece goods and rice. Like the Randeris they spoke Gujarati, and many formed close business partnerships with the Randeris. The Memons were a global diaspora and had created community endowments in other Indian Ocean cities including Durban and Port Louis Mauritius, and dominated Indian and Muslim social, economic, and political life in those cities.[32] Cholias,[33] south Indian Tamil-speaking Muslims, had been in Rangoon, Mandalay, and Moulmein since well before the colonial settlement. Suratis knew them as sellers of wares in the bazaar[34] as fellow shop owners and tenants, as neighbors, and both Suratis and Europeans knew them as the butchers and meat sellers.[35] Zerbadis were Muslims who were ethnically Burmese.

The Randeris had come to Burma after 1853 as owners of merchant vessels, and as rice and piece goods traders. Rander was a small but wealthy town in Surat "dominated by Sunni Bohras."[36] The merchants of this city in India had first benefited from the decline of Cambay after the silting over of the Gulf in the sixteenth century, when Surat came to regional prominence as a center of trans-shipment trade, particularly the pepper-trade nexus between Aceh, Gujarat, and the Red Sea.[37] Randeris were settled in Calcutta where the owner of a merchant vessel had endowed the Zakariya mosque and had established a community graveyard. Most families that came to Rangoon did so via Calcutta and business interests between the two cities were closely linked. Randeris were shrewd businessmen and the number of legal suits filed by them for rights in inheritance settlements and business ventures in Calcutta and Rangoon demonstrates that, like Parsis, community members were well versed in the principles of colonial law which protected their capital and they were highly litigious.[38] The Variao celebrated the *mawlud* whereas the Randeris did not, and the former were known in Rangoon for the fact that they had communally owned ceremonial cooking vessels which were large enough to produce food for large events and were rented out to those who needed them.

South Indian Tamil-speaking Muslims of Rangoon referred to as Cholias were part of an Indian Ocean trading community with agents on the Coromandel coast, in Johore (modern day Singapore) and Kedah and Penang on the Malay peninsula, who had dominated the tin trade into the early nineteenth century. They diminished economically in the Malayan peninsula in the nineteenth century, but remained economically influential in Tamilnadu and secured a place in the coastal area carrying trade.[39] Cholia ships started carrying to Rangoon at least as early as the first annexation of Arakan; total imports to Rangoon on Cholia vessels were estimated at between 200 and 600 tons in 1821.[40] By the late nineteenth century, Cholias were established through the country as shop owners, with a presence in remote villages as well as major towns and cities.

The range of difference in Muslim cultural and ethnic preferences certainly gave credence to the Randeri position that there was no basis for approaching the Sunnis of Rangoon as a homogenous community. However, there were ideas in play which suggested that it was possible for Muslim worshippers in a mosque to organize as a society and assert control over mosque management. The registration of societies demonstrated the prevalence of a principle of individual rights in association. Certain Muslim religious societies were registered, among these the Moslem Association of Rangoon in 1893[41] and the Cholia Muslim Association in 1912.[42] These merchants' religious associations were, in Nile Green's formulation, religious firms which sought to promote their own "proprietary Islam . . . multifarious—and indeed competing—social producers of religion."[43] In addition to creating cultural organizations, Indian migrants to Rangoon (as well as Burmese, Hindus, Europeans, and Parsis) joined the Indian Ratepayers' Association.[44] The Parsi advocate Cowasjee, who served on the municipal committee, spoke to the urgency of the organization of interests relating to capital to resist municipal rates increases. Other associations such as the Rice Traders' Association, the Rangoon Trades Association,[45] and the Advocates' Association, promoted migrants' economic interests.[46]

These associations and committees were governed by the Societies Registration Act of 1860, a piece of legislation that invited any seven or more people who were associated for a literary, scientific, educational, or charitable purpose, to register a society, its objectives and the terms of their association with the Registrar of Companies. This legal device was, in effect, a public declaration of assets, terms of membership and appointment of officers, schedule of meetings and elections, and the process for dissolution.[47] Registration of a society systemized relations between its members by setting out the terms of regular membership and those on which office was held and allowed for review of shared objectives and the terms of association.

While Muslims joined societies, control over mosque properties could not be assigned to a society of worshippers. Muslims, and those of other indigenous faiths, were differentiated from Christians in the 1880 Religious Societies Act, which was passed in response to repeated representations by members of Simla Union Church who were unable to maintain an effective body of trustees over moveable and immoveable Church properties. The Governor General's Council noted that a similar difficulty was felt by religious societies in England. As a result, the act provided that if specific property was conveyed to trustees for any religious congregation, and no special provision was made for appointment of new trustees, new trustees may be appointed by the congregation if two-thirds of its members were in agreement. The Act did not apply to Hindus, Muslims, Buddhists, or anyone else the governor general might see fit to exclude.[48]

The idea that a mosque congregation should be deemed a society that could have custodial rights over the mosque and its assets was engendered by a widely publicized case in which a congregation of Surati and other Gujarati worshippers in Port Louis, Mauritius, had overturned the claim of a small exclusive group to custodianship of a Friday mosque through appeal to the Judicial Committee of the Privy Council. Construction for that mosque was started in 1874 by Indian immigrants, and the land that was donated to and purchased for the mosque was registered to the

Katchchi Memon community which was itself registered as a society.[49] In 1903 when the society moved to have the finished mosque registered to the Katchchi Memon society, other members of the congregation objected. The Privy Council ruled in 1908 that the only society which could claim rights to a communal space in Mauritius was the congregation itself. The mosque was registered in its own name and the congregation registered as a society. A new scheme for management of the mosque required the congregation-society's consensus for appointment of custodians and did away with narrow ethnic and hereditary terms for the appointment of custodians.

Many among Rangoon's Muslims imagined themselves to be part of a transethnic and transnational community that could transcend difference and take up principles of social reform to come together for the purpose of political advancement.[50] Many followed the progress of the Muslim League in India and the Burma branch of the Muslim League was established in 1909[51] as immigrants began to feel alienated by Buddhist nationalism which centered on religion and the public space of the pagoda, excluding non-Buddhist immigrants to the region.[52] Advocates of the Aligarh movement[53] in Rangoon put forward a view that Muslims should be invited as a community to modernize and standardize education.[54]

The Educational Syndicate of Burma consulted with the Aligarh group on ways of improving the general Muslim educational condition. Charles Fox, the chief judge of lower Burma who served as president of the Educational Syndicate for much of his eleven-year membership of that organization, served as president of a Muslim Education Committee to promote integration and standardization of Muslim schooling in Burma.[55]

Ahmed Moolla Dawood, a prominent Memon trader who had founded and served as president of the Moslem Association of Rangoon and who also served as secretary of the Burma Branch of the Muslim League, led the suit for broad Muslim participation in management of the Friday mosque.[56] Dawood had become known in the West as an advocate of a modern and global Islam owing to his meeting in the 1890s with Alexander Russell Webb, ex-consul to Philippines and convert to Islam, who sought to bring Islam to the United States. He contributed 300 dollars to the cause and translated some articles for Webb to publish in his journal *Moslem World*.[57]

Dawood was closely connected to the colonial administration; he had consulted at other times with the judge of the high court, C. E. Fox, on Muslim education and took a vocal and visible position on a variety of issues concerning Indians in Burma.[58] Dawood filed the suit that challenged the identification of Moolla Hashim as the original mosque endower, proposing that the mosque had been originally supported by a colonial land grant as well as community philanthropy,[59] and that management of the trust was vested in the community for whom the mosque was made, not just in the Randeri committee.⁶⁰ The case initially went up before C. E. Fox, judge of the high court, whose judgment favored Dawood's position. This leading member of the colonial administration saw the potential in the Societies Registration Act and the Mauritius case to offer a different model of mosque management.⁶¹

A final judgment of the Judicial Committee of the Privy Council judgment was delivered by Ameer Ali in 1916. Ali argued that while all Sunni Muslim worshippers had the right of worship, members of the congregation had no innate right to participate in the management of the mosque, as participatory and representative governance of the mosque in no way affected the fulfillment of the purpose of the trust. He went on to assert that the civil courts played the role of the qazi in enforcing Islamic law, glossing over the radical transformation engendered by the new political dispensation.⁶² Islamic law, he said, stipulated that the management of the mosque should be carried out according to the grantor/benefactor's will. Therefore, the Lords of the Privy Council were bound to discern and uphold the vision of Moolla Hashim, the original benefactor of the mosque. As the trustees had not mismanaged the trust, nor committed any dereliction of duty, or introduced innovations in services that interfered with the rights of worshippers, he saw no reason to undermine their control over the mosque. The JCPC's judgment differentiated the size of individual Randeri gifts to the mosque from collective donations and rejected the example of Mauritius because that judgment was influenced by precedents in the country's Napoleonic law and incomparable with the legal circumstances of colonial India.

Rangoon Muslim efforts to create a more socially inclusive model of mosque management were inspired by models of Muslim community organization across India and as far away as Mauritius. The 1916 judgment put these possibilities for congregational participation in mosque management and public influence over managerial prerogatives conclusively to rest. Custodians were deemed to not be accountable to the congregation.

Instruction in the Rangoon Friday Mosque

Paternalistic mosque custodians controlled every aspect of programming in the mosque. The case of the Rangoon Friday Mosque allows us to focus on the social consequences of one aspect of control in particular: instruction offered through schooling and sermonizing in mosques. Mosque schools, also known as Koran schools, and in Urdu vernacular as *maktabs*, were ubiquitous but largely ignored by colonial administrators and Muslims committed to educational reform as being of minimal educational consequence as their curricula were centered on Arabic reading literacy. Mosque schools, which appeared to provide a service but not an education for an apathetic Muslim society, and their structure and governance received little attention. But the Rangoon Friday Mosque custodians closely deliberated what sort of instruction should be imparted in the mosque school and in Friday sermons and this school was very consequential for the community.

The trustees of the Rangoon Friday Mosque began running Urdu and Quran classes for children in one of the mosque properties in the late 1800s. This instructional activity was classed as vernacular schooling as teaching was conducted in Urdu. Until 1899, the Randeria Madrassa, as it was called, only taught reading, recitation, and memorization of the Quran in Arabic, and imparted basic literacy in Urdu. English was introduced after 1900, in an effort to "aid the material, moral and spiritual advancement of young people . . . without in any way interfering with the religious instruction which . . . formed the basis of the work,"[63] on the advice of the Director of Public Instruction of Lower Burma who advised private benefactors to introduce standards for Anglo-vernacular schools and to hire a well-qualified staff of teachers.[64] By 1908 a total of 200 Muslim students were studying at the Randeria Madrassa of the Rangoon Friday Mosque and another smaller mosque school close by.[65] By 1913 the school at the Rangoon Friday Mosque had 159 students and had become an "aided" school receiving some government support and offering secondary education.[66] This development resonated with a regional government effort to improve Muslim education by offering subsidies to teachers in mosque schools who adopted the Government of India's education standards[67] including instruction in English, elementary mathematics, history, and geography.

The custodians of the Rangoon Friday Mosque introduced the official primary and high school government curriculum for vernacular schools in 1909.[68] The government curriculum could be delivered in two ways: one that favored teaching and learning in language and text and that led to the university entrance exam and onwards to employment in the civil services, and the other "of a more practical and less literary character," an approach encouraged by the Government of India to prepare students for applied studies in engineering and science. The custodians of the Rangoon Friday Mosque preferred the latter approach; the strength of the instruction remained in the field of teaching Urdu and Quranic studies, a basic education was offered in English,[69] and elementary math, history, and geography were introduced.

The custodians' position of not providing a more robust English-language curriculum and higher-level training in oriental languages set them at odds with the Aligarh influenced members of the congregation, primarily Ahmed Moolla Dawood who preferred more specialized language training and preparation for the university entrance exams. Dawood, like other participants in the Muhammadan Anglo Oriental Conference who styled themselves as Muslim modernists, was preoccupied with the reform of the curriculum of the Rangoon Friday Mosque school. This position was fueled by developments in the wider realm of Muslim politics and discourse as well. Abul Kalam Azad drew on hadith and Islamic history in one of his numerous widely circulated pamphlets to assert that learning of doctrine was an individual, internal process which needed no disciplining in social settings,[70] and that Muslims should have unrestricted access to the mosque as God's house.[71] He fiercely derided the custodians who appeared to him to exploit the control which they had gained over mosques through the founding documentation of endowment and used the incomes to supplement their own personal finances and observed scathingly that "every custodian cherishes his right to give an Islamic education to every harbinger of the devil."[72]

Local administrators had a low opinion of the Randeria Madrassa and the project of privately run vernacular education in general, reporting that Indian Mahomedan parents were generally apathetic when it came to education and paying fees,[73] and in 1912 vested far more hope in a "large and well endowed public high school under private Mussalman management, talked of for the last three years," for which they anticipated that Ahmed Moolla Dawood would provide the funds.[74] This overall low opinion of vernacular schools, and especially mosque schools, saturated education reports and was rooted in the valuation of literacy in English and studies based in rational and reasoned thought as the most important educational objectives.[75] However administrative and Muslim modernist dismissiveness of the Randeria Madrassa masked the fact that a great deal was happening in the mosque school under the control of the custodians.

Reasoning for curricular priorities was provided to and for the custodians of the Rangoon Friday Mosque by the *khatib* of the early twentieth century, Abdul Hai Kaflaytvi of Surat. Kaflaytvi was trained at Deoband and was hired directly by the custodians to serve as resident sermonizer and prayer leader and wrote a book entitled *The Muslims of Burma and Education* (*Musalmanan-i Burma aur Talim*) describing the needs in educational instruction for Muslims of Burma. The book was published posthumously in 1918 by Kaflaytvi's successor in the post of *khatib* at the Rangoon Friday Mosque. Kaflaytvi did not serve as the principal of the madrassa; between

1900 and 1927 all but one of the school's principals were British as "white skin alone commanded respect."[76] Kaflaytvi's relationship to the custodians, and therefore to the congregation and students at the mosque school, was one of advisor, a position dictated by the structure of the trust which placed all decision making control in the custodians' hands. Kaflaytvi's authority did not produce a religious interpretative position for the mosque and the Muslims who attended it; rather the custodians selected him, appointed him, retained him, and eventually replaced him.

Kaflaytvi's vision for education for the Muslims of Burma was thoughtfully articulated as a response to the Aligarh and Muslim League priorities for preparing Muslims for civil service and participatory politics. There were two prevailing motivational frameworks for Muslim education and self-improvement, Kaflaytvi wrote: *dunyavi*, economic self-advancement, and *deeni*, pleasing God with one's worldly actions.[77] Abdul Hai set himself apart from the principles of educational reform which had guided schools like Aligarh. When a student went in to such an institution of higher education, he might learn a smattering of geography, history, and speak a topsy-turvy English, but this did not allow him to achieve any sort of real success.[78] "As far as one reflects on the list of educational [achievements] of the Muslims of Hindustan," he argued, "it becomes apparent that their efforts were only towards employment." "There is no doubt," he continued, "that as far as the art of employment is concerned, they have achieved great successes, and time after time, continue to achieve this. But such success is not enough to allay the tremendously straightened circumstances of the seven or eight crore Muslims of Hindustan."[79] Kaflaytvi echoed the Deoband position that the purest form of education was the study of religion (*ilm-i din*)[80] but he could not take up the anti-utilitarianist position preferred at Deoband, imagining the madrassa to be a school purely concerned with religious philosophical inquiry and understanding.[81]

Dismissing the strategy of re-education in support of colonial subjecthood and political participation as inadequate for providing employment for the majority of Muslims, Abdul Hai was not differentiating religious from utilitarian education but rather addressing a crucial failure of the Aligarh view to address and provide a vision of economic subjecthood which served traders and other capitalists in the empire who did not seek professional employment, and earned money through investment and trade. Such interests, he said, were not served by the clamor for independence that was so great that it was impossible for a teacher or parent to put pressure on a young person to study. Were young Muslim men from Burma to go to Aligarh or Lahore College, he said, the phantom of independence would alight on them and keep them from peacefully attending to their work.[82]

Kaflaytvi gave language, concepts, and substance to the expectations of the mosque custodians and proposed a curriculum which was suitable for the children of traders. He argued that new ideas and theories should be translated into vernaculars (*mulki zaban*),[83] and principles of European trade (*tijarat*) should be well understood. Trade, after all, had brought the English to India and had made European and American merchants wealthy beyond compare, and it was a profession of the Arab lineages established in Sindh, Gujarat, Kachch, Malabar, China, Malay, and Africa.[84] At a minimum, he believed, traders should have the equivalent of a middle school education which enabled them to read and write telegrams, read letters, books, and newspapers, and comprehensively understand the rules and principles of trade.[85] In addition they also needed to learn the demeanor of respectability (*sharafat*), which elicited the trust of their customers who should buy from them, and suppliers who should give them goods on credit.[86] Where aspirants for government jobs were best served by a curriculum of the study of Arabic, Persian, classical literature, and works on conceptions of state and society, Kaflaytvi proposed an education that supported understanding of trade and business and the significance of capital, contextualized by a robust regard for divinity and the obligations of worship.

Another smaller Gujarati Muslim trust-run school also delivered primary education for its community members and favored a curriculum centered on religious instruction. The Madrassa Nurul Islam admitted children from first through fourth standard and offered classes in Urdu reading, writing, and arithmetic, some Persian at the upper level, Arabic reading and enunciation, Quran in translation in Urdu, and Quran memorization and recitation.[87] No English, science, or geography classes were offered.

This did not mean that students did not get an English-language education. Roll call lists and notations about the lessons covered each week at this school in 1917–18 were transcribed in English. A delightful note from a student's parent to a teacher, left as a bookmark in the register, was written on the back of page torn from a notebook, covered in a child's English cursive: "Harry ran into the ... Lucy, come and see! ... Lucy hearing her ... ran to him. Then he took ... into the stable ... there with four pretty white pups." For many students, education at the mosque school may have supplemented rather than replacing English-language educational and cultural exposure.[88]

Any worldly education provided in schools must, Kaflaytvi argued, be balanced by a religious education as Muslims were universally aware that worldly existence was insignificant and short as compared to the afterlife, and the only means of achieving a magnificent afterlife was by living in accordance with the laws communicated by God and his Prophet through the Quran and the hadith. Kaflaytvi believed that balance in the worldly and religious life could be achieved through instruction in childhood, and under colonial conditions, could never be achieved if religious education was not introduced early as children were exposed unwittingly to ideas and arguments that were inherently opposed to Islam. If an awareness of the pleasure of observation of divine law and the observation of injunction was not cultivated, Kaflaytvi argued, exposure to Western ideas, subjects of study, and writings would kill a child's "religious spirit and apostasy [would] take root in their souls."[89] His views on English-language education were broadly inspired by Deobandi discourse[90] and directed against an Aligarh position.[91] But a mosque school like the Randeri madrassa was not an independent institution like either of those institutions with the resources to produce its own educational traditions; it was one directed by mosque custodians who chose the subjects their students would study, equipping these young people of their neighborhoods in a manner that they deemed to be appropriate.

Kaflaytvi proposed the study of principles of Islamic law and history and enough Arabic that students should be able to interpret and absorb the Quran and "achieve balance in their dispositions." Muslims embodying religious values should deliver all childhood instruction, Kaflaytvi argued. European teachers could have no interest in tempting Muslim kids toward or emphasizing the importance of religious worship and young students instructed by Europeans would spend their whole educational careers of eight to ten years in the freedom of not reading their ritual *namaz*, nor hearing any words of encouragement to do so, and after being released from such an education would not be inclined to observe religious obligations.[92] The intention, Kaflaytvi said, is that "Muslim children should remain Muslim while gaining an English education. . . . The poisonous germs of science will not be able to pollute the blood of their faith and belief."[93]

Mosque schools like the Randeria Madrassa were the most ubiquitous places of instruction for the Muslims of north India and were counted as primary schools from the 1880s to inflate the numbers counting as provisioning for indigenous education.[94] In the Punjab, village schools were convened in mosques, and in other religious establishments for Sikhs and Hindus.[95] Of the 11,000 Koran schools with 183,000 students counted across Bengal, Punjab, the United Provinces, and Bombay,[96] the vast majority were attached to local mosques.[97] Very few such madrassas grew into places of specialized advanced instruction by highly trained teachers, like the madrassa attached to the Rangoon Friday Mosque and the Ramzan Ali mosque in

Calcutta.[98] Most were led by a single teacher who offered undifferentiated instruction to a group of boys and possibly some young girls, of diverse ages and abilities.[99] Colonial administrators dismissed the activities that took place in mosque schools as being of little consequence, but together such schools were a mainframe of education across Muslim north India and Kaflaytvi's writings demonstrate that teaching in such schools could be profoundly ideologically motivated and of professional consequence even where it did not advance religious, scientific or governmental objectives.

Instruction in the Rangoon Friday Mosque school had a counterpart in instruction in the congregation hall. The *khatib* offered interpretation and application of religious precepts in the ritual Friday sermon, describing dogma and making reference to matters of contemporary concern, modeling the way in which Islamic injunction resonated with immediate, local, and everyday life. The *khatib*'s role as advisor and guide for the congregation was enhanced when the mosque trustees established a *darul ifta*, an office staffed by 'ulama, and received questions from local Muslims concerning a range of quotidian matters from prayer to dress, work, and marriage; the 'ulama provided detailed instructions for religiously appropriate behavior.

The founder and custodians identified as Hanafis; Friday sermons were given in Arabic, and visiting speakers were always of the Hanafi religious profession; Deobandis were particularly favored as *khatibs* and visiting lecturers. The nearest indication of the orientation of the content of the Friday sermons given at the mosque comes from the remaining books of the mosque library; some 200 volumes on fiqh, *tafsir* (Quranic exegesis) Islamic history, *sirah* (biographies), and hadith bound and catalogued from 1918 to 1925 demonstrate the dominant influence of a north Indian tradition of Hanafi fiqh at the mosque.[100] The *khatib*'s published works embody prescription for piety which were entirely unlike the Ahl-i Hadith recommendations in their preferred texts, *Taqwiyatul Iman*, or *Mishkat ul Anwar*.[101] The Ahl-i Hadith recommended a wholly personal practice, interpretation, and understanding and refused any role to the 'ulama. Kaflaytvi explained that the significance of words and recitations, and by extension logic, was embedded in philosophical approaches to the understanding of the self and divinity, that inference of divine will could not be achieved through the individual intellect but had to be derived by the 'ulama from the body of Hanafi law.

The custodians' instructional preferences in the Rangoon Friday Mosque were disputed in Rangoon as they had been in Tajpur. A Variao named Kaka, influenced by Ahl-i Hadith prescriptions for ritual practice, would attend prayers at the Surti mosque and recite the *amin* loudly. When asked to desist from his vocal *amin*, Kaka quarreled with the trustees and the *khatib* of the mosque. The trustees proceeded to file a criminal suit against him and Kaka was sentenced under the penal code.[102] Had Kaka been more resourceful, he may have invoked the JCPC judgment of the Tajpur Mosque case in 1893 that declared that practicing according to one's own ritual preference in a mosque was not a nuisance, but most likely he did not have the will or the finances to pursue his suit. The custodians' control in the mosque school was even less ambiguous; they refused Ahmed Moolla Dawood's efforts to create a broadly inclusive governing body for the mosque and dashed his hopes for a modernist school curriculum in the Randeria Madrassa. They also initiated and won legal proceedings against a man who had an argument with the teacher over his son's behavior.[103]

The fact that Kaflatvi the *khatib* crafted a meaningful position on education and Hanafi law was made possible by the legal structure of the trust which placed the custodians in a position to establish instructional objectives and protected them from the congregation's expectations as parents and as worshippers. Mosque schools were governed by the structure of the mosque trust and under the direct control of the mosque custodians who were not accountable to a Muslim public or government and yet made arrangements for pastoral guidance and childhood instruction which imparted a philosophy of self and prepared young people for employment. They were, in this respect, entirely unlike mission schools whose pedagogies were put in place by and informed by members of the Church associated with the mission itself. The difference between Islamic instruction directed by the 'ulama and the delivery of instruction endorsed by laymen will not be lost on any scholar of South Asia; most simply put, teaching in mosque schools cannot be presumed to follow broader tends in religious scholarly interpretation, but rather to be constituted by individual preferences in them. This individual preference was influenced by place, language, access, and familiarity. Custodians of the Rangoon Friday Mosque crafted, endorsed, and anchored their own Islamic preferences through their hiring practices for the school and could do so with the full strength of the law behind then.

Conclusion

In 1909 the Rangoon mosque custodians were named in a feature on Islam in India in the journal *Revue Du Monde Musalman* which profiled the waqf as among the most important mosques and madrassas across India.[104] They were also regularly featured in the school's own yearbooks and colonial records on education in Rangoon.[105] In the years after the conclusion of the suit, the standards at the Randeria Madrassa continued to improve and it reached "a high level of efficiency" measured by the numbers of passes in the Vernacular VII Standard examinations.[106] This success eventually set it apart in the minds of colonial administrators from other Mahomedan vernacular schools in which "ignorant *mullas* . . . incessantly preach to the ignorant people the uselessness of secular education. They themselves being unqualified to teach in recognized public institutions, prevent others from establishing them for fear that they may lose their chance of keeping inefficient small *maktabs*."[107] The custodians crafted something unique and, as Kozlowksi has argued in his early work on waqfs in colonial India, their custodial positions reinforced their social prominence.

In his work on Muslim endowments, Gregory Kozlowski did not account for the fact that custodial control was actively, broadly and almost successfully contested through a variety of creative social, political, and legal strategies aimed at enabling congregational participation in management. But the instrument of the English trust had been so effectively adapted to fulfill the purpose of the Islamic waqf that the alternatives, to use the model of the society or to reimagine the very nature of endowment, commanded little interest among the jurists who heard the suit.[108] Among these jurists, Syed Ameer Ali had publicly argued for the preservation of the instrument of the trust as it "prevent[ed] the pauperization of the well-do-do classes . . . and helped materially in the diffusion of knowledge." He was openly committed to protecting the very elite status and influence of the custodians that their challengers sought to dismantle.[109]

The 1916 JCPC judgment allowed for some congregational participation in the committee but derived imperatives for management of the trust from the first act of endowment by Moolla Hashim to assert that the majority of members must be Randeri. This judgment disallowed the principle that religious activities in mosque "trusts" must be sanctioned by democratic consensus. Instruction was the most consequential of these activities, not only because of the visibility and success of the school at the Rangoon Friday Mosque, but also because of the combined penetration and reach of all South Asian mosque schools. The Judicial Committee of the Privy Council sanctioned custodial control over mosque programming in 1916, a privileged control over instruction which has not been accounted for in the extensive body of work on Islam and education in South Asia. This story of the Rangoon Friday Mosque provides a foundation from which to reexamine Islamic thought and practice with attention to the influence of custodians of neighborhood mosques over teaching and learning by socially diverse Muslims.

Chapter 3

AURANGABAD AND KANPUR UP, 1924

THE MAGISTRATE'S CONTROL OF THE MOSQUE PERIMETER

Introduction

From 1913 to 1918 conflict spiraled into violence at two mosques in the United Provinces. These disputes took place against the backdrop of numerous conflicts at temples and on the streets of this densely populated and highly urbanized province of British India. Religious organization, political reform, and the increasing circulation of print fueled conversations, emotions, and ambitions. In Kanpur, in the east of the province, the Machchli Bazaar Mosque stood in the path of a newly planned road which would tidy the unplanned layout of the neighborhood of the fish market. Muslims across north India, highly sensitive to disregard and disrespect, spoke out in the press and travelled to Kanpur to protest the demolition of this mosque. In Aurangabad Sunnis who prayed at a local mosque objected to the vocal remembrances of the town's Shi'as as they wound their way through the narrow streets and past the mosque entrance in their annual commemorations of injustice in early Islamic history. In other towns Muslim congregants clashed with Hindu processionists, and cow protectors attacked mosques and the Muslims within. No single unified ambition or vision for Islam explained the range of motivations expressed by Muslim petitioners and protestors, but conflict signaled overlapping religious interests of Sunni, Shi'a, Hindu, and the state, and the tenor of these conflicts was ever more shrill, marking a persistence of difference through the early part of the twentieth century.

Mosque protectionists in Kanpur and in Aurangabad expressed a belief in the sanctity of the mosque perimeter in opposition to those who violated it and criticized the administrative and legal process by which religious claims on shared spaces were mediated by the magistrate's office. In Aurangabad, the Shi'as of the town filed a suit demanding recognition of their absolute and unmitigated right to religious procession on the street. In 1924 the Judicial Committee of the Privy Council ruled that the established procedures would prevail: the local government, usually represented by the magistrate, would continue to mediate claims in liminal spaces of overlapping religious and public interests. The mosque perimeter crystalized in the urban spatial imaginary and the local government asserted bureaucratic control over it, excluding it definitively from the territories and matters governed by reasoned legal principles and higher law.

Drawing inspiration from debates in urban and spatial history, this chapter identifies a liminal feature of the mosque which has never been recognized in Western scholarship although it was debated by South Asian Islamic scholars in the early nineteenth century. Muslim mosque defense movements were often perimeter defense movements. Here I move historical focus from the inspiration Muslims took from forging a political identity to the spatial context for Muslim feelings about mosques.

Mosques and Urban Environs

Vernacular architecture and town planning, literature, and public festivals featured the mosque. These cultural forms suggested a mosque-centered city made up of mosque-centered neighborhoods (*muhallas*).[1] These maps, books, pamphlets, and Islamic discourses shaped Muslims' expectations and associations, constituting an Islamic urban spatial imaginary that coexisted with the colonial spatial arrangements for cities.[2]

Urban enclaves of the United Provinces could have distinctly Islamic characteristics.[3] *Qasbahs*, administrative centers of the Mughal era which developed as marketplaces to serve the countryside, were populated by Muslim landowning gentry and political and cultural elites and were grandfathered into the colonial administrative system intact. The built environment of *qasbahs* was developed by these wealthy notables who erected fine *havelis* for their own residence and endowed mosques, madrassas, and imambargahs. Mosques were endowed, examined, designed, and defended in ways that demonstrated a social belief in their significance within the urban built environment from the very start of the colonial period.

Catherine Asher has noted that the mosques of Jaipur and Delhi were built to dominate the cityscape through elevation and location, unlike temples which were almost invisible. They also shared certain decorative qualities such as frescoes, and epigraphic references to Mughal and classical Islamic monuments. Repetitions of convention in design across the wide expanse of central and north India, along with invocations of Mughal and Islamic architecture, suggest widely subscribed norms of mosque architecture which in turn produced what Asher has called "bold," and we should also recognize as intentional, "manifestations of Islam in urban environs."[4]

Alison Mackenzie Shah tells us that the movement of processions past grand buildings affected Muslim understanding of urban space; palaces, mosques, and imambargahs and the procession routes that went past them produced an elite centered spatial order for the princely state of Hyderabad during the nineteenth century.[5] Nawab Shah Jahan Begum of Bhopal, following a tradition of urban development of Bhopal around mosques,[6] started construction on the magnificent Taj-ul Masajid, "Crown of all Mosques."[7] A bridge oriented the entry to and passage past this grand building, intended to be the largest modern mosque in India, incorporating and supporting pious self-carriage to the mosque as a feature of the city. She also built the stately Masjid Kulsum Bi in 1898, completed in 1902, at a total expenditure of 30,000 rupees. Colonial administrators greatly admired both projects.[8]

Urdu manuscripts and printed texts dealing with urban aesthetics and the mosque were circulating from at least the beginning of the nineteenth century. A body of writing already existed on mosque management which detailed rights of uses and reuses of all mosque incomes and property. The rules were exhaustive and governed cash, capital, furnishings, materials that comprised roofs and floors, down to the branches of trees on mosque land.[9] A text written in Delhi in 1849 described the importance of illuminating mosques by lamplight at night. The short tract drew on hadith and the Quran to highlight that mosques must be decorated with regard for the public experience of viewing them. The author quoted from a hadith that the Prophet appreciated a large Friday mosque that was lit up to be visible in the nightscape.[10] Sir Sayyid Ahmad Khan's *Asar-al Sanadid* which was published in 1848 described the dense built heritage of nineteenth-century Delhi.[11] Tabular lists of palaces, temples, shrines, and mosques suggested urban design constituted by ancient and modern imperial and elite building projects and communicated the excitement of thinking about mosques as part of a living heritage of Mughal power and Islam in India. The neat intersections of the concerns of the authors of these texts with the efforts of the colonial resident's office to manage Delhi's urban affairs,[12] recent adoption of oil lamps in place of candles for lighting interiors of government buildings,[13] churches,[14] and later efforts of the Delhi municipality to improve roads and sanitation beginning in the 1860s[15] suggest a degree of cross-fertilization of strategies of urban aesthetics and improvement, albeit in tense political circumstances.

An Urdu text published in Delhi in 1853, *Masail-i Thalathin*, was organized as thirty-three answers to questions about the etiquettes of worship in mosques provided by Maulvi Abdul Rab, an Islamic scholar of Shahjahanabad. The text described religiously appropriate practices of mosque attendance, congregation, and endowment, and in so doing denoted a system of social and political organization centered on the Friday mosque of Shahjahanabad where the moral and imperial authority of the king was expressed.[16] The Friday mosque was in turn orbited by a constellation of self-organizing and reasonably autonomous neighborhoods.[17] Rab suggested that a neighborhood was the area of proximate settlement by a single community, and the social order of the neighborhood relied on the mosque.

> Hazrat Ayesha related that it was a tradition of the Prophet to [ask people] to build mosques in neighborhoods. Sheikh Abdul Haq Muhaddis Dehlavi has said in his translation of this hadith, "build mosques in neighborhoods as long as there is no evidential damage to another mosque. Each community (*qaum*) should establish its own congregation (*jama'at*)."[18]

The organization of the city perceived by its Muslim denizens is depicted in the map illustrating Bashir ud-Din Ahmad Dihlavi, *Vaqi'at al-Hukumat-i Dehli*, published in 1919. In this map and its key, the city is centered by the Friday mosque and organized into neighborhoods, each of which features a mosque as well as other religious buildings[19] (see Figure 2).

Writing in Delhi before the fall of the last Mughal emperor, Sayyid Ahmad Khan and Maulvi Rab were observing a religious economy and a built environment produced by endowments and other forms of elite patronage. They produced an idealized view of the spatial order of the Mughal imperial city which inspired Muslim understandings of the city well into the twentieth century.

Indigenous architectural traditions shared principles of design and construction. An Urdu text published in 1915 and intended for wider circulation set out principles of design and materials for the decoration of mosques. It was published for the benefit of builders from "not just the Punjab, but all provinces."[20] The author also offered suggestions for adaptations of the mosque design for Sufi shrines, Sikh and Hindu tombs, and temples that served different Indian religious traditions,[21] techniques that he had been taught by his own teachers and elders and that were in danger of being forgotten (see Figure 3).

Urban geography was described through associations with historical and mythical figures in Noor Ahmad Chishti's 1867 encyclopedia of Lahore's

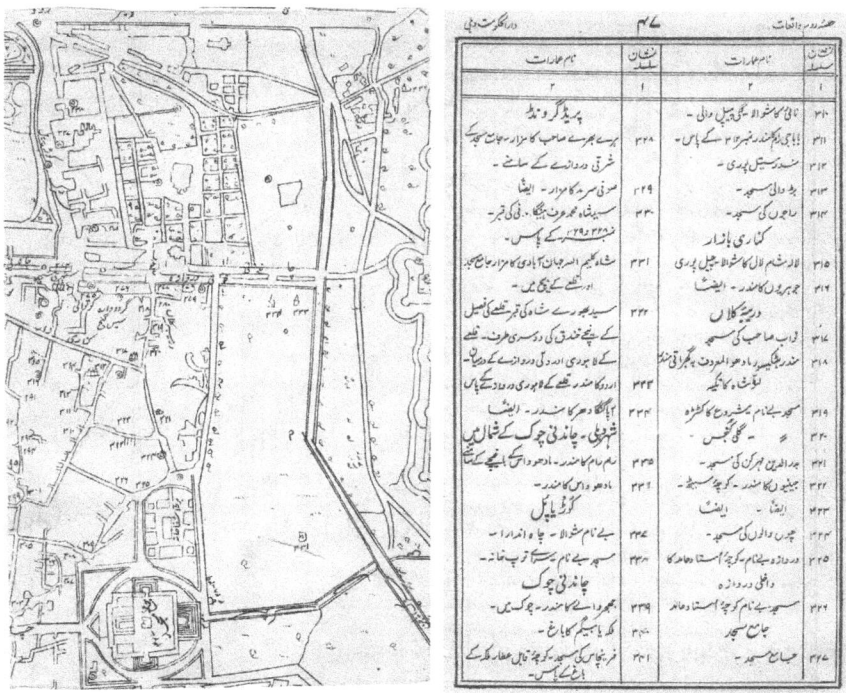

Figure 2 Center segment and key of the map of Delhi published in Dihlavi's *Vaqi'at* (1919).

history. He described particular locations in the city, including mosques, as significant for their association with saintly and political historical figures and described contemporary remembrance of those historical and mythical personalities.[22] Syed Muhammad Latif used a similar literary device in his study of *Lahore: Its History, Architectural Remains and Antiquities* in 1892.[23] Abdul Halim Sharar, the prolific writer of colonial Lucknow, mythologized the lavish cultures of the precolonial city to influence an urbane Muslim present. The literary longing for the splendors of the utopian Nawabi city shaped the literary trope of Muslim loss and decline while also emphasizing cultural priorities such as refinement and honesty.[24] History, politics, religion, the past, and the present were intertwined in these texts.

Kannhyayal, a structural engineer employed by the Lahore administration, wrote a history of Lahore's built environment in 1884 by drawing on government records, oral testimony, and his own surveys. His study suggests that mosque building by imperial householders and their elites was a strategy of development of the built and settled environment, particularly from the time of the Mughal Jahangir (1605–27) and

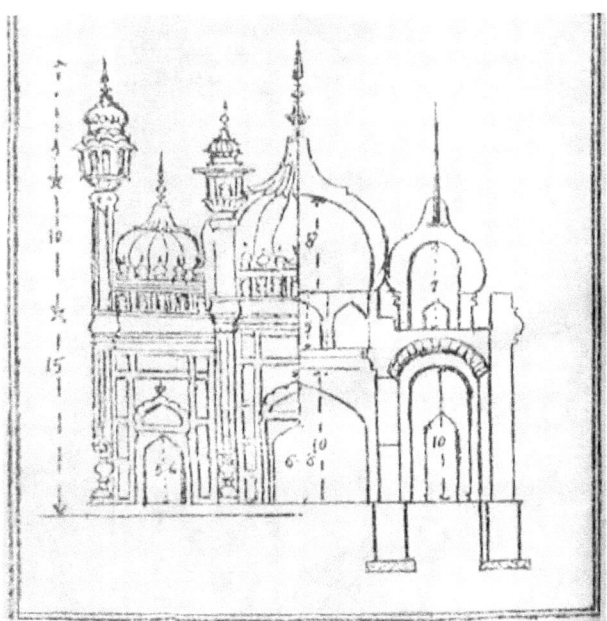

Figure 3 Design for a temple or mosque *Masjid* (1915).

continuing into the eighteenth century.[25] Jahangir's queen Mariam Zamani built a mosque at the city's Masti Darwazah in 1614,[26] a mosque was built at the city *chowk* constructed in Dara Shikoh's name during Shah Jahan's reign, and another adjoining the imperial treasury at Taksali Darwazah. In 1731, at his own cost, the governor of Lahore, Nawab Zakariyya Khan, built a mosque and sank a well in the walled Muhalla Mughalpura outside the city limits.[27] Kannhyalal frequently described neighborhoods which took the name of their mosques, suggesting the centrality of the mosque to the *muhalla*. Jahangir was said to have built a mosque as a gesture of imperial benefaction in the Muhalla Qasaban, the butchers' quarter. This walled settlement was built at Jahangir's command outside the city limits to house Lahore's butchers at a distance from the city's Hindus.[28]

The idea that the use of the street outside the mosque should be regulated to restrict ambient sound became popular in the late nineteenth century. "Zones of tradition", territories where cow protection was enforced by landlords, were emerging in Bengal in the 1890s, fueling associations of religious practice and territory.[29] Sacred spaces that could be violated through acts of disrespect or disregard for tradition were observed and defended around temples and in neighborhoods.[30] Something of a Muslim position on the ways in which noise could violate mosque sanctity emerges in the rare documentation of a private agreement between trustees of the Shi'a Mogul mosque of Rangoon and the custodians of the Shri Jain Shwetambar Jain Temple of 29th Street, behind the mosque.

"Various loud musical instruments" and a band that played in the early mornings and evenings "unreasonably interfered with the comfort of the mosque trustees and their fellow worshippers... and wrongfully interrupted the devotion at" the Shi'a Mogul Mosque. An agreement between the custodians of the mosque and those of the temple was brokered by "mutual friends . . . and by way of a friendly settlement and compromise." A document of indenture set out times and dates and manner in which noise control measures should be implemented at the temple.[31] This document demonstrated that music associated with Hindu worship was of concern where it was not part of a calendar of Hindu worship and could be heard on any day at the five times of prayer, or at times of reverence on any of the days of special Muslim worship at the mosque.

1. The Temple Trustees shall not cause or permit the playing or sounding of any musical instrument or instruments, or the ringing of any bell or bells within or near the said Temple which could be heard within the Mosque premises during the following periods of any day:
   a) From one hour immediately before sunrise to sunrise
   b) From 12.30 pm to 1.30 pm
   c) From twenty minutes after sunset to one hour and five minutes after sunset. i.e. for 45 minutes

2. The Temple Trustees shall not cause or permit the playing or sounding of any musical instrument or instruments or the ringing of any bell or bells within or near the said Temple which could be heard within the Mosque premises during the following period:-
   a) From 8 am to 10 am on Ramazan I'd
   b) From 8 am to 10 on Korban I'd

3. The Temple Trustees shall not cause or permit the playing of a band (or any collection of instruments in the nature of a band) within or near the said Temple during the following periods in any year:-
   a) From 4 pm on 9th Muharram to sunset on the 10th Moharum [sic]
   b) From 4 pm on the 12th Moharum to 6 am on the 13th Moharum
   . . .
   n) From 4 pm on the 14th Jamadiul-awal to 5 am on the 15th Jamadiul-awal.

   Provided however that if the Pachusan and the Maharum holidays happen to be on the same days the said Temple Trustees shall

subject to the provisions of clause 1 be at liberty to cause or permit the playing of a band within or near the said Temple at any time within the Pachusan holidays save and except from 4 pm on the 9th Moharum to sunset on the 10th Moharum.
4. The Mosque Trustees shall give previous notice to the Temple Trustees 48 hours prior to the occurrence of the holidays referred to in clauses 2 and 3 thereof.

This document elicited Hindu recognition of the sanctity of Shi'a Mogul Mosque and in return for this the custodians dropped a nuisance suit and also dropped objections to festivities accompanying an important Hindu festival.

Mosques featured prominently in urban imaginaries produced in vernacular traditions in north India, establishing the presence of Islam, organizing cities spatially, contributing to urban aesthetics and centering neighborhoods. Urban development in princely states, vernacular descriptions of architecture and heritage, and private agreements asserted the significance of the mosque as a feature of the built environment. These strategies were not organized, nor evenly reproduced across time and place, but suggest that in the minds of benefactors and architects, and those who were influenced by these forms of cultural production, the mosque and Muslim worship were a fixed feature of heterogeneous street life.[32]

While it may have been the intent of the authors of these numerous works, I do not seek to establish that the "abstract form" of a city derived part from historical memory, part from lived experience and part from myth[33] organized habitation in cities into the nineteenth century. However I do seek to establish that the ideal of a mosque-centered city made up of mosque-centered neighborhoods was reproduced in a variety of cultural forms through the late nineteenth and early twentieth centuries. The urban imaginary generated in a variety of cultural forms constituted a spatial context for Muslim life in early-nineteenth-century north India. Mosques were recognizable and important feature of cities and urban living and Muslims expected to see them, walk past them, and, often, to visit them.

The Perimeter of the Kanpur Mosque

As Muslims expressed the relationship of the mosque to the city in vernacular texts, discourses and building projects, the local government, including governors, commissioners, assistant commissioners, and magistrates, shaped the colonial Indian city with an intent to "promote civic and moral advancement."[34] New civic centers were defined by public buildings, an "orthogonal order," and organized space, and municipal government introduced electricity and piped water and made arrangements for trash removal and sanitation.[35] Colonial roads and buildings coexisted with older parts of the city in a complex spatiality marked by absorption, abrupt discontinuities,[36] and the preservation of monuments in a symbolic inheritance of knowledge[37] and of India's imperial past.[38] The colonial vision for the city and an Islamic spatial imaginary met and clashed at the perimeter of the mosque.

At the start of the twentieth century, Kanpur was a city of almost 200,000 with an old established weaving industry and connections to the agrarian hinterland, and a new cantonment and civil lines built after 1857. The "native quarter" with its winding roads appeared "mean" to the imperial administration, no doubt influenced by persistent representation of the city as the site of the mutiny-period massacre.[39] The colonial view of the city should make you uneasy given the histories of the emergence of Kanpur as a center of capital, new enterprise, and industry, including vernacular publishing and printing.[40]

The work of developing the urban built environment in colonial cities was consigned to municipal committees in major towns and cities, and local and district boards in less urbanized areas. A municipal committee was created in Delhi in 1863, and in Lahore in 1867.[41] These municipal bodies managed precolonial properties that were classified as *nazul* (government lands),[42] roads, tombs, bunds, graveyards, gardens, and property without legitimate heirs,[43] and buildings constructed by the colonial government including public schools set up on the European model ("normal schools"), waterworks and sewage lines, and markets and slaughterhouses.[44] The income from all these properties and facilities, collected as school fees, taxes on bazaar frontages, rents, and sales of buildings, accrued to the municipality.[45] While the mandate of municipal committees included support to the "native" city, municipal funds were disbursed in expenditures which disproportionately supported the new administration and newly planned settlements and suburbs.[46] In Rangoon a municipal committee was formed in 1874. It solicited and financed expert reports on drainage, sanitation, health, and electrification and articulated a vision and priorities for the urban built environment.[47]

From the 1880s, municipal committees and district boards charged with the "administration of non-revenue and non-military state lands" were established in the United Provinces. The work of these committees, described in annual reports, included running of local dispensaries, hospitals, schools, and sanitation systems. They also maintained trees and drains running alongside roads, provided for the administration of vaccines and repaired and maintained existing roads.[48] They were additionally charged with constructing and repairing wells, establishing and maintaining relief works in times of famine or scarcity, establishing and maintaining cattle pounds, managing public ferries, regulating camp grounds, running agricultural and industrial shows, and undertaking any works likely to promote the health, comfort, or convenience of the public.[49]

Municipal committees and district boards were controlled by the local government but included elected members. Their creation was a part of a larger process of creation of laws pertaining to the environment that produced a civic sense and security,[50] while also closely defining what that civic sensibility was. Projects for development of the urban built environment were overseen, and probably often even proposed by Indians who were the majority of members of the municipal committee, but the inspiration and the direction for them came from European ideals for urban design and engineering that favored orthogonal intersections for roads and broad, straight streets, championed by the local government.[51]

Urban redevelopment began in Kanpur in the twentieth century under the direction of the Kanpur Municipal Board, an elected body whose chairman was appointed by the district magistrate or his equivalent, and which worked closely with the magistrate's office to create bylaws and to prosecute.[52] Sewerage and drainage works were being constructed by 1905,[53] and a sanitary conference in Naini Tal in 1908 added attention to public health concerns.[54] Electric lighting was introduced in 1916.[55] And a trust was established by the central government for the opening out of congested areas in 1908,[56] providing funds for the outlays for paving, draining, and widening roads.[57]

From 1913 to 1916, the inspector general of police for the United Provinces took on a rare short-lived commitment to coordination with the municipalities and deployment of the police for the supervision of vehicular traffic, despite the resistance of inspectors and sub-inspectors to carrying out this duty.[58] The police department ran classes for instruction of police in the regulation of traffic and strongly recommended correction of road alignment in addition to provisioning for lighting, and introducing driving rules to aid the movement of motorized vehicles through the city[59] (see Figure 4).

The Kanpur mosque, as it came to be known, was to the Lt. Governor of the United Provinces an unexceptional building near a fish market on a small side street coming off the intersection of Halsey Road and the Mall in Kanpur. The main entrance was through a door above some shops on the south and a short flight of steps led up to an entrance in the north wall which admitted the entrant into an outside washing area. The courtyard was small and irregular in shape; on its west side was the triple arched

Figure 4 The Kanpur Mosque July 1913 © The British Library Board IOR/L/PJ/6/1256/2826.

and roofed place of prayer. The mosque stood among the residences of the Bisatis, small-goods merchants who appointed members of their own community as custodians of the mosque. The east side was demarcated by the wall of the adjoining house; part of this plot had been incorporated into the mosque to expand the courtyard and provide the space for a 9 by 28-foot *dalan*, a washing area.[60] The spatial history of the plot demonstrates an expansion in place through either gift, occupation, or purchase of additional land, all of which imply the direct support and interest of local residents for the growth of this building.

The Kanpur Municipal Board had been purchasing large numbers of plots, houses, and strips of land for the purpose of "widening lanes," and started road building projects in 1910–12.[61] The first notifications of plans for the new A. B. Road through Machchli Bazaar were published in 1908. In March of 1909, a petition was forwarded to the municipal authorities suggesting an alteration in the alignment of the road because under the scheme as then framed, three temples and two mosques, including the Kanpur Mosque, would have to be demolished.[62] The custodians engaged actively to advocate for the protection of the mosque through a period of dramatic urban change in the city. When the building adjoining the mosque on the eastern side was purchased by auction, the custodians approached the Municipal Board to ask that the wall of the house that was shared with the mosque would be left standing.[63] Their efforts were mirrored in Hindu representations asking that the temple opposite should not be knocked down.

In 1912 the Lt. Governor Meston visited the site; he remembered hearing a variety of opinions expressed and being particularly taken by the temple, "a building of some picturesqueness and with a pathetic story attached to it,"[64] and announced that the road should be splayed to protect both the mosque and the temple. A committee of the Municipal Board visited the bazaar in March 1913 and new plans were prepared which required only a slight alteration to the mosque: the demolition of the *dalan* to accommodate the angle of the road. This time the custodians gave their agreement to a municipal proposal to take the corner of the mosque to accommodate the alignment of the road in exchange for a small plot of land a little distance away. Although the custodians had agreed to the plan, other Muslims objected on the grounds that the land was waqf. Petitions from members of the public asked that these plans be cancelled out of respect for the mosque sanctity and deference to the "feelings of members of the Mahomedan community."[65]

The municipality responded:

> The mosque should not be interfered with but the washing place is not part of the sacred building and when a similar point arose in connection with the Lucknow improvements, the Muhammadans assented to another washing-place being given them in place of one which was required for public purposes. The present washing-place must therefore be removed. The authorities of the mosque will be asked to choose another site on which a washing-place will be built for them by the municipal board.[66]

The plans for demolition proceeded on July 1; Muslims came out on the street across region. *The Comrade*, *The Muslim Gazette* and *Al-Hilal* carried articles about the mosque, the site was visited and scrutinized and remarked upon by lawyers, politicians, one-time members of the Municipal Board of Kanpur and 'ulama, and on August 3, 1913, a citywide demonstration culminated in a meeting for prayer at the site of the mosque, and an impromptu effort to rebuild the demolished *dalan* which was under the guard of the magistrate's office. A force of 150 armed constables, military police, and mounted police opened fire discharging over 500 rounds of buckshot. In all, 16 people were killed, 28 wounded, 131 arrested. Outspoken men identified as part of the "Young Party" campaigned for awareness about the massacre. *The Comrade* and *The Pioneer* published stories that highlighted colonial violence deployed to suppress street action.[67]

A petition submitted by Shahid Husain of Kanpur and others represented to the government that this action should stop. The petitioners responded to snide references of attachment to the washing place and accusations of being motivated by intercommunal competition owing to the fact that a temple standing opposite the mosque was to be preserved. "Our community is not moved by any feeling of jealousy towards the good fortune that has attended the Hindu temple close to the mosque in question. Our community has deeply resented the suggestion that the outburst of feeling was due to the saving of the said temple. We think that it should have and has rightly been spared." Rather they objected to the fact that there had been no proper reference to the local community, no vetting of plans, and they submitted "with all the power of earnestness that we can command, that the portion demolished was sacred and was an integral part of the mosque."[68]

While there are a variety of scholarly opinions about the motivations of the Kanpur mosque "agitators," there is consensus on this at least: the process which led to the demolition of the corner of the mosque demonstrated an expectation for and a profound absence of consensus over the cultural priorities for development and regulation of the built environment. A variety of opinions were expressed about the mosque. The richness of the debate was subordinated to the weak course of action available to advocates for mosque protection: application to the municipal board and the district magistrate. The Muslims submitted a petition and after a long debate in meeting, the municipal board decided to go ahead with the plans to disassemble the *dalan* and mosque wall, but directly implicated the lieutenant governor in this decision by permitting a formal representation to him that he allow the mosque be entirely spared. The lieutenant governor refused. A deputation of Muslims asked the district magistrate for his intervention; the latter advised them not to press "what he considered to be a factious grievance."[69] It was clear to those involved in mosque defense that the objectives for urban development were produced by the central government and enforced under the authority of the district magistrate, and it was equally clear to them that if the district magistrate did not feel compelled to accommodate their request, he would not.

The debates between the 'ulama which followed distilled to the question of what process should be used to determine the fate of the mosque perimeter. Maulvi Muhammad Salamatullah of Firangi Mahal questioned why Muslims should object to the creation of the new elevated washing place as the terraced structure would provide the facility and the land below the overhang "would be preserved intact in its service to the masjid," by serving as an access to the door.[70] He stated that the municipality and the governor's office had been sensitive to the Muslim claim to the land and had demonstrated sufficient attention to *maslaha*, considering the public benefit through reference to Islamic law. The "government," represented by the governor's office, had fulfilled its duty and he argued that Muslims should not pursue any further litigation. He echoed the assertion put forward by municipal surveyors that the land that was being claimed for the *dalan* did not in fact belong to the mosque and that it did not belong to anyone.[71]

A leading Shi'a cleric of Lucknow highlighted the instances of colonial benevolence and financial support for religious sites, emphasizing that the respect that Muslims sought was already offered by the British government:

> The principle consistently followed by the British Government from the commencement of its rule in India has been to respect the sanctity of all places of worship, irrespective of creed, and to protect the buildings devoted to that purpose. Through the kindness of Government and its local officers I know of mosques which in the hands of people had been allowed to fall into complete disrepair or were being used for purposes other than that of prayer. . . . After seeing numerous instances of this kind it is hard to believe that the British Government, or any of its officers—especially Sir James Meston, of whose kindness of heart we are all aware,—would deliberately destroy a mosque or any portion of a mosque. His Honour respects not only our religious feelings but our personal ones and takes a keen interest in all old Muhammadan mosques.[72]

"The real blame," he said, "lies with those Muhammadans who, having access to the local officers, failed to warn them that the removal could not take place without obtaining a fatwa from the 'ulama."[73] He recommended acceptance of the provincial government's decision, and trust that they would do what was "according to shari'a."

The Bareilvi *Darul Ifta* issued a fatwa stating:

> the land of a mosque under any circumstances, under no circumstances, can be used for a road for railway lines or for any other purpose. Masjid, in reality, is the name of the land. A roof cannot be called its *naim ul badal* [that which is received in exchange]. And neither can this land be exchanged with any other piece of land.[74]

Was it possible, he argued, that "a dog, a madman, a pig, or even a sweeper carrying nightsoil, should pass under the roof of a mosque?"[75] To remain silent on these matters, he said, would have been a betrayal of the legal principles encapsulated in shari'a, a betrayal of justice and rights. The issues must be articulated, he argued, and they must be defended in the courts. Ahmad Raza Bareilvi, the vastly popular reformist leader, said that there was no doubt that consideration had been shown to Muslims. Even the Viceroy had given instructions in this matter and asked that when reaching a verdict the feelings and happiness of Muslims should be taken into consideration. The problem, he said, was in asking for conciliation. Muslims had the opportunity to agree with him and stay peaceful, but that would have been a betrayal of the legal principles encapsulated in shari'a, a betrayal of justice and rights. These rights, he argued, must be defended in the courts. Ahmad Raza asked all Muslims to follow this directive, to take their cases to the courts, to try to draw the government's attention to the principles underlying the debate, particularly given the government's deal with detainees, to release them if they promised not to initiate legal proceedings.[76] Ahmad Raza presented the colonial courts as the appropriate institution to govern the perimeter of the mosque and mediate its relationship with civic infrastructure.[77]

While a number of studies have highlighted the popular Muslim response to the Kanpur Mosque affair, few have noted the implied critique of the colonial bureaucracy. Meston pointed to the numerous fatwas received that sanctioned the demolishment of the *dalan* and attributed an irrational, fanatical, and competitive Muslim attachment to mosque land, deeming the spokesmen for the mosque to be leading a calculated "agitation." While some have argued that the fatwas should have been enough to placate Muslim sentiments, Ahmad Raza Bareilvi dismissed the fatwas of the 'ulama that sanctioned urban redevelopment efforts on the grounds that the cultural underpinnings of the Muslim position, the perceived sacredness of the mosque, and the impact of urban change which had led to the appropriation of mosque land and reorientation of the neighborhood away from the mosque, were not adequately addressed by the 'ulama of Firangi Mahal, nor had these matters received due consideration from the district magistrate.

The custodians and Muslim members of the Kanpur Municipal Committee themselves filed testimonials about the religious illegality of resuming waqf land. These interventions were noted alongside notes on payment schedules for street cleaners on committee minutes. A Muslim community member nominated to relate concerns about demolishment of the corner of the mosque competed for time in a tent at a one-off visit to the site by the lieutenant governor and his name was forgotten. The newspapers angrily highlighted the multiple instances of disregard for mosque sanctity. People gathered on the street outside the mosque to see, to talk, to dispute. The debate about the Kanpur Mosque, as it continued in the press, in scholarly discourses, and on the street, established a range of forums in which widely held cultural values for the development of civic infrastructure were being debated and produced.

Town planning strategies in Kanpur in 1913 required that any dispute over urban improvement projects had to go the magistrate's office, but the magistrate's office did not have the capacity to consider or respond to those concerns. Hindu expectations for the temple and the multiple Muslim responses to the Kanpur Mosque demolition were grouped together in the English-language press as evidence of myriad, fractured, and irreconcilable expectations for the public. There was no clear leader, moral authority, or forum that dominated or knitted together a vernacular discourse on civic priorities.[78] Yet there was a demonstrated shared belief that the local government asserted priorities for the civic environment without sufficiently accounting for the widely held cultural value of mosque protection.

The matter was not a straightforward instance of colonial arrogance because the perimeter of the Kanpur Mosque did not appear to officials to be either an essential part of the mosque, nor to exclusively pertain to the mosque itself. But what had emerged in the debate about the Kanpur Mosque was that the perimeter of the mosque, defined both by the boundary wall and to a lesser extent by adjacent public spaces, could be understood to pertain to the mosque and could be treated as a sacred space. People gathered on the street outside the mosque to see, to talk, to dispute.

The colonial vision for the Indian city which led to the demolishment of buildings and widening of roads met with an indigenous vision for the city at the perimeter of sacred buildings. Muslim observers of the Kanpur Mosque incident argued that the mosque perimeter was inextricably linked to the mosque and that Muslims must have religious priority in this space.

Magistrate's Control over Devotionalism on the Street

The Kanpur Mosque incident and other cases of religious claims on public roads demonstrated that the colonial state had put in place a system for mediating religiously inspired disputes over urban public spaces which was unlike other aspects of the colonial dispensation. Competing religious claims in public spaces were managed through a system of conciliatory and violent governmental interventions by the magistrate, the most powerful and ubiquitous of the officers of local government, instead of judicial deliberation.[79]

A central principle of colonial administration was that the will, logic, rationale, justice, and expectations of the empire should be represented at the district level as "local government," officers of the colonial bureaucracy. The magistrate, also known as the collector or the deputy commissioner, was typically the highest ranking officer of local government present in a district. He was an officer of the Indian Civil Service vested with powers to assess and collect revenue, judicial powers to hear and decide civil and criminal cases, and administrative powers to maintain control and order of the "public." And he served as a moral authority in the locale, intervening and reinforcing traditional and legitimate authority where needed. The magistracy was reproduced and made consistent across colonial India over the course of the nineteenth century. Macaulay, a highly influential British Whig politician and historian said in an address to the House of Commons in 1853 that

> some gentlemen seem to imagine, that he is something like a commissioner of tax or stamps in this country, while the truth is that the collector of revenue in any part of India is the sole consul of a great province the district assigned to him being about the size of one of the four provinces of Ireland, and the population therein probably about 1,000,000 human beings. . . . Such a power as that which collectors in India have over the people in India is not found in any other part of the world possessed by any class of functionaries.[80]

The magistrate's conjoined right of intervention in civil matters, criminal jurisdiction, and revenue collection was the lynchpin of control by the British Empire. Despite critiques of magisterial power put forward by elite Indians,[81] these summary judicial powers were incorporated further into the penal code in the Punjab and defended elsewhere.[82]

Mechanisms of imperial control and priorities for appointment to the Indian Civil Service changed after the reprisals and reflections of the 1857–8 period. A system of appointment to the civil service through competitive exam was introduced in 1856.[83] Politicians had imagined highly educated Oxbridge graduates filling these posts but age requirements for entry into the civil service meant that the vast majority of those who won appointments prepared at crammer schools where candidates' time and attention was distributed over the study of four or five subjects chosen from among European and oriental language, literature and history, mathematics, political science, political economy, jurisprudence, and natural and moral science and philosophy. Those who additionally managed to complete a full university education before taking the exams had to diversify their studies early on in their careers. Candidates succeeded by demonstrating intelligence, versatility, and preparedness to take up a career in India by the age of twenty-five at the latest. Their counterparts seeking traditional employment in law and academia in England would undergo painstaking training in any one subject area in the classics, social sciences, mathematics, sciences, or law.[84] Academic preparation to enter the cadres of the ICS was supplemented by two years of institutional training in England, and then minimal on-the-job instruction in India.

At the start of the twentieth century trials of all smaller revenue and criminal cases valued at less than Rs 5,000 remained in the hands of magistrates who had received only a basic academic training in jurisprudence, and whose effectiveness as judges derived from a functional knowledge of the Indian Code of Civil Procedure and the Indian Penal Code.[85] They heard all suits and applications relating to taxation and land resumptions.[86] The territories of the United Provinces and Agra and the Mughal capital of Delhi had come under the administrative control of the Government of India through a series of political and military actions from the late eighteenth century through the early nineteenth century. The governor or chief commissioner of a province oversaw financial commissioners who in turn oversaw the work of commissioners of revenue divisions. Divisions were further subdivided into districts, each one headed by a magistrate.[87] Municipal and district boards in the United Provinces in 1883–5 were directly subjected to the oversight of the magistrate's office; magistrates were "elected" as chairmen of these committees in seventy-one out of ninety-one districts where they participated in and observed the proceedings.[88] A large number of honorary magistrates served under their district magistrate to take some of the burden of case load off the latter's hands. Honorary magistrates needed only to be literate in one of the vernaculars enough to read and write in it, conduct proceedings with intelligence, and understand the Code of Civil Procedure.[89]

Legal authority was concentrated in the hands of these civil servants for reasons of expediency at home in Britain and in other parts of the empire as well. As the number and length of court hearings increased in Britain during the nineteenth century under the combined influence of a growing population, "more vigorous prosecution and more voluble lawyers elaborating defenses, magistrates took up the load."[90] Magistrates were also allowed undue discretionary and final authority in adjudicating disputes where individual freedoms and dignities collided with public priorities. Across Britain and the empire, magistrates interpreted and asserted master and servant laws which were created to make the labor supply and performance more reliable, and "especially in the case of migrant labor, cheaper than it could be obtained otherwise, if it could be obtained at all."[91] In India, magistrates interpreted inheritance laws with the effect of endorsing paternalistic and conjugal claims over women.[92] The magistrate's effectiveness as an agent of empire derived from his power to weigh public interest against individual rights and freedoms in his evaluation of evidence,[93] preventative policing[94] and enforcement of contract.

One such matter of public interest was the roads of colonial India.[95] The magistrate was charged with issuing directions to prevent obstructions of the thoroughfare or breaches of public peace[96] and issuing orders to those obstructing public ways or causing nuisances of injuring, endangering, or annoying the public.[97] From the 1860s, magistrates received requests from individual subjects of the state, community representatives, trustees of religious endowments, and municipal committees to either sanction or prohibit religious claims on roads. Sanctioned Shi'a and Hindu religious processions on public streets were scheduled and permitted accordingly. Religious claims on the road that were prohibited were subjected to temporary orders under section 144 of the criminal procedure code[98] to restrain the religious devotee from "illegally interfering with the exercise" of the right of passage on the street.[99] The magistrate's seemingly benign authority to keep traffic flowing in the interests of the public conferred on him the power to evaluate religious expectations pertaining to roads.

Requests to the magistrate to exercise his power to regulate religious expressions on the road were evaluated through reference to Hindu and Muslim calendars of religious fairs, festivals, and fasts and attention to the "prescribed customs in each district." A handy guide for the district officer in the United Provinces provided a general introduction and list of Muslim and Hindu festivals and fasts which would aid the local government in identifying events "requiring control" and making the necessary arrangements for them.[100] The guide did not provide the sort of ethnographic detail that was available in other texts such as the gazetteers; it provided explanations of Muslim and Hindu calendars and encouraged district officers to understand the routes of processions. "Trouble" arose out of the overlap of devotions in public spaces, but these devotions could be anticipated calendrically and spatially.

The twelve lunar months of the Islamic Hijri calendar and twelve to thirteen months of the Hindu Samvat calendar were identified, the latter "more stable" in its relationship with the English calendar. The manual also noted that Muslims observed the start of a day at sunset while Hindus observed it at sunrise. These calendars and times of day corresponded to ritual practices. Muslims prayed five times a day—morning, noon, evening, sunset, and night; Sunnis were more observant of congregational prayer than Shi'as.[101] The first twelve days of the lunar month of Muharram, and especially the first ten days, were "a period of mourning in memory of the assassination of Husain at the instigation of Yazid in Karbala."[102] Twenty-seven universal Hindu festivals and fasts were listed; those of a more local origin which had no meaning and significance beyond the locale were omitted as together the list would number in the hundreds. Among them, Dadh Kando, the second day after the birth of Krishna and a festival that had become important in recent years, was observed by way of processions taken out in the evening and temple worship observed on a very large scale.[103]

The manual indicated to officers which rituals were rooted in local custom.

> No special times are fixed for taking out of the [Shi'a] processions and this depends on local custom; similar custom decides the precedence of the various *taziyas*. In general the processions finish on the night of the tenth of Muharram but in certain places, for instance Agra, the *taziya* and *alam* (banner) procession is taken out on the night of the 12th Muharram. The Shi'as observe a *majlis* on the twelfth day of Muharram and in certain places continue these *majlises* [for forty days].[104]

Local community leaders provided information about the size of religious groups, prevailing customs, and procession routes through the locales.

The magistrate and the municipality dealt with most urban issues relating to thoroughfares by applying nuisance laws which otherwise provided for issuing fines for obstructions and littering and making arrests for vagrancy. Religious matters were more grave. Where he received requests for or complaints about the performance of religious devotion on the street, the magistrate was charged with evaluating the request through reference to the numbers of worshippers involved and the local history of the practice, and either permitting and enabling or prohibiting that practice with a police cordon and the use of section 144, the suspension of all regular rights on the street. He treated these as extraordinary and dangerous events, more so when more than one group submitted a petition. Magistrates did not endorse any specific priorities for or principles of religious conduct on the street, instead simply acknowledging the various forms such priorities took.

The magistrate performed such critical judicial functions without any advanced legal training by drawing on the civil code[105] What this meant was that the magistrate acted in his capacity as a judicial officer in his management of the street, but his decisions at this junction of colonial and native interests were devoid of any legal or moral reasoning. He had no ability to reconcile or rationalize the competing philosophical approaches to, or priorities for, the street. A brief and final return to the Friday mosque of Rangoon in 1893, as the cow protection movement gained ground, illustrates the way in which the magistrate's authority over the street was asserted through acts of conciliation and violence.

Eid was approaching in Rangoon and a Muslim residing on 29th Street, opposite a temple, insisted on his right to perform the ritual Eid sacrifice, to the great consternation of the Hindus of the city. After a meeting with the Muslim Yacoobji Dadu, the leading Hindu of Rangoon Bhagwan Das, and their respective lawyers in 1893, the deputy commissioner and magistrate of Rangoon, Fleming, assessed the two positions on cow slaughter. Not having the power to intervene in religious affairs meant that he could not compare Bhagwan Das's representation of Hindu custom and Dadu's representation of Muslim custom and take a moral position on cow slaughter. Instead he enumerated the support for each position, concluding that at the time of the dispute the Hindus were in majority in the neighborhood, and so he decided in their favor.

> There are large numbers of Hindus who are not amenable to reason and the fact of a cow destined for slaughter being brought past their temple, and its probable ejaculations before slaughter, are likely to excite the religious feelings of the Hindu mob. Both parties anticipate a riot if the slaughter of cattle is permitted. . . . It appears from the papers above quoted that the Hindu temple in question was built some ten years ago, and that previous to that time the majority of the residents in the neighborhood were Mussulmans. Since the temple was built, the Hindu community has increased in numbers and strength and is now in a majority.[106]

Fleming's assessment of residential patterns in the Mogul and 29th Street area drew on surprisingly detailed municipality records of residency in buildings. Hindu, Muslim, Jewish, and Christian residents were distinguished from Chinese and Burmese residents, and all of these permanent householders were distinguished from the coolies, the latter being temporary seasonal occupants. It is likely that house inspections and mandatory registrations for the purposes of tax assessments produced this data which was then represented spatially as the demographics of a neighborhood. There was little that distinguished this "neighborhood" from surrounding areas in terms of use of its streets. These streets served as passage from residences and commercial spaces on Dalhousie Mogul and Merchant Streets, southwards to the river docks, northeastwards to Shwe Dagon Pagoda, eastwards to the new industrial areas, and northwestwards to the Surati Bazaar. The purpose of this demographic representation was to determine the numbers of proximous people who would be invested enough in the issue to cause a "fanatical" uproar in response to the magistrate's order (Figure 5).

Determining the Hindus in the vicinity of the mosque to be in a majority, the magistrate employed section 144 of the criminal procedure code, thereby suspending the rights of householders within 200 feet of the temple to conduct a cow sacrifice and then deploying police to secure the area at that 200-foot perimeter. He wrote that under the present regulations this was permitted and the Mussulmans were within their rights to slaughter a cow, but

> having consideration to the consensus of opinion that a riot will take place, if their rights are exercised, and that the police force is not sufficient to check it without the probability of bloodshed, I think it right to exercise the power given me by section 144 of the Criminal Procedure Code.[107]

Section 144 of the criminal procedure code allowed the magistrate to temporarily limit civil liberties and direct subjects to refrain from acts which caused "obstruction, disturbance or annoyance," within 200 feet of the Hindu temple.[108] This action not only restricted the ability to carry out the cow sacrifice, but restricted passage on and use of Mogul Street, measuring 50 feet across, and 29th Street, measuring 25 feet across. The magistrate wrote that "any person who chose to hang about in the vicinity of a riot must take the consequences of appearing to sympathize with the rioters." The magistrate's strategy of enumeration and corresponding police deployment were enacted within the territory of the "neighborhood of the temple," criminalized the minority Muslim movements and actions in the area.

Between 1918 and 1924, there were several other instances of dispute of cultural priorities for the use of the street in the United Provinces, many of them related to Shi'a devotional practice which was becoming more organized and purposeful in claims on the street. A Shi'a *taziya* procession was opposed by the residents of a Hindu *muhalla* in Agra. A

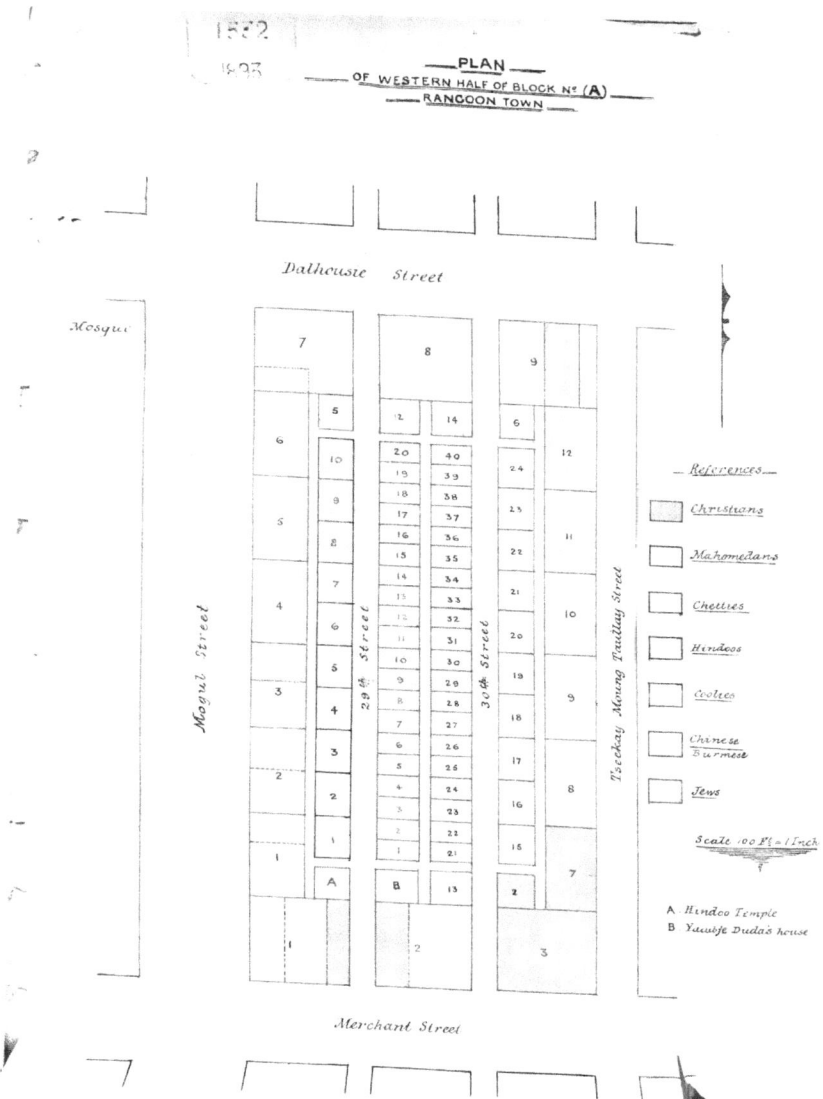

Figure 5 Residences around the Rangoon Friday mosque © The British Library Board IOR/L/PJ/6/354, File 1532.

Hindu marriage procession was opposed by the congregation in a Sunni mosque in Jhansi.[109] In Shahjahanpur, the Shi'as objected to the Hindu Dadh Kando *mela* that fell during Muharram.[110] In each of these cases the district magistrate's office issued orders for the use of the street that defined the dates and times at which processions could be taken out, access points and routes. The precision and enforcement of these directions appeared paramount; when a riot occurred in Agra, it was because a non-customary route was followed, and orders for the procession were not given promptly (Figure 6).[111]

The colonial government recognized devotional uses of public spaces, ascribing an extraordinary character to the road for the period of time and along the route that such activities occurred. Increasingly into the twentieth century, such scheduled, mapped uses of the road took place under the singular and paramount power of the magistrate's office to assess, prioritize, permit, and police the expression of devotionalism on the street.

Muslim objections to the demolition of the corner of the Kanpur Mosque were subject to the supervisory authority of the magistrate over devotionalism on the road. The robust debate about the Kanpur mosque and cultural values for the development of civic infrastructure, as it continued in the press, in scholarly discourses, and on the street, were not echoed in the decisions of the magistrate's office. Far from being based in legal reasoning or calculated to formulate or incubate consensus, the decisions of the colonial executive in Kanpur were inspired and enabled by long established imperial administrative procedures.

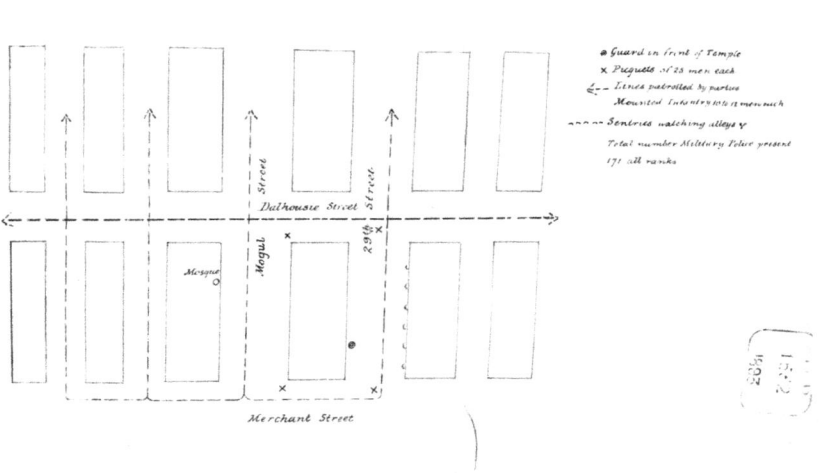

Figure 6 Police lines around the Rangoon Friday mosque in 1893. © The British Library Board IOR/L/PJ/6/354, File 1532.

Political Appointments of Magistrates

In an interesting and highly consequential parallel political development, Indians angled for the privileges that accrued to the office of the magistrate, reading the problem as the exercise of oppressive power by unfriendly officers rather than one of limitations of the legal process and excesses of bureaucratic power. The judgment confirming the overarching control of the magistrate over the street was delivered in the Aurangabad mosque case in 1924, shortly after the constitution of elected representative legislative councils under the government of India Act 1919. In the years that the case (discussed below) moved through the courts, members of the United Provinces Legislative Council offered sustained criticisms of actions taken by district magistrates' offices which curtailed religious and devotional activity in the street and often demanded that magistrates provide copies of their orders for scrutiny by that elected body. However, rather than making recommendations for a calculated reduction of bureaucratic power in favor of judicial process, the UP Legislative Council gradually accelerated demands for appointments to magisterial posts along communal lines. In other words, Hindu and Muslim elected representatives sought to appoint officers who were friendly to their communities, who could assume the privilege to make discretionary choices for street devotionalism and exercise it in the interest of their coreligionists. Proponents of religious rights abandoned legal reasoning in favor of arguments for communal appointments of Muslims and Hindus to local posts and their assumption of the privilege to choose religious priorities for the street.

A committee of the UP Legislative Council did look into the separation of judicial and executive power in 1921 to propose a scheme that was workable and "not too expensive." [112] However its authors maintained the authority of the magistrate to give orders relating the removal of nuisances, and to give prohibitive orders under section 144 of the criminal procedure code relating to "urgent cases should he apprehend danger to human life, health or safety, or disturbance of the public tranquility or a riot or an affray." The report allowed for appeal to a sessions judge, but the principles of magisterial authority to assess religious sensibilities and use extraordinary force to control religious expression in the public interest were not challenged.[113]

During the Muharram disputes of 1923–5 members of the council demanded the government act more responsively in registering complaints[114] and taking action against officers who acted improperly and in a manner that may have provoked riots. Council members were deeply concerned with the nature of the orders passed by magistrates in cases of religious dispute and scrutinized these orders in council.¹¹⁵ These orders in turn became more and more detailed. In the Hindu month of Sambhal which coincided with Muharram in 1925, maps of Muharram routes and lists of imambargahs were prepared in advance by the district magistrate of Muradabad. The magistrate took agreements from community leaders that "people would follow customary routes and times and ensure that the tail of the procession had passed the Maddeyan Temple by 4 pm and to protect the Pipal tree on the Amroha Road." In turn,

> from the 7th to the 9th of Muharram, Hindu worship of arti, ghants, dholak, baja was only permitted from 7.15 to 8.00 pm, and the hours of the customary fair of Hindu women and the Chairan fair were reduced from 12 to 5. Any violator of these terms would be sentenced to 6 months imprisonment or a fine of Rs 1,000 or both.¹¹⁶

The detail in the orders highlights the continued and perhaps even increased government reliance on magistrates to evaluate and manage devotional uses of the street.

Elected Muslim and Hindu politicians began to rely increasingly on a notion of embodied authority, jettisoning even the most basic proposals for training in jurisprudence for honorary magistrates in favor of appointing those with social influence. The source of the magistrate's authority to hear and decide civil and criminal cases was debated in council leading to a resolution in 1922 that honorary magistrates should be tested to ensure that they understood the customary "laws of the land" and that nominations for such posts should not be made until consulting the "public opinion" of the locality concerned and ascertaining "that in view of his social status and antecedents and reputation, . . . he will be a fit and desirable person to exercise the powers." It was clarified later that year that "the policy of the Government in appointing honorary magistrates and honorary assistant collectors ha[d] been to [appoint] private gentlemen who by their position, character or attainments command respect in the neighborhoods." The government produced a list of all sixty-nine honorary magistrates of Shahjahanpur and Moradabad during the disputes in that district in 1924 to demonstrate attention to these priorities.¹¹⁷ The Judicial Department stated the impossibility of designing a test that would be passable by the sorts of "gentlemen who are eminently suitable for appointment."¹¹⁸ Recommendations of training in jurisprudence put forward for early appointees to the office were abandoned in favor of identifying and inducting magistrates of personal stature and power. Because efforts were focused on appointing officers whose orders would be widely accepted and not disputed, council members unapologetically preferred social clout to legal and procedural training,[119] an embodied rather than a reasoned authority.

Political activists and community leaders sporadically tried to encourage Muslim acceptance of Hindu processional uses of the street in return for Hindu acceptance of Muslim rights of slaughter on private property, notably in a conference in Bengal following riots in Pabna and Calcutta in 1927.[120] But it was impossible to produce statutory regulations enabling religious freedoms where the debate had come to rest on the "exact extent and limit of the right of subjects to make music and their liberty to worship idols and sacrifice cows ... when music becomes a nuisance to persons engaged in lawful convocation in the neighborhood."[121] The debate in legislative councils came to focus on producing officers who internalized ideologies rather than debated the substance of the law relating to shared interests in the roads. Vernacular writings relating to street violence and conflict increasingly equated justice with preference for or sympathy toward the author's preferred religious group, and equated injustice with religious or cultural antipathy.[122] Among many other political developments in this time, the diminishing of the discussion of rights and increasing popular support for communal representation in bureaucratic appointments was deepening the divide between Hindu and Muslim.

Defense of the Perimeter of the Aurangabad Mosque

The ultimate irony of this story lies in the fact that Sunnis championed the position that the courts should decide what was permissible at the mosque-street junction in Kanpur in 1913, but Sunni efforts to defend mosque worship from disruption by Shi'a devotions on the street produced the 1924 legal judgment which confirmed the magistrate's discretionary control of the mosque perimeter. Unlike the Kanpur Mosque incident, the dispute in Aurangabad UP wound its way through the colonial legal system to the JCPC and elicited the critical judgment that consigned the perimeter of the mosque, and the passage of worshippers along it, to the discretionary and paternalistic control of the district's magistrate. There were no firm sectarian positions on mosque law, just flares of interest in particular events. The Sunni-led Aurangabad suit produced a verdict in keeping with the underlying colonial strategy for mosques: to appoint overseers of mosque affairs.

Aurangabad was a *qasbah* town of the northwestern United Provinces with an early-twentieth-century population of 5,000, governed by the district board of Bulandshahr.[123] The numerically consequential Sunnis had been used to control and leadership in local affairs,[124] and were acknowledged as such by local government. Shiʻa sayyids, those claiming lineage from the family of the Prophet Muhammad and whose ancestors had founded the town, were hereditary zamindars of Aurangabad and twenty-nine other villages across the district.[125] Other non-Shiʻa landlords also held property through mortgage and purchase. The majority Muslim population had managed differences between Shiʻa and Sunni as well as negotiating urban relationships with a Hindu population for hundreds of years. Across the *qasbahs* of the United Provinces, Sunnis, Shiʻas, and Hindus watched each other's festivals, particularly on the streets, but did not engage with the other's religious symbols or enter another's places of worship or schools. The blending of communities had limits which Raisur Rahman has asked that we attend to, but he also demonstrates that grounding in religion had produced ideas, associations, and texts which served intercommunity dialogue and discourses.[126]

In 1916 the wealthy Shiʻas of Aurangabad filed for a declaration from the court that "members of the public have a right of not only walking down a public road but also stopping occasionally in a reasonable manner and at reasonable intervals for all lawful purposes." Aurangabad's collectively used spaces included a mela which took place each year at the tomb of the founder,[127] a weekly market,[128] held on a "long spacious platform," constructed in the 1880s,[129] a hospital-dispensary, a school, and water tanks.[130] A small and architecturally unexceptional Friday mosque in a residential area that had been rebuilt at the turn of the century was one of at least six mosques in the bazaar that served the 3,000 Sunnis of the town.[131] As was commonly the case across India, the main road was a site of performance of Ashura commemoration by the town's twenty-five Shiʻa families, and of Holi and Ram Lila celebrations by the 2,000 Hindus of the *qasbah*. "*Taziyadari*," a Shiʻa witness testified in 1918, "has been observed in Aurangabad for hundreds of years."

> There are 200 or 250 Shiʻas in *qasbah* Aurangabad. The following observances take place during Muharram days: *majlises* (mourning meetings) are held, *taziyas*, *alams* (standards), *nash* (imitation of the coffin of Imam Husain), *gahwara* and *zuljenah* (a horse like that of Imam Husain) are taken out. The *taziyas*, *alams* and *zuljenah* are taken through the whole of the town (*abadi*). The *gahwara* and the *nash* are taken from one imambargah to another. Afterwards they are taken to *karbala* for burial. The *zuljenah*, *alam* and *taziya*, the three articles are taken out by roads in day time and the *gahwara* the *zuljenah* and the *taziya* are taken out by roads at night. At the said processions *marsiya* is recited and *matam* (self flagellation) is observed. There are also musical

accompanists with them. When the procession starts it does not go on marching. On the contrary people stop after each 2 or 4 paces and then *marsiya* is recited and *matam* observed.... The *zuljenah* the *alam* and the *taziya* pass by the road which is on the back of the Aurangabad Mosque. The people used to stop at the back of the mosque and the *marsiya* used to be recited and *matam* to be observed.[132]

The route of the Muharram procession along the *qasbah*'s streets began at a community-agreed point, either a private home or an imambargah, then looped around the town and returned to its starting point.[133] The processions connected families and neighborhoods through performance, sound, and movement. These processions led by a horse, carrying representations of a tomb, a coffin, a cradle of the martyred child of Husain, were also taken out[134] during the plague and cholera epidemics which ravaged this region in the early part of the century[135] and instigated a movement of populations out of cities and larger towns.[136] Where the colonial establishment promoted vaccinations and other Western medical practices to promote a sense of civic security, the Shi'a engaged in public devotional performance to reassure a frightened and debilitated urban population.

Shi'as and Sunnis shared many of the routines and rhythms of religious life across the region, from their daily prayers, to the celebration of the two Eids and commemoration of saints. Sunni observers watched Shi'a commemorations of Muharram, invited their Shi'a neighbors to their homes for tea, and kept *taziyas* in their own homes. Yet they maintained their own spaces. Sunnis managed Sunni mosques and Shi'as managed their own mosques, *karbalas*, and imambargahs.[137] One of the spatial intersections of their shared and separate lives lay at the boundary of the mosque. The Friday mosque of Aurangabad was situated in a row of buildings with a main road at its western front, and a 12-foot-wide lane at its eastern wall.[138] This lane running behind the mosque was on registered private land, a portion of 750 yards of land[139] that was owned by the Sunni Muhammad Zaman Khan but had been used as a public passage for at least the last twenty-two years and was lined on both sides with drainage that was maintained by the district board of Bulandshahr.[140] The houses adjoining the mosque were mostly occupied by Sunnis; residents of five of the houses were in government service, and four others were barbers.[141]

The defendants in the suit, the Sunnis of Aurangabad, were led by Zaman Khan and asserted that the open field and lane behind the mosque could be differentiated from the metaled and paved highway that ran in front of the mosque. Their position was that the lane was used by the public but only with the special permission of the land owner it was on. Zaman Khan admitted that the Shi'as had long used this lane for the passage of their processions, but claimed that under a prevailing (though undocumented) agreement, both sides had agreed that the site was his property and that music would stop during the passage behind the mosque.[142] He added that there were three verandas and two windows overlooking land, and two doors for the egress and ingress of the worshippers (*namazis*) and these worshippers were "in every respect, concerned with the way."[143] Zaman Khan demonstrated a longstanding concern with the management of the road behind the mosque and its relationship to the mosque, a position that was reinforced by the policy of the United Provinces administration that prevailed until at least 1915, to leave unmetalled roads to the charge of Indian members of the district boards or "influential landowners."[144]

It was not so much proprietary rights which Zaman Khan asserted, but the relationship of the road to the western frontage of the mosque. This road, which lay in the direction worshippers faced in prayer, was overlooked by three verandas and two windows of the mosque and served two entrances to the mosque. Zaman Khan stated that the mosque was "in every respect, concerned with the way,"[145] and in doing so invoked foundational principles of shari'a. The public path leading to the entrance of the mosque was pivotal to the identification of the building as a public endowment. Hanafi law, periodically invoked by the colonial courts, set out that a building could only be considered dedicated to use as a mosque if there was a fully accessible and unrestricted thoroughfare leading to its entrance.[146] Moreover, under Hanafi law, no one could obstruct any Muslim from saying his prayers in a mosque.[147] These laws were compiled by an *alim* and translated by Ameer Ali to support colonial jurists in ascertaining the validity of the creation of a trust but took on a life of their own in Zaman Khan's testimony and his defense of mosque protection efforts. Just as the public street served and defined the mosque, he saw the mosque as producing values for the streets around it: the street should allow expediency of access, it should enable pious self-presentation at the mosque, it should serve as a perimeter of sanctity for the mosque.

The Deobandi headmaster of the Islamia high school of the neighboring town testified to the doctrinal basis for a relationship between the mosque and the public spaces of the *qasbah*:

> prayers said in a mosque confer more blessings that those said in a house, and prayers said in a Friday mosque confer more blessings than those said in other mosques. According to Sunni ideas, making noise and playing instruments are improper, i.e. they are totally disallowed and in the vicinity of that mosque (also) they are totally disallowed. I have not stated all this according to my ideas. It is written in [books of fiqh].[148]

The Sunni defendants claimed that the Shi'a processions "wound[ed] the religious feelings of members of the public and interfere[d] with their worship and prayer."[149]

The Sunnis of Aurangabad asserted a right to silence and somber regard for their piety at the mosque perimeter in response to the Shi'a expectation of the right to procession, further fueled by reports that in other places in India Hindus played music outside mosques at prayer times. The conflict was a result of competition for priority of one group's devotional rights in that liminal public space just outside or abutting the built structure of the mosque at the time of prayers or celebration or mourning and during ingress or egress. The perimeter of the mosque was one of many such liminal devotional spaces in urban India. Each participant in each conflict demanded regard for the devotional values underpinning their position and a declaration of their absolute rights in these liminal devotional spaces. These positions appeared to the colonial state to be long standing, mutually irrational, fundamentally opposed, and inherently irreconcilable. Riots and attacks by Hindus on Muslims or Muslim on Hindus have been understood to constitute a "long history of violence associated with clashing religious festivals."[150] But when considered in the context of the debate about sound and its transgression across a bounded perimeter, are also a part of a wider discussion about roads, rights on and over them, and systems of urban governance and dispute management.

On the seventh and tenth of Muharram in November 1915, police sub-inspector Kishori Lal, in charge of the Aurangabad police station, accompanied the Muharram procession as it commenced from the imambargah and followed a route through the town, passing along the lane behind the Friday mosque. He presented the following statement:

> *Marsiya* (a poetic recitation) is recited at every five or ten paces. The funeral music was with the procession, that is, the musical instruments were played. In front of other mosques *marsiyas* were recited and musical instruments were played.... The procession starts from the imambargah and comes back to it. When coming back it passes by the way the back of the [Friday] mosque... the recitation of *marsiya* was stopped and the *matam* commenced. The procession came into the street at the back of the Juma Masjid with *matam* and music.[151]

On both days, Sunnis came out of the mosque and their homes and confronted the procession and the sub-inspector. Kishori Lal filed a report accordingly as a first step to making arrangements for managing the progress and the noise of the procession in the future. His report included a statement of his "apprehension that a breach of peace will take place at the back of the mosque." The following year the magistrate H. H. Shaw conducted a visit to the site and deployed armed police in Aurangabad to monitor the Ashura procession.[152]

The events of 1915 matched up with official expectations of what could happen at religious fasts and festivals,[153] and Sunni expressions of disapproval of the Shi'a procession behind the mosque elicited a magistrate's order of accommodation of their religious beliefs. The Sunnis confronted the procession and engaged directly with the police sub-inspector to establish the incendiary nature of the Shi'a devotion. They then asserted their numerical majority in the neighborhood, and witnesses testified to a history of customary local Shi'a practice that included a procession but did not include a stationary performance of *matam*. In 1916 the police issued a report for the management of the Ashura procession; in 1917, the deputy magistrate issued an order on the basis of this report, in consultation with Shi'a and Sunnis of Aurangabad, forbidding the vocal and stationary performance of *matam*, stating that "the processional *matam* of Shi'as shall not stop behind the Friday mosque of the Sunnis or within ten yards on either side."[154]

The Shi'a of Aurangabad, represented by a prominent community member Saiyed Manzur, took their contest with the Sunnis to the court at Aligarh as a civil suit. This was a form of legal activism which was a part of the effort for community formation and public organization by Shi'as across India. From the early twentieth century, *majlises* and Muharram processions were developing as platforms for "public communication and mobilization."[155] Justin Jones argues that Muharram was reformed into a catalyst for identity, politics, and community formation, as well as differentiation of Shi'a from Sunni.[156] Some Shi'a adopted the Safavid *azan*, which included a testimony to the usurpation of the caliphate by the first three caliphs, "sacralizing" public space of aural transmission. This discursive, political, and legal effort to transform public spaces was a backdrop for the Aurangabad Shi'a appeal for an outright accommodation of Shi'a devotionalism on the street.

The judgment of the first court of appeal in Aligarh was deeply sympathetic to the Shi'a position, "Everyone Indian knows of such processions. In the Hindu processions *bhajan* is sung at short halts made after traveling small distances. Nobody would regard such a user of the road as unjustified. The right to stop on the road for the object of the procession would be included in the right to carry the procession through the street." This legal reasoning, "everybody knows," was the same pragmatism which was communicated in the *Manual of Religious Feasts and Fasts*. These activities were predictable, widely subscribed, and socially consequential. Yet despite this universal awareness of public devotional practices, the accommodation of Muslim and Hindu devotionalism in public spaces was still subject to the discretionary control of the highest ranking officer of the executive in the district, the magistrate. The 1918 judgment of the court of the additional subordinate judge of Aligarh set out that "subject to the orders of the local authorities regulating the traffic, to the magistrate's directions and the rights of the public, the [Shi'as] have go the right to make short stays in the lane at the back of the Friday mosque at Aurangabad for the performance of *matam*."[157] Despite the Shi'a success in overturning the Sunni stay on their devotional activities on this particular street in Aurangabad, they did not achieve a declaration of absolute public rights of religious performance in the street and remained dependent on extraordinary measures by the magistrate including permitting and his invocation of section 144.

The magistrate and other government officers were seen by the central government to embody the culture that the state sought to foster, in stark opposition to the people using the street who embodied emotions and religious affinities. In Saharanpur in 1923, Muharram processioners carried long bamboo poles, marching in competition with one another. They triggered a response from Hindus concerned with the sanctity of the peepal trees that they passed under. There were 563 arrests in Saharanpur in connection with these events.[158] A member of the United Provinces Legislative Council asked how many respectable people had been arrested. Saiyed Ali Nabi was told by Lambert, secretary to the Government of United Provinces:

> the precise significance which the honorary member attached to the term "respectable" is not understood. It may, however, be stated that no member of the legislative assembly or of the legislative council or of the municipal or district board has been arrested, nor any darbari or title holder or lawyer of any grade or Indian officer either on the active or retired list. Similarly, no honorary magistrate or honorary munsif or member of the learned professions has been arrested.[159]

Elected representatives looked to the disengaged and dispassionate attitudes of government servants as a foil for the expression and assertion of popular devotionalism on the streets.

Saiyed Manzur appealed the verdict to the High Court at Allahabad and onwards to the Privy Council, this time stating more clearly the legal ruling that the Shi'a of Aurangabad wished to achieve:

> As members of the public inhabiting the town of Aurangabad and from immemorial use [the Shi'a] have a right not only to pass the procession through the particular street, but also to stop and perform *matam* there.

The ruling of the Judicial Committee of the Privy Council received in 1924 restated briefly and simply that while the Shi'as should certainly be able to worship on the streets, in the manner that many religious groups did, to accord them absolute rights of devotion on the street would accord others absolute rights of public devotion, leading at the very least to major obstructions to traffic. For this reason, the judgment stated that the executive alone would sanction any devotional uses of a public way and reconfirmed the role of the magistrate in the mediation of devotional performance on the street:

> Subject to the orders of the local authorities regulating the traffic, to the magistrate's directions and the rights of the public, the plaintiffs have got the right to make short stays in the lane at the back of the Friday Masjid at Aurangabad for the performance of matam.[160]

While acknowledging the widely subscribed culture of devotionalism on the street, and recognizing the mosque perimeter as a zone of legal exception as a space of intersection of devotional interests and public rights, the Judicial Committee of the Privy Council rejected evidence and argument for the production of rights derived from indigenous cultural values.[161] The public, as a body, was differentiated from collective Sunni and Shi'a organization in support of their devotional cultures. The collectivity of Shi'as and Sunnis and their cultural values for the street only had relevance in their potential to disrupt order, whether through "wounded religious feelings," or by creating obstruction. The Judicial Committee of the Privy Council confirmed the authority of the magistrate, that powerful officer of the colonial executive, to evaluate and sanction all religious devotionalism on the road and at the mosque perimeter.

Conclusion

Mosques were intimately connected to their public environs in a Muslim urban imaginary and by lines of ingress and egress of worshippers and sound. In 1913 local government plans to demolish the corner of the Kanpur mosque provoked Muslim reflection on the intersection of the devotional purpose of the mosque with the public space of the road and the instrumentality of law as opposed to bureaucratic governance in admitting devotional claims on public spaces. The perimeter of the mosque emerged as a space of conflict as Muslim and governmental expectations for the city clashed. From 1918 to 1924 the Aurangabad suit was aimed at dismantling the control of the magistrate over the mosque perimeter, a culmination of Muslim reflection on colonial law, legal activism, and possibilities for the street.

The magistrate's authority was validated by the JCPC judgment, Muslim disappointment at the failure of legal reasoning was mitigated by the success of the new provincial legislatures' political strategy for claiming religious rights on streets. After the constitution of the legislative councils in 1920, elected representatives argued for the appointment of Indians as magistrates and in the police service along communal lines. Elected representatives adopted the principle that magistrates could make decisions on streets on a case-by-case basis, embodying justice in their decision making. This marked a new public disinclination to tackle the legal problems at the heart of social and political difference. The 1924 judgment reaffirmed the full legal sanction to magistrates to give binding orders relating to any religious activity on the street, and by extension accorded local government ultimate discretionary control over devotionalism expressed at the perimeter of the mosque.

During this period the periphery of the mosque materialized into a discrete urban space, a spatial context for Muslim social life. Writers, scholars, architects, news reporters, rioters, and politicians reminded the Muslim public of its significance. Procedures consigned the periphery of the mosque to the control of the magistrate but the space remained visible and relevant to Muslims, to local government and to members of a wider public imagining the city and choosing their everyday comportment in it.

Chapter 4

LAHORE, 1940

GOVERNMENT CONTROL OVER THE LAND RECORD

Introduction

The city of Lahore had been an important seat of the Mughal Empire, was briefly under the control of the invading Afghans and independent Sikh chiefs in the 1700s, then became the capital of Ranjit Singh's short-lived Sikh empire in 1799 and finally was annexed by the British in 1849. Colonial Lahore contained the religious and cultural legacies of both Muslim and Sikh rule. The Shahidganj Mosque (see Figure 7) and its attached lands and buildings in Naulakha Bazaar, near the railway station, were claimed by both Muslim and Sikh subjects of the colonial state.[1]

The Shahidganj site included a small shrine to Sikh martyrs, a public kitchen run by Sikh religious men, a shrine to a Muslim saint, a *hammam*, and the mosque known as Shahidganj which was now a gurdwara and the abode of the Sikh holy book Guru Granth Sahib.[2] Local Muslims associated this site with a Mughal imperial past, visited to participate in rituals at the Sufi shrine, and looked upon the domed one-time mosque as they walked past the perimeter of the site in the densely populated neighborhood adjoining the central railway depot. The shrine to Sikh martyrs drew Sikh visitors and pilgrims. Sikh religious leaders called *mahants* used the mosque building as an abode for the Granth Sahib, prepared *bhang* (an intoxicating drink) for ritual events and provided food and alms for wayfarers and the poor.[3] Another 15 acres of endowment land were covered by groves and contained several multistory residential buildings with commercial frontages opening into the adjoining bazaar.

Revenue officers surveyed and recorded land rights at the site. The whole site was designated as part of the Sikh *gurdwara* during the settlement of the revenues of the Lahore district in 1850, a decision

Figure 7 The Shahidganj Mosque *Masjid Shahidganj Masjid Shah Chiragh* (1936).

which was reconfirmed in a JCPC decision in 1940. While this outcome and the associated Sikh-Muslim conflict is well known to historians of South Asia, the history of the interaction of land law and trust law which produced this outcome and Muslim opposition to the legal basis for adjudication of the Shahidganj Mosque conflict is not. This is the story of Muslim efforts to formulate a legal claim to the land and building of the Shahidganj Mosque.

The idea that a mosque could be subject to "adverse possession," or legal appropriation of title, relied on three things: its classification as a form of proprietary land, inquiry into and the documentation of occupancy by revenue officers, and the conversion of occupancy into full proprietary rights after twelve years. The same principle of adverse possession also allowed land and buildings improperly transferred by the *mahants* after 1850 to be forever lost to the endowment. A number of Muslims challenged the Lahore administration's treatment of the mosque after 1850; the last of these efforts was the "Suit for the Mosque known as Shahidganj." We typically take account of this competition and others like it as instances of interreligious competition over heritage rights. But the Shahidganj case showed that Muslims also aimed at destabilizing the notion that endowment land was property and subject to the power of revenue officers to survey and demarcate estates, to make inquiries, and to give final and bindings orders relating to rights, the very process which consigned the Shahidganj to the custodianship of the Sikh Jiwan Singh in 1850.

The Record of Rights at the Lahore Shahidganj

From 1850 to 1927, competing claims to the Shahidganj site were examined by revenue officers of the Punjab who used concepts derived from laws governing land to establish rights in the endowment. Endowments were subject to survey, inquiry, documentation, and the recording of rights under the orders of the revenue officer. Architectural observation, local testimony, and documentation of waqf provided evidence that the Shahidganj land was originally a Mughal endowment. But revenue officers recorded Jiwan Singh's custodial rights over the site based on inquiries and testimonies that confirmed he had continuously occupied, cultivated, managed, and developed this land for at least twelve years prior to annexation of the Punjab in 1849, during which time the Muslims had been "out of possession." They noted that religious and economic activities at the site were supervised by the Sikh *mahant*, Jiwan Singh. These observations were the firm underpinning of the assignment of land rights at the Lahore Shahidganj but they were a legally tenuous basis for the assignment of religious rights in land and so the dispute was revived again and again over the century of British rule in the Punjab.

Administrators of newly annexed territories in north India in the second half of the nineteenth century surveyed and documented rights in property by carrying out inquiries relating to land occupation. These inquiries verified and qualified claims of ownership or title. Lands which were documented as being dedicated to supporting religious objectives were categorized as religious trusts or endowments and exempted from taxation or "revenue" demands but were, critically, subject to the same survey and documentation of occupation and use which related to proprietary lands. In addition to forming the basis for the colonial confirmation of Sikh rights over the Shahidganj in 1850–51, manipulation of these records enabled land grabs at the Shahidganj between 1851 and 1927, demonstrating systemic flaws in the land administration system as it produced rights in religious endowments.

By the 1850s, across India, official will and administrative capacity for revenue collection had grown through a system of controls and supervision; revenue responsibilities were fixed, financial penalties introduced, and regular checks carried out.[4] The collector-magistrate was assisted by assistants, European extra assistants and Indian extra assistants,[5] and supervised Indian staff who performed a variety of functions from authenticating documents and accounts to recording ownership and occupancy of land. The combined judicial and executive powers of the collector-magistrate's office were bestowed on the deputy commissioner of the Punjab in 1872 and 1887.[6] Deputy commissioners determined tax obligations of the newly conquered population in settlement proceedings. These officers were

> carefully selected and chosen for their intelligence, zeal and energy. The native agency at their disposal is as complete as can be organized; their procedure simple, and well adapted to gain the confidence of the people with whom the officers are in close communication; no settlement officer ever thinks of limiting his knowledge to formal proceedings placed before him; he is the umpire as well as judge in the question at issue, and it is his duty to search out and ascertain its real merits. He confronts the litigants, closely and judiciously cross-examines them, places the point at issue, when necessary, before a jury of village elders, and even adjourns to the village, and to the disputed spot, in an intricate matter, for the purpose of eliciting the truth.[7]

Procedures for establishing proprietorship and occupancy of land, associated rights, and the tax or "revenue" obligations on Punjab land had been refined in northeast India close to a century earlier[8] where local government had produced various forms of documentation as a part of the process of recording and entrenching rights in land and determining fiscal liabilities. Revenue surveyors were being employed and trained in India from the end of the eighteenth century, and from the 1860s methods and expertise had evolved sufficiently to permit the colonial state to undertake detailed cadastral surveys. These surveys empowered the executive to define the rights and obligations of each landowner and identify each field.[9] Records of rights in land accompanied these maps or plans. In the Punjab, the maps, village plans, and records of rights were composed by trained district *patwaris* (land registrars), a "class of village accountants not to be equaled anywhere in Hindustan," under the supervision of settlement and then revenue officers.[10]

> When the revision of a settlement is undertaken, the maps, measurements, and records-of-rights of ownership and actual possession

are thoroughly revised by the settlement officer and a special staff of *tahsildars, naib tahsildars* and field *kanungos* (subordinate officers of the revenue department). On the conclusion of the operations these records are transferred to the custody of the Deputy Commissioner, who is henceforth responsible for their maintenance, and correction when necessary. Briefly, the system in force is this: the *patwari* makes a field-to-field inspection at each harvest, noting all changes in rights, rents, and possession, and all amendments required in the field map. The changes thus noted are recorded, after attestation by a superior revenue officer, in a revised record-of-rights which is prepared for each village every fourth year and called the *jamabandi*. The Deputy Commissioner is assisted in this duty by a revenue assistant (Assistant or Extra Assistant Commissioner), the Director of Land Records acting as his expert advisor in all matters connected with it. The staff consists of a District Kanungo, with a number of field *kanungos* and *patwaris*. In 1904 there were 7,906 *patwaris* and 386 field *kanungos* in the province.[11]

The Board of Revenue defined both procedures to be followed and the powers of the officers and staff who carried out its work. Records of rights were produced under the Board of Revenue for all land "which has been separately assessed to land revenue or would have been so assessed if the land revenue had not been released, compounded for or redeemed."[12] All documentation was maintained and archived in districts under the oversight of the district commissioners in their capacity as agents of the Board of Revenue. Deputy commissioners' reports on their districts, encompassing their carefully gleaned economic and cultural knowledge, were expanded and enfolded into gazetteers and census reports.[13] The Department of Land Records produced manuals to guide the work of the *patwaris*,[14] providing detailed instructions on the determination of ownership or tenancy. These records were subject to periodic review and revision based on prevailing occupancy and land use. Any dispute of the entry in the registers was subject to inquiry by a revenue officer who would reach his own decision and issue binding orders on what the final entry in the register was to be.[15] The colonial legal and administrative systems attached a "presumption of truth" to this record of rights.[16] No civil court could reevaluate documentation or evidence of land rights to supersede the decision of the revenue officer.[17]

While mosques and other endowments were fundamentally not proprietary land, they were subject to inquiry, surveyed, and documented as part of settlement and revenue management procedures. Revenue officers inquired into their history and evaluated their uses, gave the orders regarding classification of these sites, and produced documentation for them using the same forms, the record of rights, which conferred title in proprietary land. Yet there were few if any explicit instructions to *patwaris* and surveyors relating to the manner of recording the character of a religious site on the record of rights. Under the rules relating to land revenue and tenancy acts, published in the Punjab in 1887, revenue free estates were to be recorded in the name of grant holder, with a "note of the fact and the names, description, and shares of the grant holder (*muafidar*) in red ink in the column of Remarks."[18]

The new administration of Lahore closely examined grants of land to religious personalities and institutions and initially consciously perpetuated the political patronage of religious figures by the Lahore Darbar—the court of the Sikh state.[19] A variety of holy men who had received assignments of revenue lands or pensions from the Sikh treasury continued to receive payments from the early colonial administration at Lahore.[20] Mosques, temples, places of pilgrimage and devotion, and serais were "ornaments to the villages; they have some architectural pretension, and being embosomed in trees are often the only shady spots in the neighborhood."[21] Like many precolonial religious sites,[22] the Shahidganj endowment had perpetuated the political authority of the Sikh state;[23] Jagga Singh and his son Jiwan Singh had been recognized by the Sikh government at Lahore and awarded a village in Sheikhupura in return for their support in around 1834,[24] and again when the Sikh Khalsa Hira Singh passed through the Shahidganj site on his way to retake the Lahore fort after a coup in 1843.[25] The colonial administration of Lahore produced a verification of the land grant "enjoyed by Bhai Jiwan Singh" in 1850, collecting oral and documentary evidence of title and possession of land.

Jiwan Singh was able to produce documentation that he had been given a rent-free grant of villages in Pargana Saurian by the Lahore Darbar. His claims to the land of Shahidganj relied on testimony from local zamindars to establish that this family had occupied the site for at least a generation and that he had cultivated crops on these lands. These testimonies established Jiwan Singh's "proprietary and *jagirdari* (royal grant) rights to this land."[26] In 1855 the survey office reported that Jiwan Singh's actual landholding exceeded the acreage of titled and reported lands documented in 1850; Jiwan Singh argued that he had merely misreported the size of his actual landholding in 1850. The commissioner's office dismissed the inquiry as he was clearly in possession of the land, seeking to quickly regularize the terms of land settlement.[27]

Shahidganj was a site of religious and political significance for Sikhs and also included an active Muslim shrine within it. This shrine, of the saint

Hazrat Shah Kaku, dated to the seventeenth century. In the eighteenth century, during the reign of the Emperor Farrukhsiyar, the nobleman Mirza Qurban Beg had built a mosque at the site and appointed the managers of the Sufi shrine as custodians of the mosque as well.[28] Qurban Beg's son Mirza Falak Beg had created an endowment of just under half an acre of land at the time of his father's death to pay for the costs of the mosque and a school that was run on the premises. Falak Beg nominated a custodian and conferred hereditary rights of custodianship on him in the hopes that he may continue to impart education, keep the mosque in flourishing condition, pray for everlasting government by the family of the reigning king, and bring blessings to the memory of his father.[29] The entire endowment that had included the mosque and the shrine as well as a variety of other buildings had come under the control of Jiwan Singh's predecessor during the period of Sikh rule, and in 1850 Muslims were still visiting the shrine.

After documenting the extent of the land holding and possession, the settlement office calculated Jiwan Singh's revenue obligations. Singh presented evidence establishing that Sikh *mahants*, including Kahan Singh (d. 1854), Jagga Singh (d. ?), and his son Jiwan Singh (d. 1858),[30] had served concoctions of pepper and *sukha* or *bhang* (a cannabis based intoxicant), at the site in the early 1800s. These activities established that the Shahidganj site and Jiwan Singh's management of the landholding served Sikh religious purposes. Together the settlement inquiry and associated testimony produced a record of 15.7 acres of land at the Shahidganj site itself. The settlement office also confirmed Jiwan Singh's title to three villages, two wells, 7.4 acres in "the suburbs of Lahore" and 36 acres of land in Pargana Saurian, a combination of endowed lands associated with the Shahidganj and his own proprietary land holding. (The family disassociated the latter from the endowment in later years.)[31] The earliest land records relating to the Shahidganj recorded Jiwan Singh's name in the "name of owner" column for each portion of the estate in 1856. The remarks in the accompanying land registration stated that these plots were held as *mu'afi*, revenue demand free, by Jiwan Singh.[32]

The colonial state presumed all non-public land, whether revenue land administered by the Board of Revenue or that which served settled living and was administered by municipal committees and district boards, to be subject to ownership and gradually surveyed and documented as such. The colonial presumption of ownership favored the crown and precolonial elites during the period of the permanent settlement, and farmers during the later periods of thinking about tenancy rights. In towns and cities, title as well as occupation of land conferred proprietary ownership of land. Former elite or crown-owned lands were classified as *nazul* and assigned to the proprietorship of the colonial state.[33] Among other proprietary estates, Shahidganj, which came first under the Board of Revenue and then the Lahore Municipal Committee, was evaluated like proprietary land, recorded, and registered through the same processes and using the same documentation by way of which proprietary land was registered, and then the revenue demands on the land were "released" in a nod to the faith which motivated benefactors and devotees at this site.

The Board of Revenue's documentation of land was comprehensive; detailed field maps composed by the village accountants accompanied records of rights and topographical detail was provided for every estate in great detail.

> Not only have boundaries been sketched, but the surface of the ground has also been faithfully portrayed; every detail of cultivation of forest, grove, brushwood, of sterile waste and sand, of hillock and ravine, of pool, marsh, and rivulet, of road and path; of building habitation, and garden . . . so that each map not only presents with scientific precision the external boundary and area of each estate, but also its physical aspect and its internal peculiarities. . . . When fitted together on a small scale for entire districts, they furnish the most complete topographical information that can be desired.[34]

A plan shown in Figure 8,[35] and the accompanying entries in the land register, showed the northern and southern parts of the Shahidganj site as comprised by a number of distinct plots which made up the site and together measured a little over 3 acres (see Figure 8).

District commissioners and commissioners, acting under the mandate they were given by the Board of Revenue, conducted "extensive judicial operations" to hear suits contesting the terms of the first settlement of revenues in the Punjab.[36] These officers heard and settled up to 28,000 cases in a single division over a 5-year period; a suit filed with the district commissioner could go on appeal to the divisional commissioner's court, and from there to the Board of Administration of the Punjab in a final appeal.[37] Among these was the appeal filed by Nur Ahmad, hereditary custodian of the still-functioning shrine and occupied mosque. Nur Ahmad presented two pieces of documentary evidence: the original eighteenth-century Mughal deed of waqf of the mosque as well as a school, seven shops, a well, trees, and a *hammam*,[38] and a petition signed by a number of local prominent figures, including dispossessed landlords, which stated that the endowment belonged to Muslims.[39] Nur Ahmad's suit was admitted by the extra assistant commissioner, Kalab Abid Khan, who stated that "the proper thing, in my opinion, is that the Mohammedans have a right to the building of the mosque and whatever is attached thereto on account of it

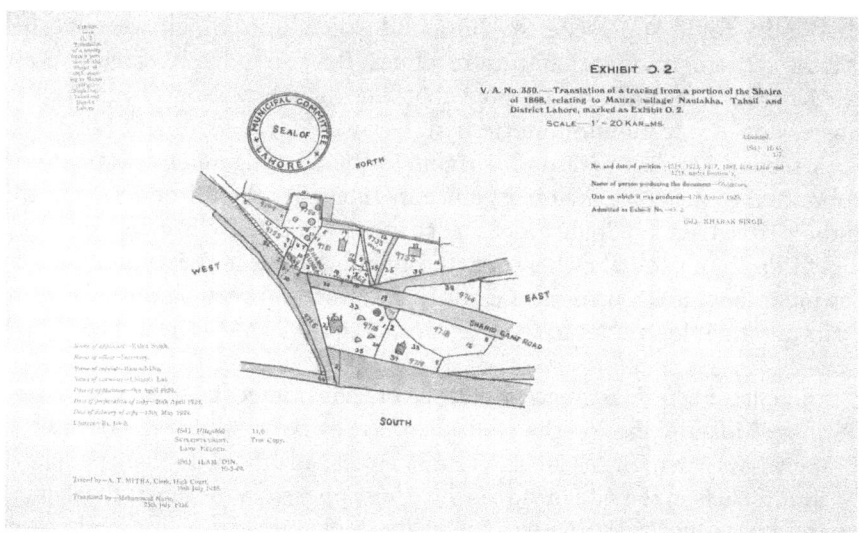

Figure 8 Extract from Record of Rights 1868.

being a religious place." However, Kalb Ali Khan's writ was limited by the principles of land law and he stipulated that

> on account of his being out of possession, his suit cannot be considered [as] the plaintiff has been out of possession for such a long time. I have no power to award possession simply because of the documents which are with him or for the reason that Hindus can have no right over a mosque or the buildings attached thereto.[40]

Despite recognizing that real moral reasoning lay at the heart of Nur Ahmed's suit, Kalb Ali Khan was bound to act under the rules and procedures set out for him as a revenue office and apply the powerful twelve-year rule, the law which had been appropriated from British law into Indian regulations to protect tenancy rights. This was the "presumption that property rights accrued after twelve-years occupancy," a law intended to encourage, productive uses of land.[41] Had there had been a record of the initiation of a suit within the twelve years required to establish rights of occupancy of the land, Kalb Ali Khan would have been able to review and award the site to Nur Ahmad.[42] But there was no such record of protest that would have had to have taken place under Sikh rule, through reference to jurisprudential, economic, and political principles which did not compare to those of the colonial period. Therefore Kalb Ali Khan recommended that Nur Ahmad take his case to the Court of the Settlement Officer, hoping that

that court could supersede the rules and procedures which were created for the settlement of agricultural revenues. But the judge referred to Kalb Ali Khan's "decision" and restated that, as Nur Ahmed had been "out of possession," he would not interfere in the case.[43]

A second Muslim petition for rights in the Shahidganj endowment was submitted to the commissioner's office in 1883 after the introduction of the Indian Trusts Act. Pir Shah, muezzin of a mosque inside Delhi gate, submitted a petition for custodial rights over the Shahidganj site at the same time that the incumbent Sikh custodian Ganda Singh, who had been paralyzed for five years and then fell victim to the plague, was confined to his deathbed.[44]

> There has been in existence a mosque of Mohammedans since the time of the Muslim kings on the roadside of Landa Bazar, which has been in the possession of the Akali Sikh Ganda Singh and others. The said people commit acts in the said mosque which are opposed to the tenets of Islam and on seeing [that] the feelings of the Mohammedan community in general are very much injured the petitioner, therefore, prays on behalf of the Mohammedan community that possession of the mosque and property attached to it might be awarded to him.[45]

A variety of motives may be attributed to these petitioners. Like Nur Ahmad, Pir Shah submitted for custodial possession of the site "on behalf of the Mohammedan community." There is no evidence that Pir Shah's suit was backed by a contractual solidarity of a variety of Muslim stakeholders in the way that Nur Ahmad's was; his suit was rumored to have been instigated by an Afghan who acted on the Afghan Amir Sher Ali Khan's concern over Muslim dispossession in India.[46] Both suits relied on a recognition of Muslim custodial rights over the endowment and both implied rather than guaranteed that their custodianship would serve a wider Muslim community. The settlement officers noted that owing to the enquiries necessary to produce correct records, colonial occupation and the judicial process revived many "dormant disputes" which were dealt with expeditiously through their own internal appeals process; the Muslim petitions for Shahidganj were treated as revival of such a dormant dispute.[47] Despite the presentation of the waqfnama and evidence of shared uses of the site, the Muslim custodians of the mosque were shown again and again to have been out of possession, and Jiwan Singh presented valid evidence that he was in proprietary occupancy for a period of twelve years around the settlement operations, evidence which conferred a valid title owing to the extension of the property regime to the Punjab.[48] Sikhs treated Muslim claims as opportunist efforts to reclaim land which had been lost through a period of political change.

Curiously, the process of survey, inquiry, and documentation of land rights provided evidence of one continued Muslim use of the Shahidganj site, albeit evidence which was of little use to the mosque-focused petitioners. Muslims had continued to worship at the small shrine of the saint Hazrat Shah Kaku. In 1884, the extra assistant commissioner reported:

> Besides the site, under the houses, about [an acre and a half] of vacant site and the agricultural land situate towards the east are attached to the mosque. In it a lodge (*khanqah*) of some Mohammedan holy man is built and therein Mohammad Baksh and others, belonging to the Khoja community, residents of Kashmiri Bazar, burn lamp and do sweeping etc., on Thursdays.[49]

The neighborhood of the shrine of Hazrat Shah Kaku had been known as the *muhalla* of the Khojas; the buildings here had been almost entirely dismantled and the residents relocated during Sikh rule.[50] Local Muslim social and religious associations with Shahidganj and the inconspicuous shrine at the site persisted into the colonial period and coexisted with Sikh rights over the site. The connections between the Muslim shrine and the Sikh practice at the site dated to at least the lifetime of Kahan Singh, Jiwan Singh's father who had participated in Sufi teaching, learning, and worship at the shrine of Hazrat Shah Kaku. In the earliest colonial documents relating to the site, a Muslim petitioner testified that Kahan Singh was a disciple in the Sufi line of Shah Kaku and had a legitimate presence at the site.[51] Hereditary Sikh custodianship of the shrine of Hazrat Shah Kaku transferred through two generations; the memory of the saint Hazrat Shah Kaku was received through ritual performance and oral description into the 1930s, and has recently begun to be commemorated once again by a local group of the Naulakha Bazaar neighborhood.[52]

Muslim authority, ritual practice, and memory may have been subordinated to the custodial control of the *mahants* over Shahidganj, but shared land use and comfortable neighborliness between the shrine custodians and the gurdwara's custodians persisted. This was in a large part possible because the custodians of the Hazrat Shah Kaku shrine were documented as tenants at the endowment. In 1893 Ganda Singh leased the well to Imam Baksh, the custodian of the shrine, at a rent of eighteen rupees a month.[53] In 1909, the shrine keepers were entered in the municipal land registry as non-rent paying occupancy tenants of a small plot related to a "grave."[54] The Revenue Department assigned the shrine keepers rights at the site based on records of occupancy.[55]

An impassioned Sikh demand for judicial review of custodianship of Sikh gurdwaras grew in fervor from 1919 to 1921 following two decades of India-wide activism for increased recognition of worshippers' rights at religious sites and accountability of custodians. After two years of escalating demands by reformist Punjabi Akali Sikhs for accountability of custodians of religious sites, district tribunals were constituted by the Sikh Gurdwara Act of 1925, to review the claims to the Shahidganj site. This provided the opportunity for a renewed Muslim effort. Two vying claims to the Shahidganj site, Sikh and Muslim, produced two representations of the site in the 1920s (see Figures 9 and 10).

In 1927, the Lahore tribunal began to review the records of management of the Shahidganj site by Jiwan Singh's successors to establish the extent of the land grant which accrued to the gurdwara and discern whether the mahants had mismanaged the land and assets attached to the endowment.

The Sikh Gurdwara Tribunal of Lahore found evidence that in 1879 Ganda Singh wrote a will in which he bequeathed portions of the site to his wife Musammat Khem Kaur, his daughter Makhan Devi, and his grandson Attar Singh. This bequest corresponded in part to plot 14 on the 1929 site plan, and to other shops and buildings within the contiguous religious site and jagir, including plots 25 and 27.[56] Ganda Singh also made two sales of land, totaling close to half an acre, to a Muhammad Sultan Contractor in 1860 and 1868.[57] In 1915, an Aslam Khan purchased plot 10, an old mill, and shops built by Ganda Singh, and, in 1922, plot 15,

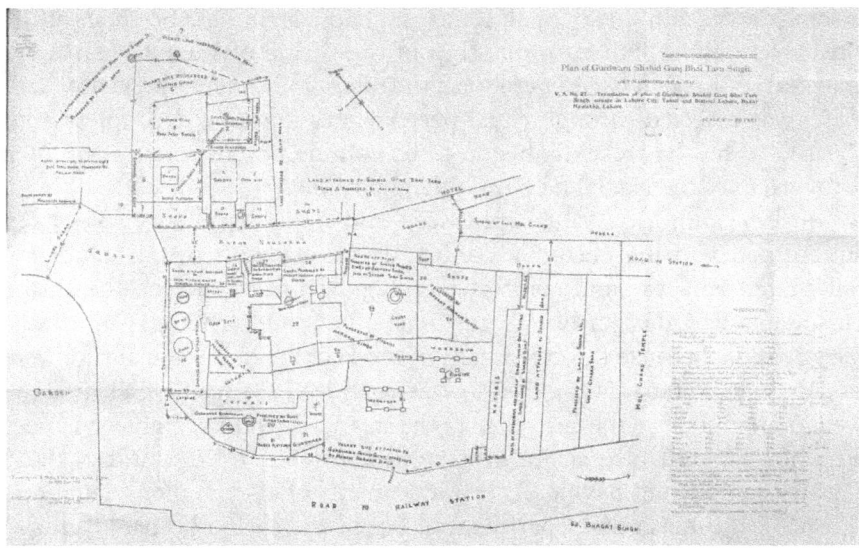

Figure 9 Plan of Gurdwara Shahid Ganj Bhai Taru Singh 1927. *The Mosque Known as Shahidganj v. SGPC* JCPC Case Papers. © The British Library Board PP 1316.

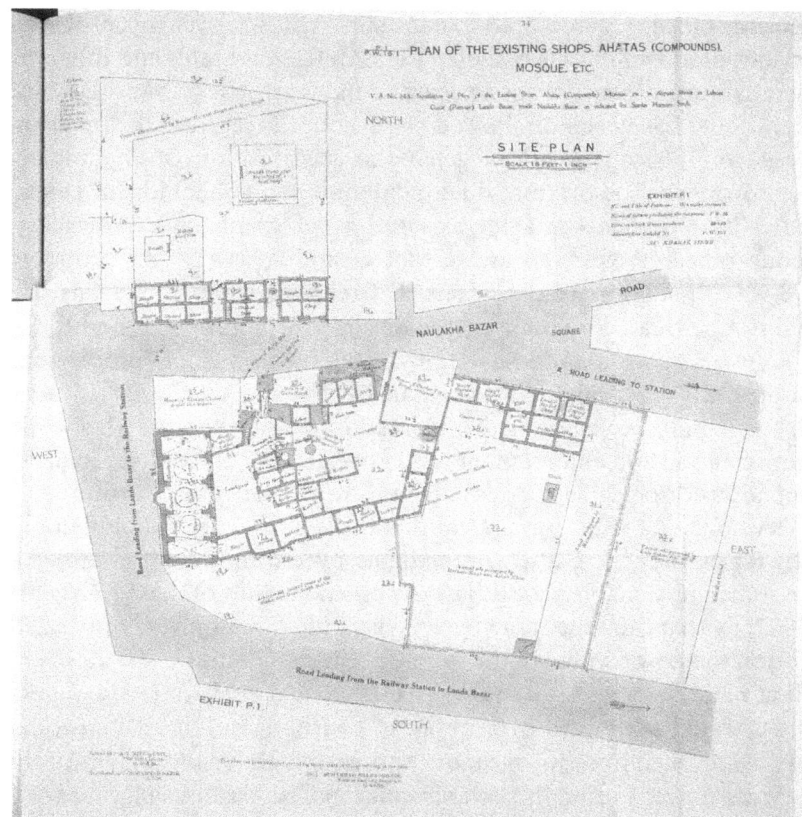

Figure 10 Plan of mosque and other buildings at Shahidganj 1929. *The Mosque Known as Shahidganj v. SGPC* JCPC Case Papers. © The British Library Board PP 1316.

residential or commercial buildings along Naulakha road. In 1925, part of Hari Singh's land was sold in a court auction; Aslam Khan also bought half of plot 30 and portions of land leading down to the southern road.[58] The hamam was dismantled and its materials were sold to a Mewa Ram.[59] In 1896, a Hindu called Lala Mul Chand bought a section of the northeastern portion of the site and built a Shiva temple there.[60] Jiwan Singh's grandson sold a plot inlcuding nine shops, in 1919.[61] His other grandchildren sold a shop, number 27 on the plan, in 1897.[62] In 1913, another great grandson sold part of plot 29 which had been willed to his father by Ganda Singh in 1879.[63]

Under land administration rules inheritance, purchase, mortgage, or gift was reported to the *patwari* who created a new entry in the record of rights.

A revenue officer was required to maintain oversight over this process and carry out inquiries in case of a dispute.[64] All the land sales and inheritance which had taken place over the years of management of the site by Jiwan Singh should have been disallowed by revenue officers and the magistrate/deputy commissioner's office, given the classification of Shahidganj as an endowment. The original documentation of the Shahidganj generally alluded its religious character as *"mu'afi"* of grant land. *Patwaris* and revenue officers were well aware that custodians were not proprietors; there was already broad consensus that religious endowments, as trusts, could not be treated by their custodians as private property, and those in the *patwari's* office should have known the misnomer of "proprietor" to be a problem of working with standardized forms. Yet these transactions had been quite easily carried out, made possible because the work of documentation and enforcement was carried out by petty bureaucrats with tremendous discretionary powers who were almost entirely immune from prosecution. And while it was clear that these transactions should not have taken place, they were also irremediable by the time Sikh communities were sufficiently enabled by the law to demand review of these transactions in 1927; by that time the same twelve-year rule now conferred proprietary rights on the new owners of the once-endowment land.

That records of rights in religious sites existed at all and were regularly being updated in processes of survey and administration; that custodians' names were listed in the proprietor column; that the religious uses of those sites were noted ad hoc in remarks columns, proprietor columns, or not at all; and that even without a valid claim of title, occupancy of a site or title could be established through testimony, made religious endowments extremely vulnerable to sale, occupancy, and adverse possession.

The Shahidganj was one of many religious sites across India subjected to adverse possession under the twelve-year rule. In Delhi, the proprietary rights of an occupier over a piece of land containing the remains of a "rude wayside mosque" were confirmed in 1850 as no claims for waqf were brought within twelve years of his first registration of title and the case served as a major precedent in an early compilation of Anglo-Muhammadan Law.[65] The site of a mosque which was endowed by a Mughal emperor in the eighteenth century but had become disused and destroyed for materials sometime prior to 1849 was resumed by the collector's office of Delhi whose rights over it were reconfirmed in the absence of evidence of prayer at or possession of the site by Muslims in the previous twelve years.[66] The 1849 decision of the Court of the North Western Provinces that the disappearance of a mosque building (allegedly at the hands of the local Hindus) and the impossibility of prayer at that site invalidated the waqf and the state was in its rights to resume this land served as a precedent on this point.[67] A mortgagee of temple property registered his occupancy and defended his full proprietary rights over that land under the twelve-year rule.[68] In Madras, the custodian of a temple who took office in 1893 was unable to recover lands which had been sold by his predecessor more than twelve years prior.[69] Lenders to the custodian of another Madras mosque took possession of the mortgaged lands in 1874 and successfully defended their adverse possession of this land in 1888.[70]

Instances of adverse possession of religious sites tended to involve either corrupt or misguided custodians who sold endowment lands themselves or did not exercise sufficient vigilance over their heirs', tenants' or lenders' dealings with the land revenue office. A highly vigilant and engaged community of worshippers may have been able to prevent such mismanagement and erosion of religious sites, but lawsuits were expensive and worshippers had long been conditioned to leave management of their sites to the all-powerful custodians of the trust. A more vigilant district administration would have also prevented such instances of adverse possession as political officers often communicated their preference for outcomes in religious affairs to communities.[71] But in the absence of such effective defense, often in political circumstances which did not favor expressions of "preference" for Muslims, the documentation of new uses of land legitimized—*legalized*—the appropriation of land. The power of revenue officers, to survey and demarcate estates and then exercise discretionary powers to make inquiries and give final and bindings orders relating to rights over endowment land, enfolded dramatic and corrosive patterns of change into procedure.

Scrutiny and inquiry intended to prevent illegal land sales, alienation through inheritance, and illegal occupation of religious sites was carried out by petty bureaucrats of the district office whose primary job for the Board of Revenue was to produce documentation of land use and occupancy. These revenue officers and their staff had demonstrably permitted and enabled the illegal alienation of endowment land by registering the possessors of endowment land, but they had done so while carrying out their duties of regular survey, inquiry and documentation. Unchallenged, their notations superseded documentation of bequest and conferred new rights over endowment land. Registration of possession of land on the basis of political preference, errors, oversights, and misdeeds were all possible only because of the underlying conceptualization of endowment land as fundamentally subject to proprietary claims.

Rights to Mosques on Municipal and Nazul Land

Not all mosques were subject to the review based on inquiry and documentation by officers and staff working under the Board of Revenue. Significant numbers of South Asian mosques stood on land administered by municipal or district boards and on *nazul* (government owned) land. Public demands for government consideration and sensitivity relating to such mosques could be indulged far more easily.

Faced with demands for building sites, encroachments on infrastructure,[72] and governance, urban administrators established title to land and, as the survey of Delhi *nazul* lands demonstrated, also demarcated government or state-owned land. Town planners produced maps on which religious sites were clearly marked, accounting for indigenous views of the sacred in their plans for redevelopment.[73] In one important report and city survey of Lahore of 1917, a single plan was devoted to the "religious topography of Lahore, with its temples, mosques, tombs and processional ways, *dharmsalas*, schools and their playgrounds."[74] Mosques and other religious buildings were understood to be part of a sacred landscape rather than proprietary land. Yet mosques were still documented through the record of rights forms and entered in land registers alongside proprietary plots.

Some city surveyors provided more creative approaches to characterizing endowment land. The papers relating to the exquisite Sunehri Masjid of the old city of Lahore contained the following identification in the proprietor's column of the plot measurement records during the municipal survey of 1907–8: "Charitable purposes; Golden Mosque. Mutawalli: Bashir Ali Khan, son of Deputy Barkat Ali Khan."[75] This document was presented when the Shahidganj case came to trial in 1936, submitted by the Quran teacher of the Sunehri Masjid who was also gave the Friday sermons at the mosque at Bhati Gate; he believed this entry should serve as a template for classifying mosques.[76] Such efforts extended well beyond Lahore; an extensive descriptor for a "mosque built of pucca masonry . . . under the management of Hussain Khan" had been entered in the proprietor's column for a site in Gujranwala in 1933.[77] A journalist of Lahore produced documentation of a mosque in Bijnor in which the proprietor's column disclosed detailed financial and custodial arrangements: "*muʿafi* for charitable purposes waqf in the name of mosque situate . . . under the management of Musaaman Amir Begam, wife of . . ., residents of Bijnor, Mohalla Marohgan."[78] Similarly descriptive entries in records of rights relating to religious sites were provided as samples in the Berar land survey manual updated in 1941.[79] Increasingly into the twentieth century, government officers acting independently and on official instructions did try to prevent endowment land grabs through the language of notation on the record of rights.

Mosques constructed without authorization on undeveloped municipal land were flashpoints for Muslim organization for mosque defense. In Lahore in December 1934, the organization Anjuman-i Islamia organized a group of local Muslims outside the walls of the old city of Lahore to raise the edifice of a mosque overnight. The mosque came to be known locally as Masjid Shab Bhar, the mosque of a single night, although the inscription over the entrance to the mosque names it Masjid-i Shaheed. In the history of this mosque related orally by Qari Abdul Sattar, the present day caretaker of the mosque, the site was occupied by a Muslim who operated a snack stall there but was also claimed by a Hindu stall owner and neither had any documented land rights. A magistrate was due to visit to make a final decision about ownership of the site.[80] The overnight mud and brick mosque construction became an effective claim to the site; the lower floor of the mosque was fashioned as two shops with frontages on the road and were occupied by the Muslim entrepreneur in return for a rent to the mosque. The municipality, under the authority of the deputy commissioner/magistrate, regularized the sale of the site to the Anjuman-i Islamia for a payment of Rs 1,500,[81] at a discount from the market value of the land.

Nazul[82] lands were civic lands of precolonial cities which "neither came under the Board of Revenue, nor the Forest Department, nor Military, Postal, Telegraph, or any other purely imperial department" but were managed by the collector (also known as district magistrate or deputy commissioner).[83] *Nazul* lands came to the local government through escheat of lands belong to the precolonial states and elites.[84] By extension, mosques were among the many buildings which became property of the colonial state. During the early colonial period, in some cases the local administration took charge of management and supervision of mosques on *nazul* land,[85] and administrators condemned the corruption of elites in mismanaging public property in tones of moral outrage.[86] In other cases mosque lands and buildings were treated as real estate and were occupied, auctioned off, or managed for rent by specially trained *nazul darogha* officers.

After 1863 the colonial government sought to unburden itself of responsibilities of mosques on *nazul* land while having also fueled a popular debate and demands for the conservation of religious monuments.[87] The hereditary custodians of the occupied imperial mosque of Lahore had submitted numerous petitions to the Lahore administration from the time of the takeover of the city in 1849. in 1876 the Anjuman Islamia of Delhi presented an announcement of its establishment to Victoria, Queen Empress in an exquisite embroidered silk envelope and signed by 200 "respectable men of Delhi" asking that the state should "guard endowments and all property in general situated in the city."[88] The signatories objected to the treatment of certain buildings after the conflict of 1857 on the grounds that under prevailing Islamic cultural norms, waqf was "not private property" and therefore could not be subject to confiscation, occupation, or resumption on that basis.[89] At this time, rights of ownership of urban sites through *mu'afi* and the twelve-year rule were admitted for those who sought proprietary title to graveyards and some shrines.[90] However a very different policy was applied to mosques on *nazul* land: they were "returned" to Muslim petitioners or the basis of architectural identification and popular testimony that they were mosques.

The colonial administration returned mosques to a variety of Muslim petitioners in Delhi including the Kalan mosque and the Fatehpuri Mosque, which had been auctioned off as reprisal in 1857.[91] In Lahore the imperial Badshahi mosque was "returned" to Muslims,[92] as well as several other mosques on *nazul* land including the pre-Mughal Masjid Gumti Bazaar, the Mughal-era Sunehri Masjid, Masjid Dai Lado, Masjid Hamam Wali, and Masjid Taksali Darwazah.[93] The consignment of mosques on *nazul* and municipal land into the hands of Muslims became a significant counterpart to the Board of Revenue's production of records of rights for occupied mosques. The colonial executive and land surveyors were at liberty to take much more favorable views of Muslim rights in mosques in instances where they did not have to reconcile competing religious or proprietary rights; district officers' inquiries and determination of interests in land could fully accommodate Muslim demands. This was a further example of the elasticity of rules and procedures, the powers of the executive to offer favor and indulgence. Conciliatory processes did not, however, provide legal reasoning for Muslim rights in mosques. Muslim efforts to reclaim mosques on government and *nazul* land did not produce an alternative legal basis for assigning religious rights in mosques.

God's Land

An idea that mosques were God's land, sacred, eternal and distinct from those forms of land which were subject proprietorship, developed through the nineteenth and twentieth centuries. This discourse was amplified in Urdu texts, newspapers, and political statements and developed in direct response to colonial application of land law to land pertaining to mosques. A number of scholars have attended to the Shahidganj mosque defense efforts, notably David Gilmartin and Naveeda Khan who have highlighted the emotive intent of Muslim professions about the sanctity of the mosque.[94] I argue below that the press and politics related to the Shahidganj matter was primarily a Muslim effort to redefine legal norms and procedures relating to the mosque.

Some 'ulama sanctioned the resumption of mosque lands, validating government exercise of eminent domain. But a line of argument that the bequest was enduring, even beyond the life of the community which lived around it and its own use as a mosque, persisted. The colonial-era jurist Syed Ameer Ali translated the *Qanun-i Masajid*, a sourcebook of principles of Hanafi law on mosques published for the benefit of jurists in the Calcutta High Court, and provided a jurisprudential basis for disallowing the repurposing of mosque lands: "[Even] if the surrounds of a mosque become desolate, it will remain a mosque forever until doomsday." The author conceded that this principle was not absolute but was debated in the sources as the authorities concurred that a mosque was always a mosque, but the state had the right to assess the requirements for land, development, and resettlement.[95] This principle was elaborated further in another work on Hanafi jurisprudence published by a Bareilvi press in 1898 in which the author argued that if the entire area around the mosque become deserted, it would fall to the community which practiced at the mosque or the custodian appointed by the endower to take the matter to a qazi to make a decision about the resumption of mosque lands.

> The sale of belongings of a masjid, including its land and erected buildings, is not possible under any circumstances, but when a masjid, God forgive me, becomes deserted, and no trace of its dwellers remains, then according to one tradition, a qazi of the shari'a, by the dictates of Islam, may sell [the masjid's] belongings and spend the proceeds in support of another masjid. In a time of need, recourse to this tradition is permissible.[96]

These juristic principles were never invoked in twelve-year rule cases which were simply barred by limitation and so the opportunity to present the case according to shari'a never arose. The principle of the resumability of mosque land by the government was often invoked to validate the government reappropriation of one-time mosque lands and buildings for the purpose of urban redevelopment and government use. In late-eighteenth-century Allahabad, which had a British garrison and British financial administration from 1765 before it was directly administered from 1801, a Friday mosque which had been built by the Mughal emperor Aurangzeb in the seventeenth century was given by the local ruler, the Nawab Wazir of Awadh to a Colonel Hyde on the principle that it was no longer in use as a mosque.[97] During the occupation of Hyderabad in Sindh in 1843 where the estates of the defeated and vanquished Talpur rulers were occupied by military and civil administration. A narrow mosque,

17 meters long and 4 meters wide, adjoining Nur Muhammad Talpur's zenana and within the perimeter of his estate, was given over to the arsenal. Another "small elegant mosque" of burnt brick with lime-washed walls and floor in an adjoining area was used as storeroom for knapsacks.[98] And then again, during the urban redevelopment of Delhi at the turn of the twentieth century, a number of old or remarkable mosques were razed to be treated as little more than real estate and the vocal opposition of local intellectuals dismissed as being contrary to the Islamic law on the point.[99]

But many continued to believe that land once dedicated to a mosque could never be used in any other way again. Even if the site were to become disused, the only use that could be made of it was to rebuild the mosque. The idea of unresumable land which was forever beyond the reach of the market and capital took shape under the nomenclature of "God's land," *khuda ki zameen*.[100] In principle, trust law enabled the classification of the mosque as God's land. Ameer Ali wrote,

> when anyone has resolved to devote his property to religious purposes, as soon as his mind is made up . . . an endowment is immediately constituted; his act deprives him of all ownership in the property, and to use the language of Mahommedan lawyers, vests it in God in such a manner as . . . the appropriator's rights in it are extinguished, and it becomes a property of God.[101]

As a "property of God," waqf land was considered to have become inalienable, removed from the reach of capital. But we have seen that the administration of endowment land was careless and ridden with contradictions. And as the next chapter will demonstrate trust law did not in fact have the effect intended as the legal strategies for protection of endowment land from mismanagement, encroachment and the reach of the market were complicated and expensive. In the face of myriad challenges to the principle that the mosque, once endowed and prayed in, was God's land and therefore could never again be subject to occupation or possession, an ideal of reclaiming and reinstating lost mosques took shape, rejecting even Hanafi jurisprudence where it suggested the repurposing of mosque land to be permissible.

Efforts to reinstate one-time mosques resonated with efforts to protect historic buildings and sites. In an early example from Buriya in east Punjab in 1834, the political agent received Muslim petitions for an empty urban plot of land in the center of a Hindu dominated bazaar on the grounds that a mosque had once stood there but had been demolished during the period of Sikh rule in the Punjab.[102] The political agent, inspired to examine the truth of the claims, uncovered the foundation and was left with no doubt that this had been a mosque and awarded the site to the Muslims of the town. This decision triggered communal tensions as "demonstrations of triumph" on the part of the Muslims were a cause for the Hindus to close their shops and shut down the bazaar. The political agent reverted to the "neutral" arrangements that had prevailed before the excavation, refusing control of the site to either community.[103]

Widespread advocacy for protecting mosques and mosque land from resumption began after the Kanpur mosque incident. Three mosques in the princely state of Bharatpur, built by men of the irregular troops of the Maharajah's army, were scheduled for demolition as the Maharajah reorganized his army.[104] In the press, this issue was emphasized as being communally motivated.[105] The Khilafat Committee also spoke out strongly about several mosque demolitions in the press, emphasizing that they violated basic principles of waqf. The Karachi-based Sindh Mahomedan Association wrote to the provincial administration to condemn the acquisition of one mosque and the accidental demolition of another during the Sukkur Barrage development:

> The commissioner is aware Mussalman religion forbids demolition or exchange of religious waqfs and more particularly Masjids. Nor can any individual become the owner of such a waqf. In this case it is alleged that a Mulla was taken as owner of the Masjid and he was given compensation therefore. The amount received by him, I understand, has been returned.[106]

This discourse of opposition to government resumptions of mosque lands took shape in print, in texts written for a wider reading public. A writer making recourse to "only a few texts on fiqh and the fatwas of the 'ulama" published a book in 1946 entitled *The Injunctions Relating to Mosques* which he elaborated and republished in 1961.[107] He described the debate over the resumption of mosque land, particularly with reference to Muslim settlement and residence in a neighborhood:

> When such circumstances are presented that the Muslim population in a place disappears, like in times of war or revolution, or they are forced from a place because of circumstances, or all of them have died, for which reason the mosque is no longer used for prayer, or the walls of the masjid have fallen in and there is no one to carry out repairs, or the entire country is in a state of abject poverty. Even under all of these circumstances, it must be remembered that a mosque will remain a mosque. No other occupancy [*tasarraf*] by anyone is permissible. Nor can this mosque be sold. Nor can it be auctioned. Nor can it be sold in

order that the proceeds of the sale be put towards the construction of another mosque.[108]

The prohibition on return of the land of the mosque to the market or for possession or development for any other purpose than the mosque itself was stated in no uncertain terms.

This opened up the problem of how to classify land pertaining to mosques where all other land was understood for its control either by individuals or the state. The Deobandi alim Mufti Muhammad Shafi composed a text in Karachi in 1948 in preparation for a conference of 'ulama on "the classifications of land according to shari'a, and on the truth of the Quranic injunctions relating to land." He expanded and published this discourse in 1979. Shafi argued that all land should be divided into the subcategories relating to its capacity to be put to productive uses by either an individual or the government, whether it could not be put to use at all like mountains and jungles, whether it was awaiting proprietary development, or it had already been cultivated or developed to generate revenues, or it supported infrastructure to meet the general needs of people. Unlike all other land, he placed waqf land in a separate category altogether, stating it "could not be included within any individual or government's property (*milkiyat*)." For this reason the "mosques, madrassas, khanqahs, hospitals, orphanages, graveyards [and other such waqfs] of the Muslims . . . are truly God's land, (*milk-i khudawandi*)."[109]

The concerns which were being presented in these discourses were inspired by occupied mosques and conceived circumstances in which Muslims were unable to finance and defend the adverse possession of mosque land within twelve years. Under colonial trust law, Muslims were empowered to litigate as beneficiaries of the trust to claim back alienated endowment land. The circumstances being highlighted were past periods of Muslim disempowerment or lack of will to act under law, or possible future circumstances in which Muslims had either left an area or were so legally disempowered, impoverished, or ideologically unmotivated as to fail to actively defend the alienation of land from an endowment. These were not hypothetical constructs; they referred back to recent pasts, like in the Punjab, where many mosques had ceased to serve Muslim worship under Sikh rule, and penned in the 1940s amid rising communal tensions. The idea of God's land challenged the principle that mosque land could be repurposed under the twelve-year rule. Recategorizing the land related to the mosque trust as altogether beyond the reach of capital and redevelopment would mean that any administrative review of land disputes relating to mosques would not rely on evidence of ongoing active litigation by Muslim worshippers or communities initiated within the twelve-year period of limitations to uphold the documentation of waqf.

The discourse of God's land had a profound impact on key Muslim intellectuals of twentieth-century Lahore. The literary imaginary of the poet Iqbal, ideologue of Muslim nationalism, a close ally of Jinnah and Muslim statesmen of the Punjab, came to be shaped by the debate over the legal status of mosques. Iqbal visited the mosque of Cordoba in 1931 and wrote one of his most famous poems directly after that, describing the mosque both as an eternal act of inspiration and eternally inspiring for all Muslims.

> But in that shape there is the aspect of eternal stability-
> [that shape] which some man of the Lord would have made complete
> the action of the man of the Lord—through passion, the possessor of
>   radiance
> passion is the source/essence of life, for its death is forbidden
>
> Oh holy place of Cordoba! from passion, your existence
> passion wholly eternal, in which there's no going and coming
> whether it be color or brick and stone, whether it be the lute or word and
>   voice
> the manifestation of miracles of art is from the blood of the liver[110]

Popular Muslim interest in Shahidganj increased after the decisions of the Sikh Gurdwara Tribunal were announced in 1930. Among many others, Iqbal took up the cause. He did not endorse the populist efforts to rally a following but focused on the principle of the nature of the mosque as a "Khana-i Khuda" or house of God, arguing that a law which could allow a mosque to go into adverse possession, and thereby lose its very nature and its sanctity, was "completely incorrect and should be eliminated."[111]

In 1935, Iqbal signed on as a litigant in the suit filed in the name of "The Mosque Known as Shahidganj." This suit went on appeal to the Judicial Committee of the Privy Council and produced the JCPC verdict reaffirming application of the twelve-year rule. As the case made its way through the courts, Iqbal simultaneously worked with Malik Barkat Ali, custodian of the Sunehri mosque and a member of Punjab legislature, to draft the Punjab Muslim Mosques Protection Bill, attempting to create statute which would make the judicial precedent in the matter unnecessary should the suit fail. The bill was intended to reclassify mosques so that laws applying to land could no longer apply to the mosque:

An Islamic mosque, which has been endowed under the shari'a, has been removed from mundane uses and is fully and in its entirety endowed for the purpose of worship of God. The word "property" cannot be applied to it with the meaning and intent with which this word [property] is currently in use in the laws of India and the Punjab.[112]

Iqbal and Barkat Ali's Mosque Protection Act drew on the inspiration of Jinnah's Mussalman Waqf Validating Act of 1913. This statute pertained to private trusts and as such had no direct bearing on the interpretation of the public mosque trust, but was a statute which superseded JCPC judgment. Iqbal and Barkat Ali's bill would have added a new dimension to colonial law rather than working within its confines, by introducing a classification of a mosque fundamentally different to all other public, private, and endowment land. As it was, amid growing communal tensions in the Punjab and the very real risk of backlash and similar demands being put forward by Hindus in Muslim minority provinces, Barkat Ali was unable to summon the necessary support for his bill.[113] He was opposed by leading Muslim members of the Punjab legislative assembly who had grave concerns about the legitimacy of statute intended to override the decision of the highest court in the province,[114] and was unable to get Muhammad Ali Jinnah's overt support.

The idea that the mosque was God's land, a principle derived from Shari'a, was developed in texts and discourses which articulated Muslim responses to the application of the twelve-year rule to mosques. God's land was taking shape as a legal classification for land and buildings associated with the mosque which was distinct from all other categories of land and buildings. The effort to do away with the twelve-year rule anticipated a more profound impact on the South Asian landscape than just the resurrection of the Shahidganj as a one-time mosque. The principle was to remove all mosques from subjection to laws governing land and, by extension, documentation by government officials, making it impossible that a mosque should ever again be anything but a mosque and fixing those architectural testimonies to and spaces for Muslim devotionalism in the landscape forever. Had these efforts succeeded, they would have introduced a political anachronism and exacerbated communal tensions by reinstating mosques which had been abandoned, occupied, or repurposed over time, disrupting a politics of historicism which prevailed across India and even penetrated law.[115]

As it was, the jurist of the JCPC reviewed the extensive records of land use at the Shahidganj and enunciated in the final ruling on the matter in 1940, "it is idle to call upon the Courts to apply Mohammedan law to events taking place between 1762 and 1849 [when it was not then] the law of the land recognized and enforced as such."[116] Indian courts' legal responsibility for Shahidganj only dated to 1849, and at that moment, the jurists of the JCPC ruled, all appropriate procedures had been followed. They did not address the critical underlying legal question of who the land belonged to, if not to God. But they were not required to do so.

The Suit of "the Mosque Known as Shahidganj"

The Shahidganj Mosque affair is primarily understood as a twentieth-century urban movement because the legal battle was elevated to the higher courts and highly publicized during this period. The Sikh Gurdwara Tribunal of Lahore delivered its verdict in 1930; after defeating the now dispossessed mahants in a battle in the Lahore High Court, new Sikh custodians demolished the building of the mosque in 1935, attempting to put an end to Muslim claims to the mosque once and for all.[117] Almost immediately Muslim litigants, among them the poet Allama Muhammad Iqbal, filed the suit to resurrect the mosque and to restore Muslim rights of worship in it; the suit was admitted and made its way through a system of appeals to the Judicial Committee of the Privy Council eliciting the verdict in 1940.

The suit filed by "The Mosque Known as Shahidganj represented by its next friends," has been widely read as a performance of symbolic Muslim association with the Shahidganj site.[118] The personification of the mosque in the suit was, however, conceived to overcome the twelve-year rule. The litigants named the mosque itself, recently demolished, as a subject of colonial jurisprudence with rights, therefore not subject to occupation. The ghostly appearance of the now demolished Mosque Known as Shahidganj suggested its perpetual nature and refuted its classification as land on the principle that a mosque, "belonging to no one but God, dedicated to Him," could never lose its character, even if it should fall into ruins or become desolate or should be used for other purposes other than that those for which it was originally founded. "Even though the site should be ploughed and sown or trees planted," it could never be the subject of adverse possession.[119]

The suit of the Mosque Known as Shahidganj loosely borrowed a principle underlying a landmark case in which the Privy Council conceived a Hindu idol to be the subject of a bequest. That 1869 ruling "inaugurated the status of the deity as owner of the property," and subsequent rulings conceived custodians to be managers of the idol's property. The ruling in this suit allowed the alienation of land as necessary for the service of the idol.¹²⁰ The 1869 precedent on Hindu temples and the suit of the Mosque Known as Shahidganj had effectively personified the mosque as the subject of the Shahidganj bequest in order to create a perpetuity.¹²¹

There was a great deal of pressure on the judiciary to demonstrate a friendly attitude toward Islam. A judge of the High Court of Lahore whose judgment had been a basis for the appeal to the Judicial Committee of the Privy Council opined that admitting Islamic law in the matter would be "in consonance with the principles of justice, equity and good conscience."¹²²

The jurists of the JCPC reassured the Muslim petitioners that they had "ever sympathy with religious sentiment which would ascribe sanctity and inviolability to a place of worship."¹²³ However they could not accept the contention that it was more than just a building and could not be subject to adverse possession. If an occupier managed to take over a mosque and turned it into "a building of his own," claiming it as his own property under land management practices of the colonial state, he had rights over that property, the Lahore High Court ruled.¹²⁴ As rights in the mosque were inseparable from rights in the land on which it was built, this meant that "the personal law of Mohammadans has been modified by the Punjab Laws Act and the Limitation Act."¹²⁵ This ruling restated the principle that claims to contested sites would be governed by land rights conferred at the time of settlement or subsequent practices of land management, reconciling Anglo-Mohammedan law with land administration practices, denying the litigants a reclassification of the mosque as something other than property.

The success of the suit would have enabled the resurrection of the Shahidganj and the resilience of other mosques, as "a special kind of waqf and that differs from all other kinds of waqfs,"¹²⁶ within the landscape of colonial India. As it happened however, the Judicial Committee of the Privy Council reinforced the role of petty and powerful government officials, acting in their capacity as revenue officers and urban administrators, in recording rights in mosques. Rather than reaffirming a state neutrality in matters relating to religion, this principle concentrated power and influence in the hands of *patwaris* and surveyors whose records had to capture the nuance of religious land use and had the potential to confer new title over endowment land, and in the collector-magistrate-deputy commissioner's office, charged with inquiry and review of occupancy and land use. Fundamentally dependent on district officials and their ongoing documentation of land and land use, the mosque remained classified as a form of property and therefore vulnerable to hostile possession, or else administrative vigilance.

A key feature of the Shahidganj affair, one which has been overlooked in earlier work on the subject, was this intent and failure of Muslim efforts to introduce a new legal conceptualization of mosque land into colonial law. Neither the concept of God's land, nor the subjecthood of the mosque was recognized through the legal process. The conceptual limitations but administrative usefulness of permitting occupation-based rights in religious sites persisted.

Conclusion

This chapter has explored a history of colonial land management practices, their place in legitimizing mosques in Lahore, and alternative concepts presented by proponents of Muslim control of Shahidganj. In 1940 the two colonial land management practices, recognition of the successful and persistent occupation of land for religious uses and conciliatory administrative return of religious lands, were both reaffirmed as procedures for establishing religious rights of worship at a site. The failure of Muslim efforts to overturn the first principle by proposing the idea of "God's land" does not make this history any less significant. Rather they draw attention to the persistent and unresolved resistance of Muslim thinkers to the classification of all land as fundamentally proprietary.

The ideas relating to the classification of religious land continued to be disruptive after 1940. In Lahore the governor returned another Mughal mosque[127] "in appreciation of the great restraint exercised by the Muslim community generally in the Punjab and especially in Lahore" in the aftermath of the Sikh demolition of the Shahidganj mosque.[128] Proponents of the resurrection of the Somnath temple at the site of the Babri Mosque in Ayodhya sought to elicit administrative recognition of Hindu rights in the Ayodhya site from 1949.[129] Eventually an Indian Supreme Court ruling returned the site to Hindus in 2019 after extensively debating the same legal principles of adverse possession and limitation of restitution of land rights[130] which were raised in the Shahidganj matter from 1849 to 1940. In Pakistan the establishment of mosques through the forcible occupation of land became commonplace.[131]

The land underlying the mosque was subject to a body of law which was unrelated to trust law and Anglo-Mohammedan law but was interacting with it in powerful and disruptive ways. The law and policies related to the administration of land enabled the authority of the colonial executive over the mosque. Like the mosque perimeter, the ground beneath the mosque was governed in the interests of a general public but without the consensus of twentieth-century Muslim thinkers.

Chapter 5

KORA JAHANABAD, UP, 1947

MUSLIM ASSOCIATIONS WIN BACK
CONTROL OVER MOSQUES

A Hindu courtier in the late-eighteenth-century Awadh state converted to Shi'a Islam and took the name Haider Bakhsh. He built a mosque and an imambargah, a building for Shi'a congregation during the Muharram month of ritual mourning, on the lands of his *mu'afi* estate in Kora Jahanabad, some 26 miles south of Kanpur. Haider Baksh spent his life at his estate with a disciple whom he adopted as a son, his son's wives and children, his Hindu brother, and his nephews. Shortly before he died in 1837, Haider Bakhsh instructed his nephews to purchase two villages and to use their incomes to offset costs of the mosque and imambargah. Over the next fifty years descendants of one of Haider Bakhsh's Hindu nephews took over custodianship of the mosque and imambargah while Haider Bakhsh's Muslim family became impoverished and alienated from the site. As religious conflict increased in the volatile political climate of late-nineteenth-century UP, the incongruity of Hindu custodianship of a mosque and imambargah appeared ever more surprising to Muslims.

The Hindu custodians perceived and asserted personal, proprietary claims to the site, threatening the continued existence of the waqf. In the early 1900s the waqf was gradually closed off to Muslim religious use and to public access. The custodian of that time recorded the land and buildings as a private proprietary estate, denying that the site included a public mosque and imambargah at all and disputing Muslims claims that the two villages were given in waqf for defraying the expenses of the mosque and imambargah.

Worshippers' confidence in the colonial legal system was at a low ebb at the start of the twentieth century. Jurists had affirmed the paternalistic control of prayer leaders, custodians and officers of the state over places of worship while the press highlighted offenses to and denial of Muslim religious sensibilities. Amid this, UP Muslims were unable to bring the custodian of Kora Jahanabad to account through the legal process owing to the land record which denoted the site as a private estate. Muslims elected after the political reforms of 1919 worked with Muslim associations to formulate a strategy for regulating waqfs in general and for claiming the Kora Jahanabad waqf in particular. The petitioners in the Kora Jahanabad suit successfully presented the testimony of an officer of a Muslim association in court in 1934. A long history of legal, political, and social activism for worshippers' rights in mosques in colonial India culminated in the systematic involvement of expert Muslims in governance and regulation of waqfs.

Heterodox Associations and Muslim Custodial Rights at Kora Jahanabad

Political change from 1747 to 1900 had fostered heterodox associations with the Kora Jahanabad waqf. This was not syncretism; Muslims performed distinctly Islamic rituals here and while many Hindus attended *majlis*, meetings to remember the martyred family of the Prophet, none worshipped in the mosque. Muslim and Hindu neighbors formed social relationships which were fostered by activity on endowment land. Hindu and Muslim family members of Haider Bakhsh became increasingly hostile to one another as the Muslim family claimed custodial rights over the endowment land. The language of religious difference was a legal device in the suits put forward by Muslim descendants of Haider Baksh and presented to Government officials for sanction.

Haider Baksh had risen to eminence in the orbit of the Awadh court during the eighteenth century. He converted to Islam and in 1788 the Nawab Asaf ud Daula awarded him full[1] rights over 100 bighas of *muʿafi* land in Kora Jahanabad, at the southern edge of his empire, an award which was reaffirmed by the state revenue officer Almas Khan[2] in 1797. He reproduced something of the material culture of the Awadh state on his own lands adjoining his *haveli*. The main gated entrance to the estate was adorned on either side by the Awadh state crest. The gardens contained a covered pavilion or *baradari* constructed in a style common to Shiʻa endowments of Lucknow, Faizabad, and Kanpur and numerous *chabutras*, cisterns, and tanks. The imambargah had central halls as well as storage rooms adorned with lattice shutters and chandeliers and women's meeting rooms and courtyards. Ornate stone gateposts and two gilded *alams*, traditional Shiʻa flagstaffs, marked the main entrance to the whitewashed mosque and external stairs led to a flat rooftop prayer space. The eastern and western wings of the imambargah flanked the mosque and grove. When he died in 1837, Haider Baksh was entombed in the gardens, beside the imambargah.³

After Haider Baksh's death, his family regarded the mosque, the imambargah, the vessels, cloths and ceremonial objects in the imambargah, the grove enclosed by these buildings, and the villages that paid their expenses to be waqf. The whole came under the custodianship of Haider Baksh's brother's grandson and then the great grandson Lal Bahadur, and was financially and legally managed as a Muslim place of worship until the end of the nineteenth century. There were a number of proprietary claims against the grove and the revenue villages. Lal Bahadur's uncle tried unsuccessfully to partition a share of the two villages in 1853, and successfully mortgaged a share in the two villages shortly after.⁴ Muslim descendants of Haider Baksh's adopted son claimed inheritance rights over this land and denied it was a waqf at all.⁵ However a revenue court ruled in 1861 that this was endowed property,⁶ and the suits instituted by Haider Bakhsh's descendants through his adoptive son were barred on limitation.⁷ The most significant proprietary claim to the lands was the one held in reserve by the custodians themselves; Lal Bahadur, his father before him, and his son after him, were entered as proprietors of the villages in the settlement records and paid revenue on the incomes from the land, but managed the waqf for close to seventy years, testifying to this in 1875 and 1876 when they had the revenue of the two villages recorded in the documentation of land use prepared by the collector's office.⁸

The assumption of custodial responsibilities and land rights at the site by male heirs in the line of Lal Bahadur was an outcome of the land redistribution that occurred after the events of 1857. Haider Bakhsh's adoptive son was dispossessed of his own personal *mu'afi* which included the grove, imambargah, tank, and *haveli* at this time, and land and title was conferred on Lal Bahadur in return for his faithfulness and service "protecting the town of Jahanabad from looting and marauding by the rebels."⁹ Rather than typifying a past tradition of syncretism, Hindu custodianship was an outcome of political change under the colonial state. While these changes destabilized the Muslim family's claims to land and title, they did not affect the classification of the trust as a waqf, and by all accounts the agricultural income from the two villages was used in the service of Muslim worship until the end of the century. The Hindu custodians paid the expenses of rituals of meeting and public mourning in the month of Muharram including food and the fees of the *zakirs* and the maulvi who led the rituals. Income from waqf villages also paid for the upkeep of the imambargah, the mosque and the grove, a sacrificial goat on Bakr Eid, *khir,* dates and spices on the 21st of Ramadan, and commemorative events on Nauroz, Nauchandi and Shab-i Barat.[10] The uses of incomes from the lands for the purposes of "*taziyadari* during Muharram and repairs to the imambargah and the mosque" were entered by Lal Bahadur in the records of land use for the villages in 1875–6, creating a legal foundation for classifying the lands as waqf and protecting them from inheritance claims by Haider Baksh's many descendants.[11]

Lal Bahadur's family appointed Muslim managers who would take the valuable *taziyas* and other objects out of storage and make arrangements for food and *zakirs* and maulvis on religious occasions. These acting managers had abiding associations of their own at the waqf. Ashiq Hussain[12] resided in a property outside the boundary wall enclosing the mosque, grove, and imambargah; the site and size of Ashiq Hussain's home suggests that he most likely occupied the *haveli* of Haider Baksh's dispossessed adoptive son. The grave of another of these managers, Hasan Askari, who held the important position of reciter of elegies at the imambargah,[13] stood alongside Haider Baksh's, marking his importance. Both Hasan Askari and Ashiq Husain were prayer leaders at the mosque and gave the call to prayer. Their associations with the waqf coexisted easily with Lal Bahadur's custodianship of the site because they had no legal basis for claiming proprietary interests over the grove, imambargah, mosque, and revenue villages.

There were few Shi'a Muslims in Kora Jahanabad; the five families present in the town in the twentieth century were described as descended from the servants of Lal Bahadur, his son and grandson.[14] These few families were the most closely and consistently associated with the waqf. Managers of the waqf were appointed from among these families who also granted permission to anyone wishing to hold a *majlis* at the imambargah. Up to sixty people would participate in religious activities at the imambargah, up to half of them were local Hindus.[15] Hindus and Muslims attended the Muharram *majlises* together to hear stories and to receive food, fruit, and sweets.

Hindu associations with the shrine were a product of social relationships with Shi'as. Munna Lal, a Hindu and a seller of clothing, attended *majlises* because he was invited. "We could go to one, or as many as we liked. Some people would not go at all."[16] A Hindu landowner with marital ties to Lal Bahadur's family was invited to the Muharram *majlises* by the custodians themselves.[17] These invitations were a product of close interpersonal relationships between Muslims and Hindus in the locale. A Muslim landlord who had worshipped in the mosque and imambargah called the Hindu custodian "brother" and was deemed a brother in return. His mother did not observe purdah with the Hindu custodian and the Hindu wife of the custodian did not observe it with the Muslim landlord.[18]

Hindu participation in *majlises* in Kora Jahanabad in the nineteenth century followed other instances of syncretic practice and sharing of sites centered on music, poetry, and recitation. In Gujarat, Hindu and Khoja Muslim devotees worshipped together in the Satpanth tradition,[19] and almost equal numbers of Hindu and Muslim pilgrims visited and honored the same saint at a shrine near Bombay.[20] In Bengal, a poet drew both Muslim and Hindu disciples and his own religious identity remained ambiguous; his life and his teaching continued to be commemorated by Hindus and Muslims at his mausoleum after his death.[21] But Hindu visitors to the Kora Jahanabad waqf did not, by any accounts, worship in the mosque.

Muslim challengers to Lal Bahadur's family's custodial control and arrangements initiated litigation in 1889 and 1923, invoking civil procedure which granted beneficiaries of charitable trusts the right to initiate a suit in the case of any alleged breach of trust.[22] However, Lal Bahadur and Iqbal Bahadur's challengers failed to meet an underlying condition: obtaining sanction of the office of advocate general for the government to initiate a suit. The government's role in providing safeguards against hostile occupation of endowments was addressed in the Shahidganj suit and was reaffirmed by that verdict. Here, the issue at stake was the power of the district officer to sanction litigation relating to endowments, a power which could be deployed to impede general religious claims for rights in endowments. The effect of this procedure was deeply felt and experienced by Hindus and Sikhs across South Asia and fueled widespread demands for legislative change from the late 1900s. In the United Province, new legislation relating to Muslim endowments was introduced between 1920 and 1923.

Mirza Muhammad Ali Khan, the son of Haider Baksh's adopted son who had demanded a proprietary share in Haider Baksh's estate in 1873, tried again to challenge Lal Bahadur's family control over the estate in 1889, this time asserting his right to be appointed custodian of the waqf or see another Muslim appointed as custodian. He based his claim in part on the principle that Islamic law called for Muslim custodianship. The judge in this suit was not in a position to interpret the principles of Islamic law, no matter how reasonable the principle may have appeared to him. He subjected the suit to the test of "validation through the presentation of authoritative religious opinion," in other words, he wanted an accompanying fatwa and without one, he could not rule on the case.

The pleaders for the plaintiffs argue that . . . a Mohammedan will be better fitted to be a custodian than a Hindu although he may be doing the work honestly. It may be so. But I do not like to express any opinion on the merits of the case, nor has any evidence been adduced before me on behalf of any party.[23]

The judge argued that he was only empowered to rule according to clearly articulated principles of law or else in favor of a party to the suit who was able to demonstrate the clear alignment of his position with religious principles. There is little doubt that Muhammad Ali's failure to arrange such testimony was based on financial limitations; the Ahl-i Hadith in Tajpur had spent many thousands of rupees arranging the testimony of 'ulama, and Muhammad Ali claimed in a pauper suit that he could not afford even the cost of the litigation. Should the suit have proceeded, it most likely would have failed for lack of resources.

More importantly, under the codes of civil procedure in place in 1889, the charge of mismanagement of the trust required the sanction of the advocate general. Muhammad Ali and his co-litigants had written to the advocate general for the United Provinces and been informed that they needed to apply to the local government for sanction. Muhammad Ali obtained a certificate from the district collector to establish the grounds for the case, but the judge deemed this authorization to be insufficient according to more recently published rules and dismissed the suit on the grounds of procedural irregularities.[24] The principle that the government must authorize a suit for worshippers' rights doomed this one, and many others like it, to fail in bureaucratic snares.

Government authorization remained elusive. In 1911, a government prosecutor named Munshi Amir Hasan Khan filed a suit challenging Iqbal Bahadur's control over the site, once again citing the principle that Muslims should control Islamic waqf property. Munshi Amir Hasan was joined in his suit by Hakim Nasrat Husain, a man well known to the court of the collector of Fatehpur, and fifteen other local Muslims. Nasrat Husain came to tragic acclaim only four years later when he traveled to the Hijaz, found the company of the Deobandi scholar Mahmudul Hasan, and was by chance arrested and incarcerated in Malta with the latter on charges of conspiracy against the colonial state and died of illness there.[25] A zamindar of Fatehpur,[26] he identified himself as someone who "spent his time in court cases," and had deep conversations with his interrogator regarding agrarian and land management issues. Nasrat Husain's participation in the suit was presumably inspired by both his religious intellectual concerns and his deep connections to landholding in the Fatehpur district. Despite the collector's encouraging notation that Munshi Amir Hasan and Nasrat Husain were both "respectable persons," the office of the advocate general once again did not authorize the suit.[27]

During or after the 1911 suit, Lal Bahadur's son represented his title to the estate as being proprietary, erasing the mention of the waqf from the documentation of land use.[28] He stopped paying for repairs to the mosque and imambargah and barred the gate to the estate and disallowed any entry to the buildings. In 1923, three Shi'a Muslims organized by the All India Shi'a Conference sued for the removal of the Hindu custodian on the grounds of mismanagement of the mosque and imambargah. In 1911, collector of Fatehpur had received an application from the local Muslims to sanction the Muslim suit challenging Iqbal Bahadur's control of the waqf, and had warmly testified to the good character of the applicants.[29] In 1923, the collector of Fatehpur wrote to the office of the legal remembrancer to say that in his opinion, the mosque and imambargah were private trusts and confided that the 1923 suit was only the latest in a series of efforts by Muslims to "get hold of the property." He recommended to the office of the legal remembrancer that they deny the request for authorization of the suit under Section 92.[30]

Contestations of Hindu control over the waqf had started out as a competition among descendants within a family line but increasingly took on communal overtones, the implication that all Muslims in the UP if not India were collectively supportive of and represented in these activities.[31] Part of Muhammad Ali's claim was framed as a general Muslim interest in the waqf; as a Muslim, he felt that the waqf should be managed by a Muslim. Munshi Amir Hasan Khan and Hakim Nasrat Husain applied as members of a "Mohammedan community with an interest in the mosque and imambargah as a public endowment."[32] The petitioners in 1923 were delegates of an organization which had established its own authority to shape Shi'a law, culture, and social identity. This pattern of communalization of legal arguments for control over the waqf mirrored the rise of Muslim identity politics in the United Provinces,[33] and the establishment of communal representation in government.[34] Communalism provided first language, then inspiration, then resources for litigation at Kora Jahanabad, and stood to be vindicated by a successful outcome.

In every instance of Muslim litigation for control of the Kora Jahanabad waqf, government officials exercised a discretionary authority which we have come to expect. The collector provided an assessment of the suit based in his local on the ground understanding of religious groups, their motives, and the most expedient outcomes which could be desired, while the advocate general's office was charged with "watching and controlling litigation."[35] Petitioners needed to establish three things to elicit legal recognition of a general religious right in a waqf: the authority of their religious position, their status as real or potential beneficiaries of the religious trust, and administrative sanction. This was the restrictive reality that underlay the legal provisioning for a general Muslim public to claim rights in the mosque under the law, "the cumbersome and expensive process which few could take advantage of," in the words of a member of the United Provinces legislative assembly.[36]

Representation of Hindu-Muslim religious difference was a legal device for Muslims aiming to securing control over the important revenue estates associated with the waqf. Muslim efforts at Kora Jahanabad were like Muslim efforts to reclaim Shahidganj in Lahore, Khoja claims of communal rights over endowment property in Bombay,[37] and Sikh claims to rights in endowments in the Punjab.[38] Communalism expressed some truths of religious difference, that Hindus did not recognize the sacrality of the mosque, for instance, but this case is better understood to be a part of a history of legal activism for Muslim rights in endowments.

Muslim Rights in Waqfs and the Reformulation of Secular Governance

Muslim mosque activism had centered on legal action against religious antagonists. After 1920 it included political activism for administrative reform which succeeded in 1936. Reform of the procedures for filing a legal suit eventually enabled Muslim claims at the Kora Jahanabad waqf.

The colonial executive had repeatedly thwarted Muslim legal activism for clarifying religious rights in devotional sites by refusing sanction for legal suits. Members of the colonial executive, like the magistrate at the mosque perimeter, had discretionary authority to sanction legal action by worshippers but were reluctant to exercise that authority as that would require taking a position on often fine points of religious belief and practice. Indian statesmen were obliged to allow the executive to remain indifferent as to what the religious principles motivating Muslim worshippers and custodians were.[39] Elected Indian statesmen conceived an alternate procedural framework, reformulating the secularism of government.

From the early 1920s newly elected Indian members of the legislative assemblies were taking account of the economic valuation of endowment land and calling for efficient and transparent management of endowment incomes in the service of community. The Sikh Akalis drew attention to the misdeeds of *mahants* across the Punjab and drew a wide following within the Sikh community, eventually establishing corporatized management of Sikh endowments.[40] The Sanatana Dharma Sabha movement encouraged the Hindu public to exercise vigilance over the managers of wealthy endowments and to expect that this money should be used to revitalize religion.[41] The colonial executive looked hard at the question of whether it should change its policy of noninterference in religious affairs.[42]

The government of India presented an account of the total annual revenue releases on endowments in the UP: 344 lakhs on Hindu religious trusts and 138 lakhs on Muslim ones;[43] in 1927, confirmed, audited incomes of United Provinces Muslim waqfs were confirmed at close to 4 million rupees.[44] The total value of waqf property in the province was debated and valued by different groups, general agreement coalescing around the figure of one crore.[45] This value, which accrued in principle to the six and three quarters of a million UP Muslim beneficiaries, was considerable.[46]

Indian politicians were trying to introduce legislation for government regulation of religious endowments from the turn of the century. Early proposals for the creation of a regulatory apparatus identified the collector's office, alternately the magistrate's or district commissioner's office, as the appropriate regulatory body for religious endowments.[47] It was not entirely inconceivable that the district officer could take on such a role. As we know, district collectors and magistrates already exercised control over intractable and violent conflict relating to religious sites. They also authorized legal suits relating to endowments. But giving institutional responsibility for identifying, evaluating and prosecuting transgress at places of worship to a district collector undermined the colonial policy of keeping their "officers entirely free from any connection to management of these trusts."[48]

In 1919, significant legislative powers were conferred on provincial legislative assemblies of elected Indian representatives and new legislation was introduced at the all-India level. The imperial legislative assembly introduced the Charitable and Religious Trusts Act of 1920 which emphasized the rights of beneficiaries of a public trust and standardized measures for its regulation and allowed that "any person could apply to the court in respect of trusts of a religious or charitable nature," notably without the sanction of local government and the office of the advocate general. The Mussalman Waqf Act of 1923 required all custodians of Muslim endowments to file public audited accounts for the previous five years with the district magistrate. Together these two pieces of legislation provided a clear route and a basis for Muslims to individually or jointly sue custodians for mismanagement of trusts.

The Waqf Act was tabled for debate in the United Provinces legislative assembly in 1924 with many members of the legislature testifying to the general interest of their constituencies in seeing it enforced. The All India

Shi'a Conference delivered a telegram to a member of the legislature during deliberations to reemphasize its support for the legislation, and other influential Muslims and members of the judiciary commended it to their representatives.[49] Maulvi Abdul Hakim, a prominent Islamic intellectual closely aligned with Deobandi 'ulama, spoke strongly in favor of the act from a position of religious authority on the matter to describe the nature of a waqf and the accountability of custodians, adding that this legislation brought waqf property "under the control of a public."[50] Shari'at derived positions on waqf, popular sentiment, and legal reform aligned in favor of enabling individual legal agency over and claims on the productive resources of religious endowments.

The United Provinces Legislative Council adopted both the Act of 1920 and that of 1923 and was able to put a framework for official regulation of waqfs in place in 1924.[51] The idea that recognizing and upholding individual Muslim rights in waqfs was not sufficient became apparent to members of the United Provinces legislative assembly shortly after the passage of the Musalman Waqf Act. A year after the passage of the act, few custodians had registered their waqfs.[52] Complaints about those who had not done so were regularly communicated to the local government, but the government had no authority to compel custodians to furnish accounts, nor was the government able to independently compile lists of waqfs and identify which custodians had failed to register and report their accounts.[53] It then appeared there were not sufficient numbers of auditors in the province who could audit accounts in Urdu; those who did charged high fees which custodians were not clear could be charged to the endowment under shari'a. In the first year of its enforcement in the United Provinces, only one suit had been brought against a custodian under the Musalman Waqf Act.[54]

By 1926, only one case had been brought against the custodians of a waqf. Some waqf accounts had been registered at the district courts, but no one had evaluated them. It was not clear to anyone how these accounts could be systematically scrutinized to assert standards of conduct for management of and access to waqfs. The audits required by the Musalman Waqf Act produced an accounting for mosque land, assets, and income, probably differentiating mosque endowments within large multipurpose religious bequests (such as conjoined mosque-shrine or mosque-imambargah complexes) for the first time. The fifty-five custodial bodies from across the United Provinces who reported their financial affairs in 1926, almost all of them appointed at one time by the government (atypical custodians who are discussed in the next section), provided the names of custodians and the income of the endowment at a minimum. The legislation had been intended to unleash a wave of private litigation against innumerable corrupt custodians of Muslim endowments, but instead had no effect at all.

During the debates over the adoption and effect of the legislation in the United Provinces, an idea that there should be official leadership and organization of legal activism began to take shape and significantly modified the enactment of the legislation in the United Provinces.[55] One member of the United Provinces legislative assembly had cautioned that by considering the 1923 Waqf Act, they were placing a very dangerous instrument in a "vicious class of man" who may try to "harass and injure conscientious and honest" custodians,[56] while others cautioned that the waqf act would open private waqfs up to scrutiny which was not its intent.[57] Above all Hidayat Husain, a more reform minded member of the legislative committee, noted the lack of general Muslim interest in "unearthing the waqfs which had been uncared for [for] such a long time."[58] Where the legislation imagined Muslim worshippers bringing suits individually or jointly, there was little consensus within the legislative assembly that this was either possible or desirable. Divided by degrees of regard for the motives and the motivations of a general Muslim public to bring litigation against custodians of endowments, perceiving a deficit of information about the extent of waqf holdings and their classification as public or private, wary of audit service providers, and feeling a profound need to define standards of accountability, the Muslims of the United Provinces legislative assembly came together to propose and then agree to the creation of a new supervisory authority for waqfs.

The idea of creating provincial- and district-level committees of coreligionists who would supervise endowments was not new; it had been imagined from the early 1900s in the early debates on religious endowments, had been considered by the imperial legislative committee during deliberations relating to the 1923 Waqf Act,[59] and was now close to approval in the legislature in relation to Hindu endowments. Hidayat Husain suggested to the United Provinces what the responsibilities of these Islamic waqf committees would be:

> Under this committee there ought to be local or district committees for the proper control, management and supervision of waqfs in the district. The functions of these two bodies should be supervision and control of the custodians in their management of the property in their charge; secondly, unearthing waqf properties and recovering them from trespassers; thirdly inspection of waqf properties; fourthly inspection of accounts and their audit. They should also be authorized to call for information from custodians, to appoint custodians in case the waqfnama or deed is silent with regard to their appointment. They should also be

empowered to make suggestion to the district judge or to the collector when there is any scheme for the management of waqf property. They should also be authorized to file civil suits or make applications under section 92.... [The Religious Endowments Act of] 1863, [Religious and Charitable Trusts Act] of 1920 and the [Musalman Waqf Act] of 1923. [A committee] will advise the government how such boards can be created ..., things ancillary for proper administration ... what amendments are required in imperial and local acts, and [how to confer] upon recognized and representative bodies of the community, powers of supervision of waqf property.[60]

Hidayat Husain's proposal imagined the committees as performing several mediatory roles: between custodians and district courts which now required filing of waqf accounts and management schemes, between custodians and the local government which documented waqf estates, between Muslim community and the government which sought to assuage Muslim anxieties, and between community and the custodians which guarded Muslim endowment property. The work of the committees did not supplement the provisions for individual litigation against custodians of shrines in the 1923 Waqf Act but superseded them altogether. Husain proposed: "no suit shall be instituted by any person without the consent in writing of the Central [Waqf] Board."[61]

While the idea of having committees was introduced by Hidayat Husain for the first time in 1924, the means of constituting the committees and their relationship to the government was not debated publicly until 1927 and the legislation was passed in 1936. By that time the proposers envisioned two central boards: a Shi'a waqf board and a Sunni waqf board, providing advice, direction, and support to district-level Shi'a and Sunni waqf committees. The majority of the members of these committees would be elected Muslim representatives to the provincial legislature and they would include 'ulama, custodians, and delegates chosen by the powerful Muslim cultural associations, the Muslim Educational Conference, and the All India Shi'a Conference (AISC).[62]

The 1936 Waqf Bill also provided, critically, for the creation of a new post in the office of local government in each district: a commissioner of waqfs whose main responsibilities related to carrying out inquiries into land rights, enumerating the number of Shi'a and Sunni waqfs and their incomes, calculating the amount of revenue release, and ascertaining whether waqfs were public or private endowments.[63] This new gazetted officer would take on responsibilities which already fell to the local government and were mostly carried out by district officers in their capacity as revenue officers. In his capacity as documenter of the value, incomes and current arrangements for waqf property, this new officer of the local government was not required to act on any religious principle but the coreligionists who served on committees were able to express and act on religious principles and priorities in making investigations and recommending and carrying out litigation, keeping the bureaucracy inured of any responsibility to religion.

This new legislation was also adopted in Bihar and Orissa, Bengal and Bombay in the 1930s and 1940s.[64] It was adopted in the Indian Punjab in 1954 and in the territories which constituted Pakistan only after 1960.[65] Each province imagined a different balance of influence of elected representatives and the bureaucracy. In Bengal, in addition to the commissioner of waqfs, the majority of the ten or eleven members of waqf boards were appointed by the local government and the minority by the legislative assembly. Provincial differences in the manner of constituting the committee did not affect the consistency of provisions which protected bureaucrats from acting on religious predisposition.

The creation of official waqf boards and committees which scrutinized arrangements and uses of funds at religious sites posed a challenge to the colonial state's secular character, a fact that the colonial executive was acutely aware of and emphasized to Indian participants in the legislative process preceding the legislation of 1920 and 1923. As new officers and offices attending to religious affairs, the boards and committees are best understood as religious programs of government.[66] Crucially, their existence allowed statutory law and the Indian code, and the work of bureaucrats and judges, to remain free of any taint of values originating in devotionalism. What the legislation had accomplished, in effect, was to create a cadre of officers who would be authorized to express Islamic values. Other secular rationalities of governance which pertained to endowments,[67] those which protected jurists and administrators dealing with endowments, land use and the public from absorbing or expressing values produced by Indian cultural and religious traditions, were untouched by the legislation.

Waqf boards and committees appropriated the part of the paternalistic religious authority the colonial executive had appropriated from the Mughal state and had always been uncomfortable with: the executive's requirement to assess Muslim claims to religious uses of land. Waqf boards were a new cadre of officers with a religious role and mandate. And with their insertion into administration, Muslims no longer had to respect and protect the indifference of their government in religious matters.

Associations and their Oversight at the Kora Jahanabad Waqf

The waqf committees and central waqf boards conceived by Hidayat Husain had their precedents in associations of expert Muslims who had taken over management of mosques and other waqfs across India and were already highly regarded by the administration. Such associations had established themselves as honest and responsible in the eyes of colonial government and the Muslim public and modeled good management of waqfs.

After the passage of the 1863 Religious Endowments Act, custodial committees were appointed to take charge of mosques which had previously been under government control. In Delhi Nawab Ziauddin Khan, who had received estates from the colonial government for his service in the Maratha Wars and was a member of the archaeological society of India, headed the committee of the Fatehpuri Mosque.[68] In Hughli Bengal a long period of government ambivalence about the worthiness of individual custodians in charge of a Shi'a imambargah concluded with the establishment of a custodial committee under the charge of the district government in 1910.[69] The officers of these associations sometimes had religious credentials, but most often they did not. They worked systematically with their colleagues, with the state, and with a Muslim public to make expert recommendations for mosques and other waqfs based on a general assessment of good governance, good uses of funds, and good religious practice. They also managed public, governmental, and community expectations for religious worship and their own conduct.

In Lahore a committee took over the imperial Badhshahi Mosque[70] on the promise not to "permit any act within the mosque to show contempt or disloyalty to the government," and to manage and fund repairs to the mosque.[71] This committee was formalized and registered as a society called the Anjuman-i Islamia Lahore (not to be confused with scores of other associations called Anjuman-i Islamia that were established all over the region).[72] The Punjab administration treated "that committee of ten principal Mahomedan residents of Lahore"[73] as community representative in matters relating to the imperial mosque.[74] The Anjuman-i Islamia Lahore was the first organization permitted to invite the Muslims of Lahore to congregate under the colonial administration. The standard preface to the Anjuman's annual reports states that "it would not be far wrong to call the Anjuman the *'umm-al majalis,'* the mother of all gatherings."[75] The Anjuman was not an egalitarian organization, nor did it seek to cultivate a democratic politics of mosque use; the Anjuman sought to increase loyalty and faithfulness toward the country and the government among a general Muslim public, and to present Muslim demands to the government from time to time.

These were two of their five foundational objectives.[76] It was so effective that it was awarded custodianship of the pre-Mughal Masjid Gumti Bazaar, the Mughal-era Sunehri Masjid, Masjid Dai Lado, Masjid Hamam Wali, and Masjid Taksali Darwazah, and the colonial-era Masjid Shahid. The Anjuman interjected a layer of authority in mosques, interceding between Muslims in congregation and the government, a role that was not just sanctioned but supported into existence by the colonial administration of the Punjab.[77]

After the passage of the Musalaman Waqf Act of 1923 and its automatic extension to the Punjab, the Anjuman-i Islamia published combined audited accounts of each of the mosques under its management. The Anjuman professionalized the office of custodian by showing this to be a salaried position of responsibility over the combined trusts. It reapportioned incomes of mosques with bigger revenue streams to pay the expenses of mosques which had less income and made arrangements for *dars-i Quran*, public reading, translation, and commentary on the Quran at all mosques under its control. Its activities homogenized and evened out the variegated and uneven terrain of religious privilege and ritual practice across the city of Lahore.

In the United Provinces a circle of Shi'a 'ulama had established the association known as the Anjuman-i Sadr-i Sadur in Lucknow to increase communal solidarity, social welfare, and cultural development. One of the two branches of the Anjuman-i Sadr's efforts was to promote a coherent and unified religious message, to which end it appointed prayer leaders (*paish namaz*) and sermonizers (*wa'izin*) who toured different cities and towns where they convened Friday prayers.[78] The Anjuman-i Sadr gave way to a successor organization, The All India Shi'a Conference established in 1907, conceived as a congress of associations, each dedicated to its own particular work, whether religious education or charitable work. The AISC fostered the growth of many of the independent associations that made up its membership, among them the Anjuman-i Tamir-i Masajid which constructed and established mosques in Lucknow.[79] The Anjuman-i Sadr-i Sadur had called for the establishment of an organization which would monitor the condition and administration of Shi'a waqfs;[80] the AISC appointed a standing committee of its own members to do so and aspired to appointing local waqf committees across India.

The head of the AISC waqf committee himself visited the Kora Jahanabad Waqf in 1926 and recorded the state of the site, particularly noting the poor condition of the buildings and the lack of public access to the gardens, the mosque and the imambargah.[81] The committee created a plan of the estate naming various features of buildings and structures within the site using an Islamic architectural typology; in addition to the imambargah, they identified courtyards, *chabutras* or covered platforms, a storage area for *taziyas*, groves, graves, and the mosque designed with a rooftop congregational prayer space. This survey would come to directly connect the fate of the Kora Jahanabad waqf to the wider Muslim effort to institutionalize waqf regulation.

Muslims were not alone in these endeavors. Congress Party members had advocated for district-level committees for each religious community with custodial authority over all endowments and advocated for direct financial accountability to members of the public between 1897 and 1908. In Madras two members of the legislative council introduced a bill which would "enforce the ethics and disciplines of modern civic relations" by requiring the publication and audit of accounts of temples.[82] In Amritsar the Shiromani Gurdwara Parbandhak Committee (SGPC) controlled the Golden Temple and sought to end the "despotism" of *mahants* over historic places which were regarded as sacred by all Sikhs and to treat them as the common property of all Sikhs.[83]

These were the associations that inspired Hidayat Husain's vision for the regulation of waqfs across India. In 1927 the UP legislative council appointed a Muslim judge of the Allahabad High Court, Iqbal Ahmad, as chairman of a special Muslim public and charitable waqf committee to "advise what steps should be taken to provide for the better governance, administration and supervision of Muslim public and charitable waqfs."[84] Hidayat Husain himself and Nawab Murtaza Husain, a member of the royal family of Awadh and a writer of renown, were also members of the committee.[85]

The 1927 committee visited Haider Baksh's Waqf in Kora Jahanabad. The visitors found the buildings and gardens of the waqf in a ruined and abandoned state. They saw a grove was mostly overgrown and untended except for small areas which had been recently cleared. They noted that the entrance to the imambargah was run through with cracks and was in imminent danger of caving in along with sections of the roof which appeared to have been unrepaired and leaking for many years. Chandeliers and other cloths and fine objects of value that they expected to see in this historic imambargah had been removed, the latticework covering the windows had mostly disappeared, a number of buildings were sinking through subsidence and had not been repaired, and there were trash heaps in places. The delegation had trouble finding an approach to the mosque because the ground was so covered in overgrowth. They found the markers of the dedication of the building as a mosque, its westward orientation and the pulpit for the prayer leader, but noted the neglect of the building, overgrowth, and the imminent danger of collapse.[86] The delegation tried to meet with the custodian Adya Singh, but he was not available and so they made their way to the house of a local, Maulvi Shah Waris Husain, who had invited them there for breakfast and presumably arranged their visit.

As the role of the Anjuman-i Islamia Lahore and the AISC through the early 1900s demonstrates Muslim associations widely and purposefully modeled a system of waqf management and oversight which had inspired the United Provinces Waqf Act of 1936, the principles of which were eventually widely adopted across late colonial India and in postcolonial India and Pakistan. Muslim associations had broad popular appeal and were actively "shaping a Muslim consciousness."[87] The work of these representative, educated, creative, upright, and consensus producing Muslims demonstrated that the secular state had produced a crisis of management of waqfs, and that the vacuum created by the state's rejection of devotional values could be filled.

Expert Muslims in Court

A JCPC verdict delivered the Kora Jahanabad waqf to Muslims in July 1947, after the passage of the UP Waqf Act and only a few weeks before the decolonization and partition of the subcontinent began. The proceedings and judgment recognized Muslim rights in this site through the authorization of the suit and the admission of testimony and evidence by expert Muslims.

In 1934, three Shi'a petitioners filed a suit to have "a suitable person" appointed as custodian of the Kora Jahanabad waqf under section 92 of the Civil Procedure Code of 1908. Saiyyid Mazhar Husain of the district center Fatehpur, with strong family connections in Kora Jahanabad and memories of visiting the imambargah and mosque as a child, was the lead plaintiff in the case. He testified that he had decided to fight the case of his own accord and had solicited financial contributions from people in the area. Yusuf Ali of the neighboring Mirzapur, a town without an imambargah of its own, was the second plaintiff. Kalbe Abbas, the honorary secretary of the awqaf section of the AISC was personally unconnected to the waqf, never having worshipped there, but represented Muslim community in the suit as he had received and acted on letters from concerned people demanding an inquiry into the waqf.[88]

The plaintiffs overcame the first major obstacle to litigation when the attorney general of the UP authorized the suit for an imambagh, a mosque, a grove, and the income from the lands rightly due "for the performance of prayers and other rituals of worship in the mosque."[89] A political and administrative establishment friendly to Muslim efforts to reclaim sites authorized the suit, the attorney general acting on the recommendation of the local government.[90]

The first two plaintiffs argued that their rights to worship in the mosque and attend *majlises* and other Muharram events at the imambargah had been violated. Mazhar Husain described the missing and damaged objects and assets of value which he personally knew to be associated with the waqf: revenue lands and fine glass objects at the imambargah.[91] Yusuf Ali, a forty-year-old zamindar of Mirzapur would go with "everyone" in his town to commemorate Muharram in Kora Jahanabad. Up until 1924, he had participated in *majlises* and processions, partook of the sugar coated cardamom seeds and sherbet distributed to the processionists and visited the imambargah lit up with candles placed in glass vessels and lanterns for four days of Muharram. He offered Eid prayers in the mosque, attended *majlises* commemorating the death of Haider Baksh and his wife, and received the food distributed from the imambargah's kitchens in Ramzan, Muharram, and on Haider Baksh's death anniversary.[92]

A plan of the site prepared by the AISC in 1927 accompanied the Muslim suit for the site. This plan gave Islamic characterization to different features of the site: a mosque, imambargah, *chabutra* (gazebo), imambagh, and tombs. Muslim production of and submission of this plan into evidence and its salience to the proceedings were important achievements. Petitioners in the Shahidganj suit and others had not been able to use Islamic characterization of buildings to establish claims to sites and dispute the land record. The evidence of witnesses and site plans together established that there was a mosque and imambargah on the site and proved "the long usage of the mosque for worship, and the imambargah and grove for Muharram ceremonies, in particular the burial of the *taziyas* after they have been carried in procession, and the later discontinuance or decline of these usages under the management of the Defendant."[93]

Both the identification of and Muslim religious rights in the imambargah, grove, and revenue villages were bitterly disputed by Lal Bahadur's grandson, Adya Saran Singh, who claimed proprietary rights over these lands and buildings. His case rested on the curious argument that Lal Bahadur had declared the land as waqf in 1861, a misrepresentation maintained by his son Iqbal Bahadur in 1875-6 to intentionally defraud creditors. He produced a plan of the site which characterized one of the structures as a temple and the others as residential and other everyday buildings.

In addition to the oral evidence of worshipping individuals at the waqf, jurists admitted the testimony of the member of the AISC testifying to general (Shi'a) Muslim expectations for the waqf, and Muslims with expertise that established the Islamic devotional purpose of the site. A model Muslim's testimony had elicited juristic acknowledgment of religious rights in the Tajpur suit in the 1880s. Now, at the end of empire, a colonial jurist stated it was not anywhere established that an officer of an association did *not* have the right to sue and made reference to other recent precedents for his inclusion in the suit,[94] The Shahidganj petitioners had not been able to file a suit in defense of the eighteenth-century Mughal building on the site which looked like a mosque but the judgments in the Kora Jahanabad suit read the evidence "all one way," as indicating that two villages were made waqf for the "upkeep of the mosque, grove and imambargah at Jahanabad and for the performance of suitable ceremonies in the imambargah and particularly *taziyadari* at Muharram."

"It is proved," stated the Lords of the Judicial Committee of the Privy Council, that the eighteenth-century Muslim courtier Haider Baksh built and provided for the upkeep of a public mosque and imambargah.[95] Such juridical reasoning was made possible by assiduous and sustained efforts of Muslims to present Muslim beliefs relating to mosques and places of worship as testimony in court. Such "expert" testimony had served to establish breakaway, reformist beliefs in Tajpur in 1891. In Kora Jahanabad in 1947, it reestablished the Muslim public's interest in their places of worship.

Conclusion

The history of the Kora Jahanabad waqf had produced a curious intertwining of Muslim and Hindu interests. Like at Shahidganj, this intertwining was rooted in shared use of the site rather than shared cosmologies. The ambiguity which was created by mutual interests in the site was most significant for prompting Muslim action, both litigation and legislation, aimed at disentangling religious associations and interests at the site.

Muslim efforts to claim custodianship of the Kora Jahanabad waqf and the history of Hidayat Husain's efforts to create an apparatus for waqf regulation were interrelated but had progressed independently of one another. The Kora Jahanabad suit marked a culmination of Muslim legal activism for rights of worship in mosques. Hidayat Husain's legislation conceived an apparatus for systematically orienting Islamic built heritage in the service of modern community. Both relied on the work of the expert Muslims of the AISC and other associations to characterize religious worship and the use of religious sites. The expertise of these Muslims (like that of their Sikh and Hindu counterparts) related to their ability to intercede between the colonial executive and the Muslim public, courts and devotees, custodians and worshippers.

Muslim rights in the Kora Jahanabad mosque were affirmed at every stage of adjudication of the suit.[96] The suit established a common legal foundation for Shi'as and Sunnis to hold the custodians of their mosques accountable. The courts also recognized uniquely Shi'a worship which produced rights to the imambargah. The Shi'a legal effort interacted in important ways with political and reformist work being carried out by Shi'a anjumans and associations across India. Muslim associations, politicians, and bureaucrats supplied people, ideas, and financial resources for legal activists, much as the Ahl-i Hadith networks had done in the Tajpur case.[97]

The story of the Kora Jahanabad suit supplies this final chapter in this history of Muslim legal activism for rethinking the status of endowments under law and in the public domain. In Tajpur, Rangoon, Aurangabad, Lahore, and finally Kora Jahanabad colonial jurisprudence rejected values originating in devotionalism but authorized new forms of authority and control of religious expression. Over this period Muslim associations discovered opportunities to intervene in the law to claim rights in waqfs and produced a new officer of the mosque. In this final suit such representative and expert Muslims were invited to record and evaluate the religious uses of sites and communicate them to the courts. In turn the courts sanctioned their systematic involvement as representatives of Muslim worshippers in legal disputes.

AFTERWORD

Many of the stories in this book will have felt unfamiliar to you at first. Pragmatic Sikh-Muslim and Hindu-Muslim cohabitation at the Lahore and Kora Jahanabad mosque sites in the late 1700s and early 1800s, Omed Ali's insistence that he should lodge his guests at the Tajpur mosque in the 1880s, and Ahmed Moolla Dawood's modernist ambitions for the mosque school of Rangoon in 1910 fit uncomfortably with our understandings of doctrinally ordained worship. Many of the stories were familiar, stories you already knew, such as the story of Shahidganj, or found unsurprising, like the sectarianism in Aurangabad. Together these stories support a new approach to Muslim social and cultural history in South Asia; this is not a narrative of reform or revival but a history of dissimilar Muslims brought together in a search for legal solutions to a civic challenge: creating rules for congregational worship in the colonial state.

The disputes in and around mosques from 1880 to 1947 expressed the textures and variety of devotional life from Rangoon in the east to Lahore in the west. The interests of worshippers coalesced even in these varied conditions and circumstances around common concerns. Ritual in prayer halls, instruction in mosque schools, intersections of mosque with street, and the longevity and the financial regulation of mosques were debated extensively across the region through the colonial period. These features of mosques corresponded to different bodies of law and policy. Despite its single, unitary, and ubiquitous form, the mosque fractured in its service to Muslims under colonial law, each facet of its use inviting the involvement of different authorities. The history of the legal authorization of a variety of officers to manage the social uses of mosques establishes that law relating to mosques disciplined the diverse Muslim practices of worship and made them more uniform in their mutual subordination to new forms of authority.

Muslims actively engaged with the law, Islamic discourse, and community to produce new ideas and associations to intervene in mosque management. Invested with new and surprising powers in and around mosques from the late nineteenth to the middle of the twentieth century, officials disciplined Muslim worshippers. But Muslims also organized to influence the appointment of prayer leaders, custodians, magistrates, and waqf regulators.

As we track Muslim efforts to assert rights in mosques and assess the legal and political precedents which limited social rights in mosques, we can address pressing questions which have emerged from work on Islam in South Asia. The first and most pressing question is whether the mosque was a public space of the sort that engendered egalitarian and unencumbered social participation. Colonial law treated endowment as a private act of religious or charitable benefit. In Tajpur and Rangoon, colonial jurists authorized prayer leaders and mosque custodians to make ritualistic and instructional choices for the congregation and subjected dialog and debate in the mosque to the oversight and control of these officers.

Government officers regulated the street at the perimeter of the mosque and authorized religious land rights in the mosques in the United Provinces and Lahore. These government officials acted in a clearly defined public interest while maintaining their own secular outlook by refusing to incorporate devotional values in their reasoning. Muslims sought to influence these officers and the law to admit their devotional values and rights, they expressed expectations that values related to the mosque would be incorporated into the framework of law governing the public. Colonial secularism rather than the differences between Shi'as, Sunnis, and Hindus disallowed the legal acknowledgment of the sanctity of religious buildings. Government officers treated public devotionalism as special matters, to be cautiously sanctioned to placate religious communities, not as rights. The characterization of the street as public and fundamentally secular casts the mosque as a private space governed by values which were not shared by the colonial public.

Sandria Freitag and Francis Robinson, among others, have made it possible to conceptualize a Muslim public that engaged in debate and dialog in print and collected on the street. Any mosque could admit any member of this general Muslim body and after 1936 provincial waqf boards and waqf committees held custodians to account to the Muslim public for any misappropriation of funds and land. But debate in the mosque was, in principle, constrained by the instructive priorities of its managers. South Asian mosques were not public spaces during the colonial period or afterwards. They were, and remain, spaces of influence and social control.

It is significant that the 'ulama were not directly involved in negotiating these matters of everyday practice. Ahmad Raza Bareilvi's influence manifested in printed inspirational discourses providing philosophical and doctrinal matter to ground legal argument. Classical religious scholarship provided definitions of mosques, congregations, and sectarian grouping which guided colonial jurists: that mosques should have independent entrances from the street, that Muslims had unfettered rights to congregate in mosques for worship, and that Shi'as and Sunnis should pray separately. Abdul Hai Kaflaytvi produced a program of instruction in the Friday Mosque in Rangoon, and Mufti Muhammad Shafi wrote a treatise on land which he presented at an 'ulama conference. The 'ulama were not litigants in any suits. They had no part in the regulation of mosques at any time from the precolonial to the postcolonial period. They did not appear in the mosque except as worshippers or guest speakers at Friday prayer. They were not among the many officers charged by the courts with settling the affairs of the mosque. Their absence from this foundational platform of religious participation and practice should serve to qualify our understanding of their influence and measure their involvement in everyday worship comparatively against prayer leaders, magistrates, mosque custodians, and officers of associations.

Muslim legal, political, and social activism for rights in mosques produced new Muslim officers. One was the prayer leader who was boosted into significance by the Tajpur decision of 1891 which gave him the authority to establish ritual priorities for a mosque. I do not offer conjecture about the nature of influence of this new officer of the mosque and much more work can be done on this shadowy but omnipresent historical actor. The other I have casually described in Chapter 5 as an expert Muslim, for want of a better term. It would be a mistake to underestimate the influence of this officer who is already well known to us through a massive body of historical writing on Muslim anjumans, societies, and associations, and work on Hindu, Sikh, and other religious associations.[1]

A vast and important body of work establishes the ethnic and class-based associations, political strategies, and the communalist and religious discourses which inspired Muslim organization and produced these representatives and leaders of colonial South Asia. I have argued in Chapter 5 that as Muslims worked to elicit the colonial state's confirmation of collective rights in mosques, the Muslim public, government officials, and colonial jurists increasingly relied on the work of these officers of associations. Their expertise commanded the respect of government, society, and finally the colonial courts in matters of religion to effect profound changes in governance. There were 'ulama among them but it was not expertise in matters of Islamic law which conferred authority on them. They worked contextually and collectively to intercede between government, courts, and Muslim society through the colonial period.

This legal and social history of Muslim worship describes successive instances of Muslim negotiations of their rights in mosques under colonial law and concludes with an indication of how much remains to be learned about the consequences of these events. After the decision in favor of the prayer leader in Tajpur in 1891, Deobandis, Ahl-i Hadith, Bareilvis, and countless other groups claimed mosques by installing prayer leaders in them. Mosque schools continued to provide foundational instruction across the region through the colonial and postcolonial period.[2] Powerful action was taken by Hindus claiming the site of the Babri mosque in India since 1992.[3] The Pakistan government cordoned the Red Mosque and attached madrassa in 2007 when teachers and students opposed regulations for registering and regulating the institution.[4] The prayer leaders, custodians, government officials, and regulatory authorities in each of these cases operated with legal sanction for their discretionary and overriding authority in mosque affairs. Such events deserve renewed attention taking into account the underlying hierarchies of rights in mosques.

Government regulation of the financial affairs of mosques was extended to the whole of India by the Waqf Act of 1954 and to the NWFP, Punjab, and the rest of West Pakistan between 1949 and 1960, and provincial regulatory bodies worked to develop varying degrees of control over the lands, incomes, and hiring relating to mosques.[5] Naveeda Khan's work provides important insights about the ways in which Pakistani Muslim aspirations were expressed in their expectations and demands relating to mosques,[6] and Hilal Ahmed has studied the importance of mosques in postcolonial Muslim discourse in India. Sufia Uddin indicates some ways that mosque-centered activity and discussion have featured in a historical imaginary and in pious and globalizing efforts in Bangladesh.[7] But we know far too little about regional regulations, patterns of administration, and emergence of consensus about and for mosques in postcolonial states.

Together the stories in this book establish a pattern of adjudication of mosque affairs by paternalistic officers who used their discretion to control congregational worshippers. Unable to infer or produce religious law, the colonial courts would repeatedly authorize such authority in the mosque. And as a result South Asian Muslim congregational worship became fragmented and enclaved as robust debate about the shape it should take continued unabated.

Glossary

Allah-hu Akbar God is great
Amin Amen
Aqamat Convening a congregation
Arti, ghants, dholak, baja Aural elements of a Hindu procession
Ashura The tenth day of Muharram on which the martyrdom of Husain is commemorated by Shi'as
Azan Call to prayer
Badshahi masjid Imperial Friday mosque
Bani Benefactor
Bhajan Hindu ceremonial recitations
Bhang Intoxicating drink
Bid'at Religious innovation (heresy)
Bigha 1,600 square yards / approximately 0.35 acres of land in late Mughal Bengal
Chabutra Gazebo
Chowk Intersection
Dalan Outdoor washing area
Darbar Imperial court (also used to refer to a Sufi shrine)
Darul ifta Office staffed by 'ulama providing religious counsel on request
Dawat-i tabligh Inviting people to join the preaching mission
Deeni Concerning religion
Dharamsala A Sikh place of congregational worship
Dunyavi Worldly
Eid (Bakr Eid) Biannual Islamic festivals; the Bakr Eid is celebrated with a ritual sacrifice of a cow or goat as well as special prayers
Eidgah Pavilion for the biannual eid congregation
Fasad Turmoil
Fatwa Order based in religious reasoning
Fiqh Islamic legal tradition
Granth Sahib The Sikh holy book
Gurdwara Abode of the Sikh holy book the Guru Granth Sahib
Hadith/Ahl-i Hadith Verified reports of the sayings and doings of the Prophet Muhammad/Participants in an Islamic movement for modeling everyday practices on the hadith

Hamam Bathhouse
Haveli Mansion
Ilm-i din Study of religion
Imam A term from the hanafi tradition for a prayer leader authorized by the emperor to lead the Friday prayer and give the sermon
Imambargah A building dedicated for collective Shi'a ritual commemoration of the tragedy of Karbala
Jagirdari Grant based land rights
Jahil Wild/uncultured
Jama' masjid Friday mosque
Jama'at Congregation
Karbala The name for a site in which part of the Muharram ritual is carried out
Khadim Servant of the mosque
Khanqah Sufi lodge
Khatib A prayer leader who gives the Friday sermon
Khuda ki zameen God's land
Lakh Hundred thousand
Lakhiraj Land on which the state waives its right to collect taxes because its incomes are committed for religious, cultural, or charitable uses
Madad-i mash Mughal era perpetual hereditary grant
Madrassa School
Mahant – Sikh priest
Majlis Shi'a gatherings for hearing religious recitations and sermons
Maktab Mosque school or Quran school
Marsiya A poetic elegiac recitation
Masjid Mosque
Matam Ceremonial self-flagellation in the Muharram procession
Maulvi Man with some Islamic scholarly credentials
Mawlud/milad Celebration of the birth anniversary of the Prophet Muhammad
Milk-i khudawandi God's land
Milkiyat Territorial claims
Mu'afi Tax free land grant
Muezzin A prayer leader who gives the call to prayer
Muhalla Neighborhood
Muharram A month of the Islamic calendar; the anniversary of the siege of Karbala
Mulki zaban National languages/vernaculars
Mulla Religious teacher or preacher; term can have pejorative implications
Munsiff Subordinate judge of a district court
Musafirkhana Innovation/heresy
Mutawalli Custodian
Naim ul badal Something received in an exchange
Namaz/namazi Prayer/someone offering prayer
Nazūl Government lands; the colonial government of the India inherited the term of reference from the Mughal state

Patwaris District level land registrar
Peshnamaz Prayer leader
Qasaban Butchers
Qasbah Mughal-era town which retained Muslim characteristics in the colonial period
Qaum Nation or community
Qazi: A law officer of the Mughal state; his role was gradually reduced by the colonial state and then abolished altogether
Rafadain Vocalization of God's name during prayer
Sanad Mughal deed of grant of land or title
Serai Resthouse/inn
Shaitani Wrongdoing
Sharafat Respectability
Shirk Renunciation of the faith
Sirah Biography
Sukkha/bhang Cannabis based intoxicant
Tafsir Quranic exegesis
Tahsildar, Naib tesildar, Kanungo Subordinate officers of the revenue department
Takbir The call "Allahu Akbar"
Taqlid Following established authority in matters of religion
Tasarraf Occupancy
Taziyas and alams; taziyadari Ornate models of the tombs of Hasan and Husain and banners; carrying taziyas in Muharram processions
Tijarat Trade
Waqf Bequest structured on Islamic norms
Waqfnamah Deed of waqf
Zuljenah A ceremonial horse led in the Muharram procession

NOTES

Introduction

1. H. Thirkell White, Esq., CIE., Commissioner of the Pegu Division, to Chief Secretary to the Chief Commissioner of Burma, July 25, 1893 in *Riots between Mohammedans and Hindus at Rangoon* IOR/L/PJ/6/354/1532.
2. Telegram from Viceroy to India Office explaining that a riot occurred in Rangoon, Simla, June 27, 1893, in Report of a riot in Rangoon in connection with the Bakra Id festival IOR/L/PJ/6/351/1252.
3. "Wednesday Report," in *Rangoon Gazette Weekly Budget*, June 30, 1893, LOC/sn89049418.
4. Muhammad Qasim Zaman, *The 'ulama in Contemporary Islam: Custodians of Change* (Princeton: Princeton University Press, 2010); Muhammad Qasim Zaman, "Nation Nationalism and the 'ulama: Hadith in Religio-Political Debates in Twentieth Century India," *Oriente Moderno*, 21, no. 82 (2002): 93–113; Muhammad Qasim Zaman, *Modern Islamic Thought in a Radical Age: Religious Authority and Internal Criticism* (New York: Cambridge University Press, 2012).
5. Gregory Kozlowski, *Muslim Endowments and Society in British India* (Cambridge: Cambridge University Press, 1985).
6. Michael Anderson, "Islamic Law and the Colonial Encounter in British India," in *Institutions and Ideologies: A SOAS South Asia Reader*, ed. David Arnold and Peter Robb (New York: Routledge, 1993), 165–85. On work on Anglo-Muhammadan Law as a domestication of the Islamic Shari'a tradition, see Faisal Chaudhry, "Rethinking the Nineteenth-Century Domestication of the Shari'a: Marriage and Family in the Imaginary of Classical Legal Thought and the Genealogy of (Muslim) Personal Law in Late Colonial India," *Law and History Review*, 35, no. 4 (2017): 841–79.
7. See Sana Haroon, "Contextualizing the Deobandi Approach to Congregation and Management of Mosques in Colonial North India," *Journal of Islamic Studies*, 28, no. 1 (2017): 68–93.
8. Julia Stephens, *Governing Islam: Law, Empire and Secularism in India* (Cambridge: Cambridge University Press, 2018).
9. This purpose being individual engagement with state systems and apparatus. See Humeira Iqtidar, *Secularizing Islamists: Jama'at-e-Islami and Jama'at-ud-Da'awa in Urban Pakistan* (Chicago: University of Chicago Press, 2011).
10. Cassie Adcock, *The Limits of Secularism* (New York: Oxford University Press, 2013).

11 Nandini Chatterjee, *The Making of Indian Secularism: Empire, Law and Christianity* (London: Palgrave Macmillan, 2011), 51.
12 Teena Purohit, *The Aga Khan Case* (Cambridge: Harvard University Press, 2012), 25.
13 Ali Asani's work on modern Ismailis disallows any simple reading of Khoja Ismaili identity; he has demonstrated that Khoja's engaged Vaishnav, Sufi, and Bhakti literary traditions to communicate the idea of the imam. Ali Asani, "From Satpanthi to Ismaili Muslim: The Articulation of Ismaili Khoja Identity in South Asia," in *A Modern History of the Ismailis*, ed. Farhad Daftary (London: I. B. Tauris, 2011), 95-117.
14 Mithra Sharafi, *Law and Identity in Colonial South Asia: Parsi Legal Culture 1772-1947* (New York: Cambridge University Press, 2014), 6.
15 Nile Green, *Terrains of Exchange: Religious Economies of Global Islam* (New York: Oxford University Press, 2015), 207-19, 250-66.
16 Kozlowski, *Muslim Endowments*, 4.
17 Ibid., 41.
18 Haynes argues that the public culture of Surat emerged in the colonial period and was shaped in a dynamic engagement of the city's notables with British officialdom, through philanthropy, participation in municipal affairs and performance of civic-imperial rituals. Douglas Haynes, *Rhetoric and Ritual in Colonial India: The Shaping of a Public Culture in Surat City* (Berkeley: UC Press, 1991), 272.
19 J. Barton Scott and Brannon Ingram, "What Is a Public? Notes from South Asia," *Journal of South Asian Studies*, 38, no. 3 (2015): 357-70.
20 Sandria Freitag, "Ambiguous Public Arenas and Coherent Personal Practice: Kanpur Muslims 1913-1931," in *Shari'at and Ambiguity in South Asian Islam*, ed. Katherine Ewing (Berkeley: U. C. Press, 1990).
21 Sandria B. Freitag, "Exploring Aspects of the Public," *South Asia: Journal of South Asian Studies*, 38, no. 3 (2015): 512-23.
22 Dale Eickelman and Armando Salvatore, "The Public Sphere and Muslim Identities," *European Journal of Sociology*, 43, no. 1 (2002): 92-115.
23 Stephens, *Governing Islam*, 125.
24 Sandria Freitag, *Collective Action and Community: Public Arenas and the Emergence of Communalism in North India* (Berkeley: University of California Press, 1989), 224-5.
25 Francis Robinson, *Separatism Among Indian Muslims* (Cambridge: Cambridge University Press, 2004), 211-12.
26 Gregory Kozlowski, "Community Building and Communal Control of Muslim Endowments (waqfs) in Modern South Asia," *Revue Du Monde Musalman et de la Méditerranée*, no. 79-80 (1996): 201-14.
27 Hilal Ahmed, *Muslim Political Discourse in Colonial India: Monuments, Memory, Contestation* (New York: Routledge, 2015).
28 S. Jamal Malik, "Waqf in Pakistan," *Die Welt des Islams*, New Series, Bd. 30,1/4 (1990): 63-97.

29 A useful definition is supplied by the Indiana University Islamic Studies Program workshops on Authority in Islam: "the recognized capacity of an individual or an institution to sanction the undertaking of religious acts, both private and public." https://islamic.indiana.edu/research/localization/index.html, accessed May 21, 2020.

30 Kozlowski reads the frequent assignment of income from family endowments to the maintenance of religious buildings as "proclamation[s] of preeminence." Kozlowksi, *Muslim Endowments and Society*, 51. Sayyid Ahmad Khan (1817–98) had suggested Muslims use the laws permitting charitable endowments to protect family estates from subjection of Islamic Law under British Courts. Highlighted particularly in David Powers, "Orientalism, Colonialism and Legal History: The Attack on Family Endowments in Algeria and India," *Comparative Studies in Society and History*, 31, no. 3 (1989): 557.

31 Gregory Kozlowksi, "Imperial Authority, Benefactions and Endowments in India," *Journal of the Economic and Social History of the Orient*, 38, no. 3 (1995): 355–70.

32 1 bigha=1600 square yards=0.35 acres in late Mughal Bengal.

33 Shahabad Collectorate, Firman 13 Rajab 1058 AH [July 24, 1648] Basta no. 41 in Kalikinkar Datta, *Some Firmans, Sanads, Parwanas (1578-1802)* (Patna: State Central Records Office, 1962), 1.

34 Ten bighas of cultivable land granted in Hukumnama dated 1 Shawal 1011 Fasli/May 19, 1596 and Parwana dated 19 Shawal [May 15, 1598], Basta no. 815. Datta, *Some Firmans, Sanads, Parwanas*, 126–7.

35 *Kulb Ali Hoosein v. Syf Ali*, in *Cases Determined in the Court of the Sudder Dewany Adawlut*, ed. W. H. McNaughten, vol. 2 (Calcutta: Bishop's College Press, 1827), 110.

36 In Rajshahi district in Bengal, custodians of an endowment authorized repairs and renovations to the mosque, imambargah and tomb of the saint Muhammad Shah Rooposh that cost 700 rupees in the 1840s. The sizeable nature of this sum is apparent in comparison to the rents collected on the entire endowment that totaled Rs 237 in that same year. *Mahomed Buksh v. Sujat Ali*, in *Zillah Decisions, Lower Provinces (Bengal) 1849 Patna, Purneah, Rajshahye, Rungpore, Tirhoot, Twenty-four Pergnnahs* (Bengal: Zillah Courts, 1849).

37 At the very end of the eighteenth century, Muhammad Takee of Rangpur Bengal endowed a mosque with 5 villages with a total annual income of 8,501 rupees and named his wife Hyatee Khanum as custodian of the waqf trust in a will, thereby disinheriting his son and creating a secure lifetime stream of income for his wife. *Musammat Hyatee Khanum v. Mussummat Koolsoom Khanum* in *Cases Determined in the Court of the Sudder Dewany Adawlut 1799-1811*, vol. 1 (Calcutta: W. H. McNaughten, 1812), 214.

38 Deposition of Elahi Buksh, November 19, 1894, Part 8 Remand of the File of the First Court, 103–4. *In the Privy Council, on Appeal from Bengal, Fuzal Karim and another v. Haji Mowla Buksh (alias Kinya) and others, Fort William Bengal*, 1891, decided February 21, 1891. Privy Council Cases with Judgments, BL PP 1316, [Hereafter *Fuzal Karim v. Mowla Buksh* JCPC case papers].

39 Ibid., 103.
40 Written Statement of Omed Ali and Others, August 11, 1882, Part 1 Pleadings and Proceedings in the Court of the First Munsiff of Muzaffarpur, in *Fuzal Karim v. Mowla Buksh*, JCPC case papers, 5.
41 Sarkhatnama [letter of appointment] Granted to Hafiz Sheik Mowla Buksh, Safar 1 1279/July 29, 1862, Remand File of the First Court Part A, Exhibits, in *Fuzal Karim v. Mowla Buksh* JCPC case papers, 84. The full text reads:

> I, Syed Ramizuddin Ahmed, qazi of the pergunnas Saresa and Balaguch, and custodian of the mosque, have appointed you on a pay of Rs 2-1 a month, as per detail below . . . it will be your duty to be present in the said mosque at the five (prayer) times every day, call to prayers at the five times, say and lead prayers, sweep the mosque and do the service of the said mosque, render proper service to and the taking care of travelers visiting the mosque. [S]hould you remain absent from the mosque . . . refuse to carry out my just orders, I shall have the power to dismiss the muezzin in the presence of, and according to the enquiries made by the servants of the mosque. The expenses on account of travelers who may come to alight at the mosque, at 6 pie per head, with the charges for large and small water-pots, lamps, wicks, oil, will be borne by me, they have nothing to do with the muezzin or his pay.

42 Deposition of Elahi Buksh, 103.
43 One of the plaintiffs in Tajpur complained:

> There is a reservoir in my mosque. It contains about 6 garhas of water. The water of this reservoir is used for ablutions. The plaintiff Mowla Baksh performs ablutions with this water. On several occasions this water became polluted. On one or three occasions rats fell into it. On one occasion a frog fell into it. The mouse and musk-rat fell in it and died there . . . a pup fell into that well. On three occasions I saw Mowla Baksh performed ablutions with and drank the water of the well.

> The matter of the polluted water came up in two other depositions as well. Stephens identifies discussions about the purity of water for ritual ablutions in mosques as a rhetorical device used by Hanafi ʻulama when framing critiques of Ahl-i Hadith ritual preferences.

See Deposition of Hossein Ali November 24 and 26, 1884, Part 8 Remand File of the First Court, in *Fuzal Karim v. Mowla Buksh* JCPC case papers, 110–12. On Hanafi critiques on the Ahl-i Hadith see Stephens, *Governing Islam*, 122.

44 Anderson, "Islamic Law and the Colonial Encounter," 173.
45 Radhika Singha, *A Despotism of Law: Crime and Justice in Early Colonial India* (Oxford: Oxford University Press, 1998), 7–8.
46 Haroon, "Congregation and Management of Mosques," 6–9.
47 Maulvi Muhammad Ibrahim Raza Khan Sahib, *Al-Tahrir al-Jayyad fi Haq al-Masajid* (Bengal: Matbuʻa Ahl-i Sunnat wʻal Jamaat Bareily Waqai Astanah Aliya Rizviyya, 1315/1897). Maulvi Abbas Ali was resident in Hatyam, Noakhali.

48 William Glover, *Making Lahore Modern: Constructing and Imagining a Colonial City* (Minneapolis: University of Minnesota Press, 2008), 13.
49 On the desecration of the tomb of Mir Mannu, Mughal governor of Lahore, see Jadunath Sarkar, *Fall of the Mughal Empire* (Calcutta: M. C. Sarkar, 1932), 248. On the *muhallas* outside the walled city see Rai Bahadur Kannhyalal, *Tarikh-i Lahore* (Lahore: Katoriya Press, c. 1886), 89–95.
50 Syed Gardezi, *Badshahi Masjid* (Lahore: Insaf Press, 1962), 15. Ahmed Nabi Khan, *Development of Mosque Architecture in Pakistan* (Islamabad: Lok Virsa, 1991), 129. See also "Copy of a Firman of Maharajah Ranjeet Singh dated 18 Bhadon, 1880 Bikrami," in Gardezi, *Badshahi Masjid*, 29.
51 Gardezi, *Badshahi Masjid*, 148–52.
52 Kannhyalal, *Tarikh-i Lahore*, 182.
53 Ibid., 177–8.
54 Ibid., 186.
55 Ibid., 184.
56 Herbert Benjamin Edwardes, *A Year on the Punjab Frontier: 1848-49*, vol. 2 (London: Richard Bentley, 1851) 254.
57 Muhammad Ayub Qadri, "Introduction," in *Ahd-i Bangash ki Siyafi Ilmi aur Siqafati Tarikh*, tr. Ayub Qadri (Karachi: Academy of Educational Research, 1965), 11.
58 Sayyid Altaf Barelvi, *Life of Hafiz Rahmat Khan*, tr. Muhammad Hamiduddin Khan (Karachi: Academy of Educational Research, 1966), 325.
59 Barelvi, *Hayat-i Hafiz*, 325–30.
60 William Irvine, "A History of the Bangash Nawabs of Farrukhabad, 1713-1857," *Journal of the Royal Asiatic Society*, 18, no. 1 (1879): 148–50 and 72. The original estates in 1738 included 116 villages including Kanauj, and the Nawabs added Khairabad to this before 1750.
61 Ibid., 155.
62 Veena Oldenburg, *The Making of Colonial Lucknow: 1856-1877* (Princeton: Princeton University Press, 1984), 11–13.
63 The following discussion is based on Hussein Keshani, "Architecture and the Twelver Shi'i Tradition: The Great Imambara Complex of Lucknow," *Muqarnas*, 23 (2006): 219–50.
64 Kozlowski, *Muslim Endowments and Society*, 38–9.
65 Political letter from Bengal October 18, 1809 in The Magnificent Well Belonging to the Jama Masjid at Delhi IOR/F/4/312/7126.
66 The main beneficiary in the case of Pilibhit was a man called Incharam who bought most of the wall, a gate on the bridge, and three shops. Thirty-eight shops were sold together to a Mahomed Ally Khan, but he could not fulfill the terms of payment and these were resold. Statement of nazool property H. Batson Acting Collector, 1811 in Sale of Certain Government Property IOR/F/4/701/19025.
67 Political Letter from Bengal October 18, 1809 IOR/F/4/312/7126.
68 Approximately 208 Pounds Sterling based on the exchange value of 0.1-0.092 Pounds Sterling to a *sicca* or *sonat* rupee. I work from Matthew

Edney's useful note on East India Company Coinage. Matthew Edney, *Mapping an Empire* (Chicago and London: University of Chicago Press, 1997), xvii.

69 It was noted that repairs to the attached shops were not sanctioned and remained the responsibility of the king. Further Papers Regarding the King of Delhi IOR/F/4/1476/58000.

70 Extract Judicial Letter from Bengal November 3, 1820. IOR F/4/701/19025.

71 Persian Secretary to Agent to the Governor General at Bareilly, December 27, 1826. Expenditure of 2500 Sonaut Rupees on Repairing the *Idgah* of Khaja Amuddin at Bareilly IOR E/4/745.

72 Approximately 240 Pounds Sterling.

73 Sylvia Shorto, "A Tomb of One's Own," in *Colonial Modernities: Building. Dwelling and Architecture in British India,* ed. Peter Scriver and Vrikramaditya Prakash (New York: Routledge, 2007), 166.

74 Faridah Zaman, "Colonizing the Sacred: Allahabad and the Company State, 1797-1857," *Journal of Asian Studies,* 74, no. 2 (2015): 351.

75 Rs 10,000 in payments by Saunders and approximately Rs 70,000 in payments under the authority of the commissioners of Delhi and Panipat. Statement of Sums Paid for the Support of Mahomedan and Hindoo place of Worship in the Districts of the Delhi division in B. Saunders Commissioner Delhi to R. Temple Chief Commissioner Punjab June 9, 1858. Punjab Archives, General Department File 2584, Nos. 6–7 and B. Saunders Commissioner Delhi to the R. Temple Chief Commissioner Punjab July 14, 1858, Punjab Archives, General Department, File 2668 Nos 123–4.

76 Abstract translation of a letter from Bunnoo Begum to the address of the late Resident at Delhi, received on September 21, 1831, and extract from a Bengal Political Letter February 12, 1834, Bengal Government reject the request of Bannu Begam IOR/F/4/1509/59294.

77 G. E. Fryer, *Handbook of British Burma* (Maulmain: T. Whitman, 1867), 340.

78 Grants given free for Religious purposes in the Town of Rangoon, prepared by Shoay Hline, Appendix II, Record No. 79, p. xviii. *In the Privy Council, On Appeal from the Chief Court of Lower Burma between Mahomed Ismail Ariff and Ors, and Hajee Ahmed Moolla Dawood and Ors,* JCPC Appeal Nos. 79 and 80 of 1914, decided May 15, 1916 BL P.P.1316 1916 [hereafter *Ismail Ariff v. Ahmed Moolla Dawood* JCPC case papers].

79 An 1870 enquiry into land granted to religious communities that led to the revocation of the 1862 land grant to the Sunni Surati Mosque made reference to "land granted to the Parsi community for a church." Deputy Commissioner of Rangoon to Commissioner of Pegu, August 6, 1870, appendix to Judgment in the Chief Court of Lower Burma, May 29, 1912, Record No. 79, 153–4, *Ismail Ariff v. Ahmed Moolla Dawood* JCPC case papers.

80 Geo Hugh, Assistant Commissioner for the Chief Commissioner of Rangoon, May 26, 1862, Grant of C1 Square First Class Lot No. 12, in exhibits tendered by defendants 8 to 11, Record No. 79, 84–5. *Ismail Ariff v. Ahmed Moolla Dawood* JCPC case papers.
81 Sandria Freitag proposes that we can study the public as an arena, a space of collective performance, adapting Jurgen Habermas's theory of a unified and unifying public sphere to a colonial South Asian context. This framework has salience in precolonial colonial South Asia also; the term is particularly useful here, highlighting the local and potentially bounded context of use and governance of mosques. Sandria Freitag, "State and Community: Popular Protest," *Culture and Power in Banaras: Community, Performance and Environment* (Berkeley: University of California Press, 1992).
82 Richard Eaton, *The Rise of Islam and the Bengal Frontier 1204-1760* (Berkeley: UC Press, 1996), 239.
83 This term is a permutation of the Persian compound *la ikhraj*, meaning untaxed.
84 *Final Report on the Survey and Settlement operations in Darbhanga 1896-1903* (Calcutta: Bengal Secretariat Press, 1904), 22–4. Malavika Kasturi also takes note of Francis Buchanan-Hamilton's 1811–12 survey of Bihar and Patna in which he found that an "extraordinary proportion of revenue-free land was gifted to temples and ascetic orders." Malavika Kasturi, "'Asceticising' Monastic Families: Ascetic Genealogies, Property Feuds and Anglo-Hindu Law in Late Colonial India," *Modern Asian Studies*, 43, no. 5 (2009): 1050.
85 On the interaction of Indian traditions of endowment and European ideas about philanthropy and the resulting transformation of the culture of gift giving in nineteenth-century India, see Douglas Haynes, "From Tribute to Philanthropy: The Politics of Gift Giving in a Western Indian City," *The Journal of Asian Studies*, 46, no. 2 (1987): 339–60.
86 Abu Muhammad Waheeduzzaman, "Land Resumption in Bengal, 1819-1846," PhD dissertation, University of London SOAS, 1969, quoted in Eaton, *The Rise of Islam*, 239–40.
87 *Survey and Settlement Operations in Darbhanga*, 23.
88 William Theobold, *Acts of the Governor General in Council from 1834 to the end of 1867* (Calcutta: Thacker, Spink and Co., 1868), 293–301. Hathi Trust Digital Library http://hdl.handle.net/2027/uc2.ark:/13960/t5bc3wg8 3. Scott Kugle argues that Anglo-Muhammadan law was the embodiment of the "cumulative experience of the British rulers in India, as they both appropriated and rejected the Mughal polity which they conquered." Scott Kugle, "Framed, Blamed, Renamed: The recasting of Islamic Jurisprudence in Colonial South Asia," *Modern Asian Studies*, 35, no. 2 (2001): 257.
89 Nile Green locates the origins of this impulse in the mercantilist attitudes of the nineteenth-century colonial state and offers an immersive look at Bombay Muslim institutions and society in the period following these reforms. Nile Green, *Bombay Islam: The Religious Economy of the Western*

Indian Ocean 1840-1915 (Cambridge: Cambridge University Press, 2011), 11–12. Nandini Chatterjee's work locates this imperative in the ontology of colonial secularism. Chatterjee, "Regulating Trust: Law and Policy of Religious Endowments in India," *The Makings of Indian Secularism*, 51–74.

90 Kozlowski, *Muslim Endowments*, 38–40.
91 Muhammad Qasim Zaman describes the jurisdiction of the court of the qazi in the Mughal state and the 'ulama's adaptation to the colonial abolishment of these courts to provide mediation and decision making for Muslim society in religious matters. Zaman's discussion has important resonances with the intent of this book which is to examine the adaptations of mosque administration in the wake of these legal and procedural changes. Zaman, *The 'Ulama in Contemporary Islam*, 18–30.
92 Act XII of 1880 The Kazis Act, *The Legislative Acts of 1880 of the Governor General in Council* (Calcutta: Thacker Spink and Co., 1881), 76–8.
93 Chatterjee, *The Making of Indian Secularism*, 51. Chatterjee's important study sets out the involvement of Christians in advocating for and shaping the "policies, practices, and above all, a political culture" that constituted Indian secularism.
94 Deposition of Mahboob Ali November 8, 1884, Remand File of the First Court, 91–2. *Fuzal Karim v. Mowla Buksh* JCPC case papers.
95 Commissioner Delhi Letter no. 21 of January 5, 1859, "The C. C. apprehends that if a careful review of grants was carried out many of the recipients will be found to have misbehaved." Punjab Archives, General Department File 2939 No. 36.
96 Kozlowksi, "Imperial Authority, Benefactions and Endowments," 359.
97 H. S. Hartnoll Judgment on Appeals 59 and 60 of 1908, May 29, 1912 in Record No. 79, 158–61. *Ismail Ariff v. Ahmed Moolla Dawood* JCPC case papers.
98 Judgment in the Deputy Commissioner's Court Rangoon, July 12, 1870, Civil First Appeal Nos 59 and 60 of 1910, in ibid., 152.
99 Act III for Local Self Government, List of Districts in which Act III is in force, Darbhanga notified in 1887, *The Bengal Code in Two Volumes*, vol. 2 (Calcutta: Superintendent Government Printing, 1890), 801, 1064.
100 Ritu Birla, *Stages of Capital: Law, Culture and Market Governance in Late Colonial India* (Durham: Duke University Press, 2009), 104.
101 Ibid., 4.
102 William Fischer Agnew, *The Law of Trusts in British India* (Calcutta: Thacker Spink and Co., 1882), 1–15.
103 Chatterjee, *The Making of Indian Secularism*, 54.
104 Eric Lewis Beverley, "Property, Authority, and Personal Law: Waqf in Colonial South Asia," *South Asia Research*, 31 (2011): 160, 168.
105 The Judicial Committee of the Privy Council ruled on the impermissibility of waqfs that were not "dedicated in substance to religious and charitable purposes" but instead to the maintenance of family. Private trusts were permitted in 1879, restricted by a judgment of the Privy Council in 1901,

and the Muslim Waqf Validating Act of 1913, reinstated the use of waqf to create private family trusts. See David S. Powers on Kozlowksi's discussion of Jinnah's important legislation tabled in 1911 and the JCPC judgment of 1900 Powers, "Orientalism, Colonialism and Legal History," 562, *Judgment of the Lords of the Privy Council on the Appeal of Musammat Mujib-un-Nisa and Others delivered December 8, 1900* in The Judicial Committee of the Privy Council Decisions, [1900] UKPC 65.
106 *Abdul Rahman v. Yar Muhammad* [1881] ILR 3 ALL 636.
107 *Muhammad Umar, v. Ram Chand* [1892] Punjab Record 27 301.
108 *Kazi Hassan v. Sagun Balkrishna* [1899] The Indian Decisions 12 171.
109 Examples of public purpose of a trust in English law were "repairing roads, supplying water for the inhabitants of a parish, repairing bridges over any stream or culvert" and charitable benefits were "giving alms, founding hospitals, providing for people with disabilities," Agnew, *The Law of Trusts*, 19–20.
110 Birla, *Stages of Capital*, 77–8.
111 On Ameer Ali, see Beverley, "Waqf in Colonial South Asia," 155–82. On Muhammad Ali Jinnah, see Kozlowski, *Muslim Endowments*, 177–91.

Chapter 1

1 John F. Richards, James R. Hagen and Edward S. Haynes, "Changing Land Use in Bihar, Punjab and Haryana, 1850-1970," *Modern Asian Studies*, 19, no. 3 (1984): 699–732.
2 Kumkum Chatterjee, *Merchants, Politics and Society in Early Modern Bihar* (Leiden: Brill, 1998), 212.
3 Stephen Henningham, "Bureaucracy and Control in India's Great Landed Estates: The Raj Darbhanga of Bihar, 1879 to 1850," *Modern Asian Studies*, 17, no. 1 (1983): 35–55.
4 The carpet weavers of Obra and Daudnagar feature prominently in Tirthankar Roy's account of innovation and conflict in the artisanal workshops of colonial India. Tirthankar Roy, "Out of Tradition: Master Artisans and Economic Change in Colonial India," *Journal of Asian Studies*, 66, no. 4 (2007): 963–91.
5 Imtiaz Ahmad, "The Mughal Governors of Bihar and Their Public Works," *Proceedings of the Indian History Congress*, 59 (1988): 383–92.
6 Stephens, *Governing Islam*, 105–31. Julia Stephens describes the dismantling of a legally enforceable, unified, and relevant Islamic jurisprudential tradition by colonial law and policy.
7 Francis Robinson's work on the formation of the print public and the ensuing erosion of the authority of the 'ulama has served as a starting point for considering social and discursive change among Muslims: Francis Robinson, "Technology and Religious Change: Islam and the

Impact of Print in South Asia," *Modern Asian Studies*, 27, no. 1 (1993): 229–51. Qeyamuddin Ahmed and Barbara Metcalf attended to the political consequences of the Ahl-i Hadith's mosque-centered reformism in their work which laid the foundations for thinking about reformism as reshaping Indian Muslim society outside of the influence of the Hanafi 'ulama. Qeyamuddin Ahmed, *The Wahhabi Movement in India* (Calcutta, 1966) and Barbara Metcalf, *Islamic Revival in British India: Darul Ulum Deoband 1860-1900* (Princeton: Princeton University Press, 1982). The consideration which I offer here of the JCPC ruling in the Tajpur mosque case establishes that colonial law eroded the unity of Muslim discourse relating to worship.
8 Christophe Jaffrelot, Bernard Haykel, Manan Ahmad, and Michael Laffan offered a valuable feedback on an early version of this paper presented at the Princeton Workshop "Islam and Its Divisions in South Asia," November 2015.
9 *Fatawa Alamgiriyya*, tr. Amir Ali ,vol. I (Lucknow: Nawal Kishore Press, n.d.), 7.
10 Muhammad Abdullah Khan, *Masail-i Thalathin* (Shahjahanabad: Matba' Mustafa Muhammad Hussain Khan, 1270/1853), 4–8.
11 Sajida Alvi, "Religion and State during the Reign of Mughal Emperor Jahǎngīr (1605–27): Nonjuristical Perspectives," *Studia Islamica*, 69 (1989): 103.
12 Ibid., 112.
13 Abdullah Khan, *Masail-i Talathin*. BL OIOC VT 128.
14 Anne Marie Schimmel, *The Empire of the Great Mughals: History, Art Culture*, tr. Corinne Atwood (London: Reaktion Books, 2004), 126.
15 Abishek Kaicker, "Unquiet City," PhD dissertation, Columbia University New York, 2014, 417–20, 429.
16 Ibid., 389, 427–8; Kaicker's preference for the term "body politic" to refer to the rioting congregation is rooted in an examination of texts that treat the rioting crowd as a product of imbalance in the humoral body of society.
17 Alan M. Guenther, "Hanafi *fiqh* in Mughal India: The *Fatawa-i Alamgiri*," in *India's Islamic Traditions 711-1750*, ed. Richard Eaton (Oxford: Oxford University Press, 2003), 209–29.
18 The muezzin's role was to call prayer. *Fatawa Alamgiriyya*, vol. 1, 69–70.
19 Ibid.
20 Ibid., 75.
21 This stricture was taken from the Hanafi text *Tabiyul Tabiyyin*, ibid., 76.
22 Ibid., 71–4.
23 "If some people of the masjid convene a congregation and pray in the mosque and the muezzin and imam and the rest of the congregation only enter the mosque after that, then the latter congregation will be authorized (mustahib) and the first will be disapproved of (makruh) of but not invalidated." Ibid., 74.
24 Ibid., 97.
25 Refer to the Sarkhatnama appointing Mowla Baksh Introduction, fn. 40.

26 Sana Haroon, "Reformism and Orthodox Practice in Early Nineteenth Century North India: Sayyid Ahmed Shaheed Reconsidered," *Journal of the Royal Asiatic Society,* 21, no. 2 (2011): 177–98.
27 Robert Travers, *Ideology and Empire in Colonial India* (Cambridge: Cambridge University Press, 2007), 136–8.
28 Eliza Giunchi argues that such interventions distorted the nature of Hanafi *fiqh* which had been an instrument of legitimation and moral reference. "The Reinvention of Shari'a Under the British Raj: In Search of Authenticity and Certainty," *The Journal of Asian Studies,* 69, no. 4 (2010): 1119–42.
29 Anderson, "Islamic Law and the Colonial Encounter," 174.
30 Ziaul Haque, "Muslim Religious Education in India and Pakistan," *Islamic Studies,* 14, no. 4 (1975): 271–92.
31 Robert Ivermee, *Secularism, Islam and Education in India 1830-1910* (New York: Routledge, 2015), 62.
32 See Rachel Sturman on the relationship between civil administration and personal law in colonial India, and the state's intent to render the "category of social life as a residuum of the politico-legal domain, where matters of ritual significance would remain operative, but to which they would also now remain consigned." Rachel Sturman, *The Government of Social Life in Colonial India: Liberalism, Religious Law and Women's Rights* (Cambridge: Cambridge University Press, 2012), 10.
33 A number of 'ulama of Bihar were in involved in this project; among them Maulana Saadat Hussain of Bihar entered the Calcutta Madrassa in 1879 and proceeded to gain the title of Shamsul 'ulama in recognition for his commentary on Mir Zahid and *Risalah Fi'l Batal.* Abul Kalam Qasimi Shamsi, *Tazkirah 'Ulama Bihar* (Sitamarhi: Shuba Nashar-o Isha'at, 1995), 113.
34 Guenther, "Hanafi Fiqh," 218–19.
35 Mouez Khalfoui, "Together but Separate: How Muslim Scholars Conceived of Religious Plurality in South Asia in the Seventeenth Century," *Bulletin of the School of Oriental and African Studies,* 74, no. 1 (2011): 87–96. Khalfoui argues that South Asian Hanafi jurists were more permissive of pluralism and difference than their Middle Eastern counterparts.
36 Abdul Ghafur Muslim, "The Theory of Interest in Islamic Law and the Effects of Interpretation of This by the Hanafi School Up to the End of the Mughal Empire," PhD dissertation, University of Glasgow, 1974.
37 Ali Altaf Mian, "Mental Disability in Medieval Hanafi Legalism," *Islamic Studies,* 51, no. 3 (2012): 247–62.
38 Kaicker, *Unquiet City,* 48–50.
39 Under the Mughal state, the legal and social relevance of Hanafi law had long derived from the authoritative qadi "whose moral probity and knowledge of local arrangements could translate precept into practice." Anderson, "Islamic Law and the Colonial Encounter," 173.
40 Stephens, *Governing Islam,* 121.
41 R. D. McChesney describes this as a comingling of a formal scholarly education and pir-murid practice in his study of the transmission and

transformation of Islamic culture in Afghanistan in the early modern period. R. D McChesney, "Earning a Living: Promoting Islamic Culture in the Sixteenth and Seventeenth Centuries," in *Afghanistan's Islam from Conversion to the Taliban*, ed. Nile Green (Los Angeles: University of California Press, 2017), 89–104.

42 Hazrat Shah Muhammad Ramzan Muhimmi, "Wasiyatnama" transcribed Muhammad Ibrahim (1261/1845). National Archives Islamabad.
43 Guenther, "Hanafi Fiqh in Mughal India," 220–1.
44 Metcalf, *Islamic Revival in British India*, 264–96.
45 Sayyid Ahmad, Shah Ismail, and others were accused of conspiring to overthrow the colonial state. They started teaching in small discussion circles in Delhi, then travelled from town to town between Delhi and Calcutta, preaching, made a pilgrimage to Mecca, and then returned to Calcutta and declared their intent to travel to the Pashtun northwest to start a jihad against the Sikhs. They extended invitations to people to join them in their stops along the way; one of these stops was in Patna, Bihar, where Inayat Ali and Wilayat Ali of Sadiqpur, profoundly deeply influenced by their mission, followed Sayyid Ahmad and Shah Ismail to the Sikh-controlled northwest. Others who remained in Bihar provided funds for their mission. This history has been recounted multiple times. An early and useful account is Mohiuddin Ahmad, *Saiyid Ahmad Shahid: His Life and Mission* (Lucknow, 1975).
46 Harlan O. Pearson, *Islamic Reform and Revival in Nineteenth-Century India: The Tariqah-i Muhammadiyah* (New Delhi: Yoda Press, 2008). Martin Riexinger, "Ibn Taymiyya's Worldview and the Challenge of Modernity: A Conflict among the Ahl-i Hadith in British India," in *Islamic Theology, Philosophy and Law: Debating Ibn Taymiyya and Ibn Qayyim al-Jawziyya*, ed. Birgit Krazietz and Georges Tamer (Berlin and Boston: Walter de Gruyter, 2013), 497–9.
47 Muhammad Fazal-ur Rehman Salafi, *Maulana Abdul Aziz Rahimabadi: Hayat-o Khidmat* (Mumbai: Farooq Brothers, 2001), 24–5. Deposition of Ibn-e-Hossein November 13–17, 1884 in Remand File of the First Court, 98–101. *Fuzal Karim v. Haji Mowla Buksh* JCPC Case Papers.
48 He used the term "amil bil hadith" Deposition Sheik Ahmedulla, 107.
49 Here, my assessment of aurality in reformed Muslim practice differs from Charles Hirschkind's consideration of the deliberative and disciplinary aspects of listening to cassette sermons in Egypt. My analysis here does not preclude the emergence or development of such disciplinary aural cultures in the Ahl-i Hadith tradition, or indeed the reconstitution of unified legal and political authority within the tradition. Charles Hirschkind, "Cassettes and Counterpublics," *The Ethical Soundscape* (New York: Columbia University Press, 2006).
50 See this argument first presented in Sana Haroon, "Reformism and Orthodox Practice: Sayyid Ahmad Shaheed Reconsidered," *Journal of the Royal Asiatic Society*, 3, 21, 2 (2011): 177–98; Muhammad Ismail

Shaheed, tr. Sikander Bhopali, *Sirat-i Mustaqeem* (Lahore: Shaikh Ahmad, 1319/1901), 73, 89–94.
51 Bhopali, tr., *Sirat-i Mustaqeem*, 88.
52 Ibid., 76.
53 Evidence of this practice does not suggest that it was a deliberative and disciplinary vocalization or listening described by Charles Hirschkind in his study of cassette sermons in Egypt. Charles Hirschkind, Chapter 4: "Cassettes and Counterpublics," in *The Ethical Soundscape* (New York: Columbia University Press, 2006).
54 Mufti Sayyid Abdul Fatah al-Hussaini al-Qadri, "Tuhfa-yi Muhammadiyyah" (Calcutta, 1849), 3–4. Karachi National Museum Archive N. 93.
55 Ibid., 27.
56 Ibid., 22–3.
57 Article by Maulvi Hakim Ahmad Sahib, published in the *Majmu'a Akhbar-i 'Ainah-yi Giti Numa* 13 Jamadi-ul Awal, 1261/20 May 1845, in al-Qadri, "Tuhfa-yi Muhammadiyya," 5–16.
58 Ibid., 22–3.
59 This is not discussed in "Tuhfa-yi Muhammadiyya" but was a point debated in subsequent litigation.
60 *Fatawa Alamgiriyya*, vol. 1, 97.
61 Ibid., 23.
62 Ibid., 69–79.
63 Ibid., 48–59.
64 Ibid., 80–99.
65 Ibid., 69.
66 Stephens, *Governing Islam*, 122.
67 *Queen-Empress v. Ramzan and Others* [1886] ILR 7 All 461.
68 *Ata-Ullah v. Azim-Ullah* [1890] ILR 12 All 494.
69 Quoted in Metcalf, *Islamic Revival in British India*, 289.
70 "Kinya is the servant of the pleader Mahomed Ehya, the said pleader Mahomed Ehya prepared to help your petitioners." Petition on behalf of the defendants Ramjani and others, September 13, 1884, in Supplement to the Record of Privy Council Appeal, iv. *Fuzal Karim v. Haji Mowla Buksh* JCPC Case Papers.
71 Written Statement of the Defendants Omed Ali and others, August 11, 1882, In the Court of the First Munsiff of Muzaffarpur, 7–8. *Fuzal Karim v. Haji Mowla Buksh*, JCPC Case Papers.
72 Ibid., 6.
73 Plaint July 3, 1882, In the Court of the First Munsiff of Muzaffarpur, 3. *Fuzal Karim v. Haji Mowla Buksh* JCPC Case Papers.
74 Deposition of Omed Ali, May 30, 1882, In the Court of the First Munsiff of Muzaffarpur Part II, 35–7. *Fuzal Karim v. Haji Mowla Buksh* JCPC Case Papers.

75 Plaint July 3, 1882, 1–5. *Fuzal Karim v. Haji Mowla Buksh* JCPC Case Papers.
76 Deposition of Sadruddin November 11, 1884 in the Remand File of the First Court, 94. *Fuzal Karim v. Haji Mowla Buksh* JCPC Case Papers.
77 Numbers tallied from costs listed at the end of each judgment in *Fuzal Karim v. Haji Mowla Buksh* JCPC Case Papers.
78 "A field was granted to Mowla Baksh in lieu of his salary." Deposition of Sheikh Ahmedulla, 107. *Fuzal Karim v. Haji Mowla Buksh* JCPC Case Papers.
79 The amount of the salary was stipulated by Mowla Baksh in his Deposition, Record in the Court of the First Munsiff of Muzaffarpur, 62. *Fuzal Karim v. Haji Mowla Buksh* JCPC Case Papers.
80 Sheikh Ahmedullah testified that the salary was personally taken care of by the *mutawalli*, in Record in the Court of the First Munsiff of Muzaffarpur, 107. *Fuzal Karim v. Haji Mowla Buksh* JCPC Case Papers.
81 Deposition of Hafiz Mowla Baksh, February 26, 1883. Record in the Court of the First Munsiff of Muzaffarpur, 62. *Fuzal Karim v. Haji Mowla Buksh* JCPC Case Papers.
82 Deposition of Sheik Ahmedulla in *Fuzal Karim v. Haji Mowla Buksh* JCPC Case Papers.
83 Ibid.
84 Deposition of Mahboob Ali November 8, 1884, and Deposition of Sadaruddin November 11, 1884, in Record in the Court of the First Munsiff of Muzaffarpur, 90–2, 95–7. *Fuzal Karim v. Haji Mowla Buksh* JCPC Case Papers.
85 Deposition of Sheikh Ahmedullah in *Fuzal Karim v. Haji Mowla Buksh* JCPC Case Papers.
86 Petition of Appeal February 9, 1888, In the High Court of Judicature Fort William Bengal, 147–8. *Fuzal Karim v. Haji Mowla Buksh* JCPC Case Papers.
87 Attested copy of a judgment of the Judicial Commissioner Punjab, June 27, 1876. Criminal Revision case No. 274 of 1876 in Remand File of the Lower Appellate Court, 128–9. *Fuzal Karim v. Haji Mowla Buksh* JCPC Case Papers.
88 Copy of a Fatwa dated 26 Zilhaj 1298/1881 with the seal of the Court of the Commissioner and Superintendent Delhi Division, In the Court of the First Munsiff of Muzaffarpur, 39–41. *Fuzal Karim v. Haji Mowla Buksh* JCPC Case Papers.
89 Plaint dated June 29, 1882, in Record of Proceedings in the Court of the First Munsifff of Muzaffarpur, 2–3, in *Fuzal Karim v. Haji Mowla Buksh* JCPC Case Papers.
90 Barbara Metcalf describes this as a surprising deviation from colonial policy. Metcalf, *Islamic Revival in British India*, 286–8.
91 Anderson, *Islamic Law and the Colonial Encounter*, 173.
92 Judgment of the Sadr Munsiff of Muzaffarpur, February 28, 1883 in the Record of Proceedings in the Court of the First Munsiff of Muzaffarpur, p. 66 in *Fuzal Karim v. Haji Mowla Buksh* JCPC Case Papers.

93 *Judgment of the Lords of the Judicial Committee of the Privy Council on the appeal of Fuzal Karim and another v. Haji Mowla Buksh and others from the High Court of Judicature at Fort William Bengal delivered 21 February 1891* in The Judicial Committee of the Privy Council Decisions [1891] UKPC 13.
94 Memorandum of Appeal filed on March 5, 1893, 70–4 in *Fuzal Karim v. Haji Mowla Buksh* JCPC Case Papers.
95 Ritu Birla argues that this legislation created a new model of public philanthropy and marks the discontinuation of precolonial systems of religious patronage. Birla, *Stages of Capital*, 29.
96 Birla problematizes the fetishization of idols as legal subjects under law, as subjects of trusts. Birla, *Stages of Capital*, 80–7.
97 Judgment of the Second Subordinate Judge of Tirhoot July 5, 1883, in The Lower Appellate Court File, 76. *Fuzal Karim v. Haji Mowla Buksh* JCPC Case Papers.
98 Judgment of the Second Munsiff of Muzaffarpur December 27, 1884, in Judgment and Decree of the Lower Court, 116. *Fuzal Karim v. Haji Mowla Buksh* JCPC Case Papers.
99 Judgment of the Second Munsiff of Muzaffarpur, December 27, 1884; ibid., 117–18.
100 Judgment of the Second Subordinate Judge of Tirhoot, July 5, 1883 in The Lower Appellate Court File, 75–77. *Fuzal Karim v. Haji Mowla Buksh* JCPC Case Papers.
101 Ibid., 133.
102 Kali Coomar Bose concluded his judgment stating

> The defendants object that the Plaintiff No. 1 having adopted new forms, of worship, namely those of the Wahabi sect, which are against their principles of religion, they are not bound to follow him or to admit him as their leader in the prayers. This point not being of a civil nature, but purely a religious one, I consider that this Court has no jurisdiction to try it.

Judgment of the Sudder Munsiff of Muzaffarpur and Judgment and Decree of the Lower Court, In the Court of the First Munsiff of Muzaffarpur, 66. *Fuzal Karim v. Haji Mowla Buksh* JCPC Case Papers.
103 Our understanding of colonial secularism has relied on intellectual history and the history of law in South Asia. The Tajpur mosque dispute shows colonial secularism at work in the courts where people regularly professed religious basis for their reasoning.
104 Fatwa 1298/1881.
105 Abstract from the Alumgiri p. 860, Record in the Court of the First Munsiff of Muzaffarpur, 44. *Fuzal Karim v. Haji Mowla Buksh* JCPC Case Papers.
106 Judgment of the Additional Subordinate Judge of Muzaffarpur, March 15, 1886 in the Remand File of the Lower Appellate Court, 130. *Fuzal Karim v. Haji Mowla Buksh* JCPC Case Papers.

107 Deposition of Nurul Hossein, September 7, 1884 in the Remand File of the First Court, 86. *Fuzal Karim v. Haji Mowla Buksh* JCPC Case Papers.
108 Decree of the Court of the Additional Subordinate Judge of Muzaffarpur March 15, 1886 in the Remand File of the Lower Appellate Court, 134. *Fuzal Karim v. Haji Mowla Buksh* JCPC Case Papers.
109 Stephens, *Governing Islam*, 125–7.
110 Ibid., 128.
111 JCPC Judgment [1891] UKPC 13, 1-3. The custom referred to in this judgment was the custom of the mosque itself which was established through testimony and not text.
112 In this case, Omed Ali and others stated as a pretext in their written statement that the suit had arisen out of a religious dispute "but on the remonstrance of a few respectable persons, it has come to light that it was clearly scandalous and prejudicial to your petitioners in this world and injurious to the cause of religion, to go, on the pretext of religion, into a mosque which is a place of worship, and to create useless disputes with the plaintiffs." (Petition on Behalf of the Defendants Sokur and others, August 22, 1884.)

"The petitioners have no objection to the imamate and towliat of the plaintiffs being upheld and confirmed; . . . pray that illegal acts contrary to Mahomedan law which would interfere with the rights of the imam and mutawaliship of the plaintiff be issued, as prayed for by the plaintiffs." (Petition on behalf of defendant Ramjani and others, September 13, 1884, in Supplement to the Record of the Privy Council Appeal, iii–iv. Fuzal Karim v. Haji Mowla Buksh JCPC Case Papers).

Chapter 2

1 I discuss this body of work in the Introduction and Afterword.
2 A full discussion of the status of mosques as trusts under colonial law is presented in the Introduction in the section "A Private Act of Religious or Charitable Benefit."
3 Kowlowski, *Muslim Endowments*, 37.
4 Last Will and Testament of Moolla Hashim of Mogul Street, May 13, 1878, in Record of Proceedings, 49–53. *In the Privy Council, On Appeal from the Chief Court of Lower Burma, between Moolla Cassim bin Moolla Ahmed and Moolla Abdul Rahim and others*, JCPC suit No. 1 of 1904, 1905 Decided July 26, 1905. Privy Council Cases With Judgments, BL PP 1316 [hereafter *Moolla Cassim v. Moolla Abdul Rahim* JCPC Case Papers].
5 Ibid., 51–3.
6 Akbar Shahib and Jainullabdeen. V. M. Nainar Mohamed, "The Brief History of the Cholia Mosque of Rangoon," compiled January 1, 2014, 1. Documents of the Cholia Mosque, 114/140 Bo Sun Pat Street, Yangon.

7   Ibid., 2–3.
8   Deposition of Ebrahim Esoofjee Cassoo March 22, 1910 in Deposition of Witnesses for the Defendants, 32. *In the Privy Council, On Appeal from the Chief Court of Lower Burma Between Mahomed Ismail Ariff and others and Mahomed Ismail Ariff and Others Appellants, and Hajee Ahmed Moolla Dawood and Others and Mahomed Suleiman Ismailjee and Others Respondents*, JCPC Suits No. 79 of 1914, No. 80 of 1914, 1916, Decided May 15, 1916. Privy Council Cases With Judgments BL PP 1316 [Hereafter *Mahomed Ismail Ariff v. Moolla Dawood* JCPC Case Papers].
9   Ibid.
10 The Shi'a Mogul Mosque does not hold the original document of grant of land or plots on which the mosque stands, but some institutional memory is anchored in an excerpt from B. R. Pearn, "A History of Rangoon," (1936) archived with a set of documents collected by the trustees of the Mogul Mosque in the 1980s in an effort to document the history of the mosque.
11 Lot 61 of F-3 in 40th street was purchased from Khateeza Bibi in 1922. Lot 40, Lot 39 in D-1, in 30th Street Rangoon 1930 was acquired by purchase at a public auction. Agreement between Khatiza Bibi and trustees of the Mogul Shi'a Mosque dated December 8, 1921, and Indenture dated January 18, 1922, Certificate of Sale of Land July 8, 1930, and Certificate of Sale of Land May 18, 1931. Important Documents [Salvaged], File 18, Documents of the Mogul Shi'a Ja'may Masjid.
12 Moshe Yegar, *Muslims of Burma: A Study of a Minority Group* (Wiesbaden: University of Heidelberg, 1972), 40–1.
13 Scheme for the Regulation of the Trusts Connected with the Shi'a Mosque in 30 Street in the Town of Rangoon, October 27, 1910, in Important Documents [Salvaged] File 18. Documents of the Mogul Shi'a Ja'may Masjid.
14 H. S. Hartnoll Judgment on Appeals 59 and 60 of 1908, May 29, 1912, in Record of Civil First Appeal, Record No. 79, 158–9. *Mahomed Ismail Ariff v. Ahmed Moolla Dawood* JCPC Case Papers.
15 Deposition of Moolla Abdul Rahim March 30, 1910 in Depositions of Witnesses for Plaintiffs, Record No. 79, 62. *Ismail Ariff v. Moolla Dawood* JCPC Case Papers.
16 Observed in a site visit to the mosque in July 2016.
17 Kozlowski, *Muslim Endowments*, 39.
18 H. Thirkell White, Esq., CIE., Commissioner of the Pegu Division, to Chief Secretary to the Chief Commissioner of Burma, June 25, 1893. IOR/L/PJ/6/354/1532.
19 The 1872 purchasers made the plots over to themselves by way of indenture to themselves as custodians of the land. They restricted future custodial rights over the plots of land to members the Randeri community, the "Randheer Sunnat Jummauth Worra Punchayet." The mosque trust deed read:

> The building that is hereinbefore [sic] termed or called the "Soonyee Jumma Musjid" this dedication is signified in the Arabic (in native character) and

it is under the full meaning of that term that this declaration is made. No one however could lay exclusive claim now or at any time in the future to the liberties and privileges, easements, profits, Emoluments, hereditaments whatsoever to the said pieces or parcels of Land.

Thereafter, full tax was assessed and paid on mosque revenue properties, including eight shops and the function hall. Registered at pages 23, 24, and 25 of the Register of Town Lots C1 dated March 19, 1872. H Exhibit C1, Documents Admitted in Evidence for the Plaintiffs, Record No. 79, 98–99. *Mahomed Ismail Ariff v. Moolla Dawood* JCPC Case Papers.

20 In the deed of indenture of land for the Eidgah associated with the mosque, the *mutawallis* of the mosque were also identified as members of the "Randeri Sunni Voraoni Panchayat." "Instrument of Indenture, 18 November 1879." In the crucial documents of indenture of 1872, the purchasers of land transferred it to the mosque waqf and reserve future management rights over these mosque lands to members of the "Rander Surat Jamaat Vohra Panchayat." "Indenture made on 16 March 1872," Exhibit O in Documents Admitted in Evidence for the Defendants, 79–80 and Exhibit C in Documents Admitted in Evidence for the Plaintiffs, Record No. 79, 98–100. *Mahomed Ismail Ariff v. Moolla Dawood and Suleiman Ismailjee* JCPC Case Papers.

21 Written statement by defendants' advocates, representing E. A. Moolla, M. A. Rahim, M. Y. Ismail and E. H. Dooply, trustees of the mosque and representatives of the Randeri community, dated December 19, 1908. Record of Civil Regular No. 333 of 1908, Record No. 79, 16. *Ismail Ariff v. Ahmed Moolla Dawood* JCPC Case Papers.

22 Judgment of S. M. Robinson, April 25, 1910, in Documents Admitted in Evidence by the Plaintiffs, Record No. 79, 131. *Ismail Ariff v. Moolla Dawood* JCPC Case Papers.

23 Other Suratis, primarily from Variao, Sunni Memons including Moolla Dawood, a few Mandalay Muslims known as Zerbadis, and South Indian Chulias. He named Ko Po Sin Zerbadi, Ngape Ko Po, and a Chulia, Chetty Ko Po. Deposition Ebrahim Esoofjee Casoo.

24 Ibid.

25 Written Statement by Defendants' Advocates, December 19, 1908 in Record of Civil Regular No. 333 of 1908, Record No. 79, 17. *Ismail Ariff v. Ahmed Moolla Dawood* JCPC Case Papers.

26 They were supported by two separate groups of Randheris who asserted their support for earlier systems of management of the mosque. In total, 120 Radheris designated 5 representatives to defend their interests in the matter.

We the undersigned Members of the Rander Sunni Vora Jamaat desire that Messrs 1) Ajam Ismailji Dankli 2) Mahomed Cassim Bharoocha 3) Ahmed Ebrahim Surma 4) Esoof Cassim Modan and 5) Ebrahim Hashim Poo should represent the entire community in the above matter. The ... nomination of certain members of the community to represent them in the suit was made known to each one of the signatories and ... on their assent to the nomination ... their signatures were obtained.

Notice December 19, 1908, and Affidavit Moolla Ajam Moolla Dawood, Ebrahim Mahomed Jasul, February 15, 1909, in Appendix I Record of Interlocutory Files of Civil Regular No. 333 of 1908, v, viii–ix. *Ismail Ariff v. Ahmed Moolla Dawood* JCPC Case Papers.

27 "Scheme for the Management of the Trust of the Rander Sunnee Vora Jamat Masjid at Mogul Street in the Town of Rangoon" in Record of Civil Regular No. 333, Record No. 79, 12–15. *Ismail Ariff v. Ahmed Moolla Dawood* JCPC Case Papers.

28 Arthur Page and H R Abdul Majid, Case on Behalf of the Appellants in Both Appeals, in Case for the Appellants, 10. *Ismail Ariff v. Ahmed Moolla Dawood* JCPC Case Papers.

29 Mahomedan in the original.

30 Civil Miscellaneous Application arising out of Civil First Appeal No. 59 of 1910, prepared by Cowasjee and Das, Petitioners' Advocates, July 31, 1912, in Record of Civil Miscellaneous Application No. 51 of 1912, Record No. 79, 171. *Ismail Ariff v. Ahmed Moolla Dawood* JCPC Case Papers.

31 O. H. K. Spate and L. W. Trueblood, "Rangoon: A Study in Urban Geography," *Geographical Review*, 32, no. 1 (1942): 56–73, and C. C. Lowis, *Census of India 1901*, vol. 12 pt 1 Burma Report (Rangoon: Superintendent Government Printing, 1902), 38–9.

32 Goolam Vahed, "'Unhappily Torn by Dissension and Litigation': Durban's 'Memon' Mosque, 1880-1930," *Journal of Religion in Africa*, 36, no. 1 (2006): 23–49.

33 This term is more commonly transliterated as Chulia in literature relating to India, but the spelling preferred and used in modern day Myanmar is Cholia, hence the transliteration I prefer here. See Yegar, *Muslims of Burma*, 41.

34 Patail made his living buying metal goods from Cholia hawkers in the bazaar and reselling them in his rented shop. Deposition of Mahomed Esaqjee Patail March 24, 1910, in Witnesses for Defendants, Record No. 79, 41–45. *Ismail Ariff v. Ahmed Moolla Dawood* JCPC Case Papers.

35 This detail emerges in a letter to the editor of a popular English language weekly. "The Choolia (Mahomedans) are determined to pay us (Europeans) out, for beef has not been obtainable in the bazaar for the past two days." "Forearmed," letter to the editor, *Rangoon Gazette Weekly Budget*, June 26, 1893.

36 This community was notably taking a lead in local Muslim nationalist politics in Surat around this time. Haynes, *Rhetoric and Ritual in Colonial India*, 270.

37 Sanjay Subrahmanyam, "A Note of the Rise of Surat in the Sixteenth Century," *Journal of the Economic and Social History of the Orient*, 43, no. 1 (2000): 23–33.

38 Ismail Ariff of Rander purchased property in Calcutta which he later argued was given in waqf. He took the case on appeal to the Judicial Committee of the Privy Council and won a decision in his favor. *Judgment of the Lords of the Privy Council on the Appeal (heard ex-parte) of Ismail Ariff v. Mahomed Ghouse, from the High Court of Judicature at Fort William Bengal; Delivered 18 February 1893* in Judicial Committee of the Privy Council Decisions [1893] UKPC 8.
39 K. Macpherson, "Chulias and Klings: Indigenous Trade Diasporas and European Penetration of the Indian Ocean Littoral," in *Trade and Politics in the Indian Ocean: Historical and Contemporary Perspectives*, ed. Giorgio Borsa (New Delhi: Manohar Publications, 1990), 36–9.
40 W. W. Hunter, *Imperial Gazetteer of India*, vol. 8 (London: Trubner and Co., 1881), 14. The Cholias were especially involved in the tin trade from the Coromandel coast. Claude Markovits, *The Global World of Indian Merchants* (Cambridge: Cambridge University Press, 2000), 14.
41 Deposition of Ahmad Moolla Dawood, March 29 and 30, 1910, in Depositions of Witnesses for the Defendants Record No. 79, 51–54 in *Ismail Ariff v. Ahmed Moolla Dawood* JCPC Case Papers.
42 Yegar, *The Muslims of Burma*, 41.
43 Green, *Terrains of Exchange*, 5.
44 The inaugural meeting of the Rangoon Ratepayer's Association was held on February 28, 1893, chaired by the Parsi B Cowasjee, and attended by Mohammed Dooply and Ebrahim Ally Moolla as well as other Gujarati traders and two Europeans. Cowasjee proclaimed that he had "every hope that membership would soon become a thousand if all who now constituted the association would lend themselves earnestly to forwarding the objects held in view." See "Rangoon Ratepayers' Association," *Rangoon Weekly Budget*, February 11, 1893.
45 This small but powerful organization represented the retail traders of Rangoon. See references to their advocacy during the Burma reforms. Burma Reforms Committee, *Burma Reforms Committee Report and Appendices* (Rangoon: Superintendent Government Printing, 1921), 12–13.
46 "An Advocates Association," *Rangoon Weekly Budget*, February 11, 1893.
47 See lists of societies registered under the Societies Registration Act 1860 at the time that the legal battle over the management of the Sunni Surati mosque was taking place in *Report on the Administration of Burma 1917-18* (Rangoon: Superintendent Government Printing, 1917), iii, 61.
48 Act I of 1880, the Religious Societies Act 1880 Passed by Governor General in Council. See Papers Relating to Religious Societies Act IOR L/PJ/6/6/257.
49 *Judgment of the Lords of the Judicial Committee of the Privy Council on the Consolidated Appeals of Ibrahim Ismael and Others v. Abdool Carrim Peermamode; and of Ibrahim Esmael and Others v. Aboo Bakar Mamode Taher, July 3, 1908*, in The Judicial Committee of the Privy Council Decisions [1908] UKPC 31.

50 The modernist project influenced by the writings of Sayyid Ahmad Khan and was one of many efforts to conceptualize Muslim unity during this period. The Khilafat movement of the 1918–24 period aimed at unifying Muslims to protect the Ottoman Caliphate was another. Naeem Qureshi, *Pan-Islam in British Indian Politics: A Study of the Khilafat Movement 1918-1924* (London: Brill, 1999). Humayun Ansari has recently revisited the career Barkatullah Bhopali to draw the link between political radicalism and militancy and transnationalism. Humayun Ansari, "Maulana Barkatullah Bhopali's Transnationalism: Pan-Islamism, Colonialism, and Radical Politics," in *Transnational Islam in Interwar Europe*, ed. Götz Nordbruch Umar Ryad (London: Palgrave Macmillan, 2014), 181–209.

51 Aye Chan, "Development of a Muslim Enclave in Arakan State of Burma," *SOAS Bulletin of Burmese Studies*, 3, no. 2 (2005): 396–420; Maulana Akbar Shah, Mohd Abbas Abdul Razak and Mohammed Farid Ali Al Fijawi, "Transformation of Myanmar Muslim Community: Singapore as a Role-Model," *Journal of Muslim Minority Affairs*, 39, no. 4 (2019): 493–512.

52 Donald M. Seekins, *State and Society in Modern Rangoon* (London: Routledge, 2011), 55.

53 See K. A. Nizami, *Sayyid Ahmad Khan* (New Delhi, 1974); Aziz Ahmad, *Islamic Modernism in India and Pakistan 1857-1964* (London: Oxford University Press, 1967) and for a more critical appraisal of the "apologetic" underpinnings of Sayyid Ahmad Khan's modernist reasoning, see Faisal Devji, "Apologetic Modernity," *Modern Intellectual History*, 4, no. 1 (2001): 67–76.

54 Rasheed Ahmad, *Report of the Twenty Third Meeting of the All India Muhammadan Anglo Oriental Educational Conference at Rangoon 29-31 December 1909 [Riport Mutaliq Ijlas Bist-o Som]* (Aligarh: Matba' Hamdi, 1910), 95–6, and *Annual Report for the Burma Educational Syndicate for the Year 1911-1912* (Rangoon: Office of the Superintendent Govt. Printing, 1912), 1–3.

55 Ahmad, *Report MAO Educational Conference*, 95–6.

56 Deposition of Ahmed Moolla Dawood March 29, 1910 in Depositions of Witnesses for the Defendants, Record No. 79, 51–53 in *Ismail Ariff v. Ahmed Moolla Dawood* JCPC Case Papers.

57 Alexander Russell Webb, *Yankee Muslim: The Asian Travels of Mohammed Alexander Russell Webb*, ed. Brent Singleton (repr. Cabin John MD: Wildside Press, 2007), 108, fn. 202.

58 When the Royal Commission on Public Services began investigating the possibility of separating the administration of Burma from that of India, Dawood, as president of the Muslim Association, wrote heatedly that the investments of Indians Burma should be taken into account. Ahmed Moolla Dawood to the Joint Secretaries, Royal Commission on Public Services March 29, 1913. "Indian Treasure and Indian Blood were poured in profusion to subjugate it (Burma) and it is the Indian labour, largely Indian Capital which have done almost all to develop it. Indians have freely mixed

with Burmans and have been principally instrumental in advancing the prosperity of Burma in general, and the Burmans as a race in particular, in spite of all that interested parties may say to the contrary. Indeed, those who inveigh against this connection of Burma with India, apparently forget that were it not for India, they would not have been here to wag their tongues as they liked." Representation of Moslem Association of Rangoon to Royal Commission on Public Services in India, IOR L/PJ/6/1242/1936.

59 C. E. Fox Chief Judge of Lower Burma, May 29, 1912 in Record of Civil First Appeal No. 59 of 1910 Record No. 79, 158–9. *Ismail Ariff v. Ahmed Moolla Dawood* JCPC Case Papers.

60 Case on Behalf of the Respondents in Record No. 79, 2–4. *Ismail Ariff v. Ahmed Moolla Dawood* JCPC Case Papers.

61 C. E. Fox, May 29, 1912, 155–7.

62 While Islamic law and trust law might have correlated exactly in deriving custodial arrangements from the will of the benefactor, the role of the civil courts did not correlate to the historic role of the qazi as religious officer for an Islamic state.

63 *Indian Education, A Monthly Record*, vol. 4 *August 1905 to July 1906* (London: Longmans, Green & Co.), 514–15.

64 Ibid.

65 A report from 1908 enumerated the enrollment for the Randeria Madrassa together with that of a smaller vernacular school on China Street at 191 students by 1908. *Report on Public Instruction in Burma for the Year 1907-1908* (Rangoon: Office of the Superintendent Government Printing, 1908), 20.

66 *Public Instruction in Burma 1909-12*, 7, 20.

67 Known as the "The Bengal System," this initiative developed in response to Hunter's theory on the causes of the Muslim revolt, *Correspondence on the Subject of Education of the Muhammadan Community in British India and Their Employment in Public Service* (Calcutta: Superintendent Government Printers, 1886), 360, quoted in Parna Sengupta, *Pedagogy for Religion: Missionary Education and the Fashioning of Hindus and Muslims in Bengal* (Berkeley: UC Press, 2011), 110.

68 Yegar, *Muslims of Burma*, 50.

69 *Revue Du Monde Musulman Publiée Par La Mission Scientifique Du Maroc*, vol. 6 (Paris: Ernest Leroux, 1908), 109. The reporter observed that "The school is divided into two departments, one of which is devoted to the study of Arabic, Persian and Hindustani; in the second, young Muslims who wish to learn English receive basic education in this language."

70 Abul Kalam Azad, *Khutbat-i Siyasiya aur Masajid-i Islamia* (Meerut: Munshi Mushtaq Ahmad, 1921), 41–3.

71 Ibid., 23.

72 Ibid., 38.

73 *Report on Public Instruction in Burma 1917-18* (Rangoon: Superintendent Government Printing, 1918), 13.

74 *Report on Public Instruction in Burma 1909-10* (Rangoon: Superintendent Government Printing, 1910), 20.
75 Latika Chaudhary, "Determinants of Primary Schooling in British India," *The Journal of Economic History,* 69, no. 1 (2009): 269–302. Chaudhary works from Clive Whitehead's argument that the conversation about education in colonial India must be refocused to identify objectively measurable outcomes of education. Chaudhary offers a clear focus on literacy as an educational objective and highlights the government's lack of funding and support for primary schooling in British India as contributing to the low literacy rates there. One argument she presents is that government support for primary education was diminished by social division which led to Indian elites convincing government officials not to invest in primary education, but to divert those resources to secondary education instead.
76 Yegar, *Muslims of Burma*, 50; Yegar refers to a 1958 "golden jubilee year" publication on the history of the Randeria High School.
77 The book was published posthumously by Abdul Hai's successor to the post of *khatib* of the Rangoon Friday mosque, Mohammed Ibrahim Randeri. M. Mohammad Abdul Hai Kaflaytvi, *Musalmanan-i Burma aur Talim* (Delhi: M. Mohammed Ibrahim, 1918), 2. British Library, South Asia Manuscripts, Urdu 19.
78 Kaflaytvi, *Musalamanan-i Burma*, 12.
79 Ibid., 7.
80 Brannon Ingram, *Revival from Below* (Berkeley: University of California Press, 201), 52–3.
81 Ibid., 52.
82 Ibid., 8.
83 Ibid., 4–5.
84 Ibid., 10.
85 Ibid., 11.
86 Ibid.
87 Class curriculum and register of attendance for 1917–18 for the Madrassa Nurul Islam. Documents of the Madrassa Nurul Islam, 26th Street, Yangon.
88 Ibid.
89 Kaflaytvi, *Musalmanan-i Burma*, 39.
90 Barbara Metcalf, "The Madrassa at Deoband: A Model for Religious Education in Modern India," *Modern Asian Studies*, 12, no. 1 (1978): 111–34.
91 David Lelyveld, *Aligarh's First Generation: Muslim Solidarity in British India* (Princeton: Princeton University Press, 1978).
92 Ibid., 38.
93 Ibid., 41.
94 Sengupta, *Pedagogy for Religion*, 109.
95 R. Nathan, *Progress of Education in India: Quinquennial Review 1897-8, 1901-02*, vol. 1 (Calcutta: Government Press, 1904), 150.

96 In Bombay the 107 Urdu schools serving 5,661 students in 1905 were most often held "within the sacred precincts of the local mosque." *Indian Education A Monthly Record 1905-1906*, vol. 4 (London: Longmans Green and Co., 1906), 648.
97 Nathan, *Progress of Education in India*, 417.
98 Ibid., 375.
99 Ibid., 415.
100 The volumes remaining in the library are too fragile to be studied closely; they include Shah Wali Ullah's *Altaf Al-Quds* in translation to Urdu, the *Hidaya*, and the *Fatawa-yi Alamgiriyya*. In his discourse on Islamic law, Kaflaytvi made particular mention of his own teacher Qazi Muhibullah Bihari (d.1291/1874–75) and the latter's Hanafi writings *Musallim us-Subut* and *Salam-ul Ulum* as the most significant writings on shari'a to emerge within the Indian scholarly tradition. Abdul Hai Kaflaytvi, *As-Sabil al-Aqwam: Sharh-i Musallam az Subut-i Urdu* (Deoband: Imtiaz Ahmad, n.d.), 6.
101 Kaflaytvi describes the components of religious thought as the principles of utterance, the synthesis of principles of fiqh by the 'ulama, and the process of juristic deliberation by the 'ulama, ibid., 8.
102 Deposition of Ismail Mahomed Bawa, March 23, 1910, and Moolla Abdul Rahim, 37–41, 62.
103 The judge intervened to ask three of the witnesses about this incident, asking if the incident had been caused by the Wahhabi proclivities of the protestor. Each defendant denied that this was the case. Ibid.
104 Mohammed Djinguiz, "Notes et Documents : L'Islam dans l'Inde," *Revue Du Monde Musulman*, 6 (1907): 85–118, 109.
105 *Madrassa Mohammedia Randeria High School, Golden Jubilee Souvenir: 1906-1956* (Rangoon, n.d.), 10, quoted in Yegar, *The Muslims of Burma*, 50.
106 The success of the Randeria Madrassa did not redeem the religious impulses which supported mosque schools in the eyes of city administrators; instead, it led to the Randeria Madrassa being nationalized in later years, in a pattern of government takeover of aided schools. Myanmar's own nationalist trajectory cast the work of the mosque custodians even further into the shadows; the Surati Bazaar, capitalized at many millions of pounds sterling was nationalized in the 1950s and recent actions against the Rohingya have led Rangoon's Muslims of Indian heritage to try to be as inconspicuous as possible. Today, you can look out at the school from the office of the present custodians of the Rangoon Friday mosque trust who nod and will tell you, "yes, that used to be managed by us."
107 *Report on Public Instruction in Burma 1921-22* (Rangoon: Superintendent Government Printing, 1922), 66–7.
108 This legal preference was rooted in cultural and legal values derived from an English context but expressed as pragmatism.
109 Beverley, "Waqf in Colonial South Asia," 164

Chapter 3

1. See Figure 2, Map of the City of Delhi (Shahjahanabad), in which the Mussulmans' and the Hindus' ancient buildings have been shown; scale 12 inches per mile; copied from the map published by the Survey of India in 1873, Bashir ud-Din Ahmad Dihlavi, *Vaqi'at al-Hukumat-i Dehli*, vol. 2 (Agra: Shams Machine Press, 1338/1919), 36–7 (scan of the map and citation provided on Francis Pritchett at the South Asia resources site).
2. I discuss the large body of work which has described the colonial vision for Indian cities in greater detail further along in this chapter and the next. I have found Jyoti Hosagrahar and Stephen Legg's work on Delhi to be most useful for understanding the spatial context for social life.
3. M. Raisur Rahman, *Locale, Everyday Islam, Modernity: Qasbah Towns and Muslim Life in Colonial India* (Delhi: Oxford University Press, 2015), 30–40.
4. Catherine Asher, "Mapping Hindu-Muslim Identities through the Architecture of Shahjahanabad and Jaipur," in *Beyond Turk and Hindu: Rethinking Religious Identities in Islamicate South Asia*, ed. David Gilmartin and Bruce Lawrence (Gainesville: University Press of Florida, 2000), 139.
5. Alison Mackenzie Shah, "Constructing a Capital on the Edge of Empire: Urban Politics and Patronage at the Edge of Empire," PhD Dissertation, University of Pennsylvania, 2005, 174.
6. The Afghan Dost Muhammad Khan, an adventurer who arrived in India in the late seventeenth century, marked his political presence by establishing the town of Bhopal in 1722. He declared himself a nawab and commenced building a fort in 1727. A mosque was built at the center of the fort, alongside the ammunition depot. In 1732, the second ruler of Bhopal established a Jami Mosque outside the fort, indicating the expansion of settlement. In the early nineteenth century, a second and then a third Jami masjid were established near the banks of the lake. Arif Aziz, *Masajid-i Bhopal* (Bhopal: Iqra Publishing House, 2003), 25–6.
7. It was left incomplete from the time of her death in 1901. Nawab Shahjehan Begum also funded the building of a mosque in Woking in Surrey. Shaharyar Khan, *The Begums of Bhopal* (New Delhi: Viva Books, 2004), 140–2.
8. Gordon Sanderson and J. Begg, *Report on Modern Indian Architecture: Types of Modern Indian Buildings* (Allahabad: F. Luker, 1913), 12.
9. On the significance of this text in contrast with later Deobandi approaches to mosque management, see Haroon, "Congregation and Management of Mosques," 5–12.
10. Muhammad Karim Allah (?), Untitled manuscript on illuminating mosques c. 1266/1849. British Library South Asia Manuscripts/Delhi/Persian/1151k.
11. On comparison of two editions of this important work, see Christian Troll, "A Note on the Early Topographical Work of Sayyid Ahmad Khan," *Journal of the Royal Asiatic Society of Great Britain and Ireland*, 2 (1972):

135–46 and C. M. Naim, "Syed Ahmad and His Two Books Called 'Asar-al-Sanadid,'" *Modern Asian Studies*, 45, no. 3 (2011): 669–708.
12 On sanitation projects, see Vijay Prasad, "The Technology of Sanitation in Colonial Delhi," *Modern Asian Studies*, 35, no. 1 (2001): 113–55. On town planning and the regulation of prostitution, see Stephen Legg, "Governing Prostitution in Colonial Delhi: From Cantonment Regulations to International Hygiene (1864–1939)," *Social History*, 34, no. 4 (2009): 447–67. On the failures of the colonial government in matters of urban administration, see Raghav Kishore, "Urban 'Failures': Municipal Governance, Planning and Power in Colonial Delhi, 1863–1910," *Indian Economic and Social History Review*, 52, no. 4 (2015): 439–61. The Resident dispersed nuzzool funds for paving and metaling the roads of Chandni Chowk, Faiz Bazaar and other parts of the old city through the 1840s. A special disbursement for lamps in the Sudder Bazaar was sought in 1857 Delhi. Despatches to India and Bengal Oct 1847-Dec 1847 IOR/E/4/794. Despatches to India and Bengal Sep 1857 IOR/E/4/847.
13 Money allowances drawn by certain civil and military officers discontinued and lamp oil supplied instead, except in certain cases. See IOR/E/4/948, 390–1.
14 Jallandar: Churches, Lighting of by Oil lamp Instead of Candles 1853–4 IOR/E/4/821.
15 Jyoti Hosagrahar, "Mansions to Margins," *Journal of the Society of Architectural Historians*, 60, no. 1 (2001): 26–45.
16 Stephen Blake identifies the *muhalla* as the dominant pattern of residential organization in his work on imperial Shahjahanabad. Stephen Blake, *Shahjahanabad: The Sovereign City in Mughal India 1639-1739* (Cambridge: Cambridge University Press, 1991), 84. It is important to note that this model was highly idealized. Grabar points to the *muhalla* as a somewhat idealized form of urban organization through attention to Ibn Khaldun's writing on mosques and the architecture of the city also identified "spacious mosques" used for festivals and cared for by the authorities, and those which served "particular quarters" of the city. Oleg Grabar, "The Architecture of the Middle Eastern City: The Case of the Mosque," *Islamic Art and Beyond* (Burlington: Ashgate Publishing, 2006), 107.
17 Khan, *Masail-i Thalathin*, 7.
18 Ibid., 14.
19 See the map at the South Asia Study Resources site run by Francis Pritchett, hosted by Columbia University, http://www.columbia.edu/itc/mealac/pritchett/00maplinks/colonial/bashir1919/bashir1919.html.
20 Mistri Muhammad Baksh, *Masjid* (1915), 2. Punjab Public Library 692.2 .mim.sin.
21 He suggested adaptations for samadhs, rozahs, dargahs. Ibid., 4.
22 Glover, *Making Lahore Modern*, 188–91.

23　Syad Muhammad Latif, *Lahore: Its History, Architectural Remains and Antiquities* (Lahore: New Imperial Press, 1892), 163, 290; quoted in Glover, *Making Lahore Modern*, 23.
24　Justin Jones, "Urban Mythologies and Urbane Islam: Refining the Past and Present in Colonial-Era Lucknow," *South Asia Multidisciplinary Academic Journal*, 11 (2015): 1–19.
25　Kannhyalal, *Tarikh-i Lahore*.
26　Ibid., 145–6.
27　Ibid., 114. Mughalpura was later called Begumpura.
28　Ibid., 112.
29　Reece Jones, "Sacred Cows and Thumping Drums: Claiming Territory as Zones of Tradition in British India," *Royal Geographical Society*, 39, no. 1 (2007): 55–65. Jones bases his analysis on evidence of Hindu landlords enforcing Hindu cultural practices on land under their control. Jones extends this evidence to argue that construction of a mosque construed a direct claim on a road as a zone of tradition, and that Hindu processions were intended to establish roads as Hindu zones of tradition suggest competitive associations with land.
30　Anand Yang, "Sacred Symbol and Sacred Space in Rural India: Community Mobilization in the 'anti-Cow Killing' Riot of 1893," *Comparative Studies in Society and History*, 22, no. 4 (1980): 576–96.
31　Instrument of Indenture dated November 1, 1917, between trustees of the Shi'a Mosque 30th street Rangoon on the one part, and trustees of the Jain Temple 29 Street Rangoon. Important Documents [Salvaged] Documents of the Mogul Shi'a Jamia Masjid File 18.
32　David Taylor offers a description of the cultural vitality of the street and colonial efforts to regulate traffic as a response to Indian street life. His work remains the defining work on colonial modernity and roads in South Asia. David Arnold, "The Problem of Traffic," *Modern Asian Studies*, 46, no. 1 (2012): 119–41, and David Arnold, "On the Road: A Social Iteration of India," *Contemporary South Asia*, 22, no. 1 (2015): 8–20.
33　Oleg Grabar proposes a model of the Islamic city using the writings of Al-Mazriqi, the tenth-century geographer who describes the hierarchies of settlements. Oleg Grabar, "Cities and Citizens: The Growth and Culture of Urban Islam," *Islamic Art and Beyond: Constructing the Study of Islamic Art*, vol. 3 (Burlington: Ashgate Publishing, 2006), 174. Grabar's inferences relating to the imperatives behind building and city planning have been meaningfully critiqued, see for instance Jacob Lassner, "Abd Al-Malik and the Temple Mount: Revisiting S. D. Goitein and Oleg Grabar," in *Medieval Jerusalem: Forging an Islamic City in Spaces Sacred to Christians and Jews* (Ann Arbor: University of Michigan Press, 2017), 81–2.
34　Glover, *Making Lahore Modern*, 57.
35　Jyoti Hosagrahar, *Indigenous Modernities: Negotiating Architecture and Urbanism* (New York: Routledge, 2005), 53, 65.
36　Glover, *Making Lahore Modern*, 2.

37 On Fergusson enacting this colonial imperative through survey of monuments, see Tapati Guha-Thakurta, *Monuments, Objects, Histories: Institutions of Art in Colonial and Postcolonial India* (New York: Columbia University Press, 2004), 12–16.
38 On the British as "dynastic heirs" of the Mughals through the possession and occupation of Mughal buildings, see Shorto, "A Tomb of One's Own," 166.
39 James Sutherland Cotton and Richard Burn, *Imperial Gazetteer of India,* vol. 9 (Oxford: Clarendon Press, 1908), 315.
40 Ulrike Stark, "An Indian Success Story: The House of Naval Kishore," in *The History of the Book in South Asia*, ed. Francesca Orsini (New York: Routledge, 2016), 164–224. "Cawnpore May Be Said to Be the Chief Center of the Vernacular Press," *Report on the Administration of the N. W. Provinces and Oudh 1896-7* (Allahabad: Government Press, 1898), 161, 188.
41 *Gazetteer of the Lahore District 1883-4* (1884; Repr. Lahore: Sang-i Meel, 1989), 191–201.
42 A more detailed discussion of "*nazul*" as a category of urban land follows in Chapter 4.
43 There is no scholarly work dealing comprehensively with this issue in the early colonial period. My assertion is based on classifications of *nazul* properties in Pilibhit, Hoshi'arpur, and Delhi, and the statements of accrual of incomes of *nazul* properties to the municipality in Delhi referenced in Jyoti Hosagrahar *Indigeous Modernities*, 137–9. fn. 45. William Glover mentions the accrual of nazul income to the municipality in Lahore, *Making Lahore Modern*, 60; fn 5. Also see Rodney Jones on *nazul* land as municipality land in Indore and Holkar, Rodney Jones, *Urban Politics in India* (Berkeley: UC Press, 1974), 142.
44 Also the washermen's riverside stations and the Cattle and Horse Fair site in Amritsar, the Ripon Hospital in Simla, and leper asylums.
45 From an extended note on the income and expenditures of the Municipal Committees of the Punjab in the *General Report on the Administration of the Punjab 1902-03* (Lahore: Punjab Government Press, 1904), 40–2.
46 In an important recent article demonstrating colonial neglect of the "old" city of Delhi, Awadhendra Sharan shows that the reliance of the old city of Delhi on well water was criticized as unsanitary, and yet the complaints of old city residents in petitions and in newspaper reports about drainage and water supply in the old city were unanswered; a "subsoil sewer from Fatehpuri masjid to Delhi Gate" was not completed till 1909. Awadhendra Sharan, "Delhi's Belly," *The Indian Economic and Social History Review,* 48, no. 3 (2011): 433, 450.
47 The population and growth of the town exceeded Fraser's estimates within ten years, and by 1876 the city limits were expanded. Than Than New, "Yangon: The Emergence of a New Spatial Order in Myanmar's Capital City," *Soujourn: Journal of Social Sciences in South East Asia*, 13, no. 1 (1998): 92.

48 These were regular areas of activity described and budgeted in each year covered in the annual administration reports. See *Report of the Working of the Local and District Boards NWP and Oudh 1891-2* to *1920-21* and *Report on the Administration of the United Provinces of Agra and Oudh 1904-05* to *1913-14.*

49 Duties of district boards as defined in Act XIV of 1883, *The N. W. Provinces and Oudh Code* (Calcutta: Superintendent Government Printing, 1892), 572–3.

50 K. Sivaramakrishnan, "Environment, Law and Democracy in Colonial India," *The Journal of Asian Studies*, 70, no. 4 (2011): 905–28.

51 Hosagrahar, *Indigenous Modernities*, 53, 65, and Hosagrahar, "Mansions to Margins," 38.

52 Nandini Gooptu, *The Politics of the Urban Poor in Early Twentieth Century India* (Cambridge: Cambridge University Press, 2001), 76–80.

53 *Report on the Administration of the United Provinces of Agra and Oudh 1906-07* (Allahabad: Superintendent Government Press, 1908), 19.

54 *Report on the Administration of the United Provinces of Agra and Oudh 1908-09* (Allahabad: Superintendent Government Press, 1910), 39.

55 *Report on the Administration of the United Provinces of Agra and Oudh 1916-17* (Allahabad: Superintendent Government Press, 1918), 19.

56 The municipality was a trustee. *Report on the Administration of the United Provinces of Agra and Oudh, 1911-12, Report on the Administration of the United Provinces of Agra and Oudh 1906-07* (Allahabad: Superintendent Government Press, 1913), 56.

57 *Report on the Administration of the United Provinces of Agra and Oudh 1908-09*, 39. In the 1920s the Trusts became independent of the Municipal Corporation and were formed by prominent townspeople elected by the District Magistrate as well as the Chairman of the Municipal Board acting ex-officio. See Gooptu, *The Politics of the Urban Poor in India*, 76–80.

58 *Report on the Administration of Police of the United Provinces for the Year Ended 1913* (Allahabad: Superintendent Government Printing, 1914), 6.

59 *Report on the Administration of Police of the United Provinces for the Year Ended 1914* (Allahabad: Superintendent Government Printing, 1915), 18.

60 Minute by the Lieutenant Governor on the Cawnpore Mosque Riot August 21, 1913. Reports on the Cawnpore Riots IOR/L/PJ/6/1256/ 2826.

61 S. P. Mehta, *Cawnpore Civic Problems: A Critical and Historical Review of City Government in Cawnpore* (Kanpur: Citizen Press, 1952), 43–5.

62 Minute by the Lieutenant Governor on the Cawnpore Mosque Riot, paragraph 5.

63 Ibid.

64 Ibid., paragraph 6.

65 Ahmad Raza Khan and Abul Ala Muhammad Amjad Ali, *Masji-i Kanpur Kay Mutaliq aik Nihayat Zaruri Fatwa* (Bareilly: Abdul Wudud, 1914), 3.

66 Minute by the Lieutenant Governor on the Cawnpore Mosque Riot, paragraph 8.

67 Francis Robinson provides the single most important account of this response, but his reading conflates street action and press coverage and determines the entire matter to be a result of instrumentalist efforts to rally Muslims through religious and cultural symbolism, Francis Robinson, *Separatism Among Indian Muslims*, 213.
68 Address by Muhammadan Deputation and Governor's Reply July 1913 in Reports on the Cawnpore Riots IOR/L/PJ/6/1256/2826.
69 Minute by the Lieutenant Governor on the Cawnpore, Paragraph 7.
70 Maslah az Lakhnao Firangi Mahal, Marsalah Maulvi Muhammad Salamat Allah Sahib Naib Mansaram Majlis Muvid ul Islam, 30 Zilqa'dah 1331 AH, in Ahmad Raza Khan, Abul Ala Muhammad Amjad Ali, *Masjid-i Kanpur Kay Mutaliq aik Nihayat Zaruri Fatwa* (Bareilly: Abdul Wudud, 1914), 2.
71 Ibid., 4–5.
72 "Mosques and Government," Minute by the Lieutenant Governor on the Cawnpore Mosque Riot, August 21, 1913, Appendix I.
73 Minute by the lieutenant governor on the Cawnpore Mosque Riot, August 21, 1913.
74 Bareilvi, *Masjid-i Kanpur*, 3, 38.
75 Ibid., 18.
76 Ibid., 40.
77 Ibid., 38.
78 Ashuthosh Varshney's work on postcolonial India argues for closer attention to the work of civic associations in producing civic priorities. Ashuthosh Varshney, *Ethnic Conflict and Civic Life: Hindus and Muslims in India* (New Haven: Yale University Press, 2002).
79 Douglas Hay differentiates the work of professional judges conducting jury trials from the "law suffered, imposed, used and resisted" in the hands of laymen acting without juries, describing the former as high law and the latter as "low law." The magistrates in Britain and across the empire were empowered by legislation and a deliberate policy of minimal supervision by the high courts. Douglas Hay, "Legislation, Magistrates and Judges: High law and Low Law in England and the Empire," in *The British and their Laws in the Eighteenth Century* ed. David Lemmings (London: Boydell Press, 2005), 59–80. Douglas Hay's writing on magistrates and master servant laws, discussed later on in this chapter, provides a fuller account of magisterial authority in interpreting and applying statute.
80 Thomas Macaulay, Government of India Bill—Adjourned Debate (Second Night), June 24, 1853. *Hansard's Parliamentary Debates* vol. 128 *13 June 1853-8 July 1853* (London: Cornelius Buck, 1853), Column 745–747.
81 *Report of the Committee Appointed to Formulate a Scheme for the Separation of Judicial and Executive Functions in the United Provinces*, 1, quoted in S. Srivastava, "Separation of Judiciary from Executive In India with Particular Reference to the State of Uttar Pradesh," *The Indian Journal of Political Science*, 25, no. 3–4 (1964): 339–46.

82 Randhika Singha, "Punished by Surveillance: Policing Dangerousness in Colonial India," *Modern Asian Studies*, 49, no. 2 (2015): 241–69.
83 From 1800 to 1856, employees of the East India Company were appointed through patronage and specialized vocational training for service at the College of Imperial Service at Haileybury. C. J. Dewey, "The Education of a Ruling Caste: The Indian Civil Service in the Era of Competitive Examination," *The English Historical Review*, 88, no. 347 (1973): 262–85.
84 Dewey, "The Education of a Ruling Caste," 269–71.
85 Thomas Metcalf, *Imperial Connections: India in the Indian Ocean Arena* (Berkeley: UC Press, 2007), 18–20.
86 This role was adapted several times and the criminal jurisdiction excluded at times before 1857, but the joint responsibilities of the district officer were reconfirmed after 1859. B. H. Badel-Powell, *A Manual of the Land Revenue Systems and Land Tenures of British India* (Calcutta: 1882), 246–7.
87 Badel-Powell, *A Manual of the Land Revenue Systems*, 9. In what were called non-regulation districts, this office was held by a deputy commissioner who had the same powers as a magistrate.
88 *Administration of the North-Western Provinces and Oudh April 1882-November 1887* (Allahabad: NWP and Oudh Gov. Press, 1887), 27.
89 L. S. White, Deputy Secretary to Government United Provinces, Judicial Department, to All Commissioners of Divisions United Provinces, Allahabad, May 25, 1923. *Proceedings of the Legislative Council of the United Provinces*, vol. 19 Sept 5-11, 1924 (Allahabad: Government Press, 1924), 38.
90 Hay, "Legislation, Magistrates and Judges," 62.
91 Magistrates summarily enforced master-servant contracts and were a lynchpin of the bonded labor system in the colonies. Douglas Hays and Paul Craven, *Masters, Servants, and Magistrates in Britain and the Empire, 1562-1955* (Chapel Hill: UNC Press, 2004), 40.
92 Singha, *A Despotism of Law*, 165–6.
93 Under the Rules of Evidence, testimony of Indians was treated as inferior to that Europeans. Elizabeth Kolsky argues that the rules of evidence were one means by which practices of white violence against Indians were permitted under an ostensibly impartial judicial system. Elizabeth Kolsky, *Colonial Justice in British India* (Cambridge: Cambridge University Press, 2011).
94 Singha, "Punished by Surveillance."
95 Following a period of development of legislation and regulation relating to infrastructure, Indian roads were likened to the king's highway in England, the Indian Penal Code, Section 283G, subject to the definition of the public in section 12. W. R. Hamilton, *The Indian Penal Code with Commentary* (Calcutta: Thacker, Spink and Co., 1895), 20, 257–8, 271–3.
96 Ibid.
97 *Indian Penal Code* Section 268.
98 David Arnold, "The Police and Colonial Control in South India," *Social Scientist*, 4, no. 12 (1976): 5.

99 Section 144 authorizes the magistrate to issue temporary orders in urgent cases of nuisance. *Indian Penal Code* Section 268 (a).
100 *Guide to Muhammadan and Hindu Festivals and Fasts in the United Provinces* (Allahabad: Government Press, 1924).
101 Ibid., 3.
102 Ibid., 7.
103 Ibid., 19–22.
104 Ibid., 9–10.
105 Metcalf, *Indian Ocean*, 24.
106 Fleming Deputy Commissioner [and Magistrate] Rangoon Town to the Commissioner Pegu Division, June 28, 1893. Riots between Mohammedans and Hindus at Rangoon IOR/L/PJ/6/354.
107 Magistrate to Commissioner Rangoon, June 28, 1893.
108 Nicholas Dirks has highlighted the early use of section 144 to police Indian traditions after missionary objections to ritual hookswinging in southern India. Nicholas Dirks, "The Policing of Tradition: Colonialism and Anthropology in South India," *Comparative Studies in History and Society*, 39, no. 1 (1997): 182–212.
109 Proceedings January 30, 1924, in *Proceedings of the Legislative Council of the United Provinces* vol. 16 *Jan 8–31, 1924* (Allahabad: Superintendent Press United Provinces, 1924), 84.
110 Proceedings December 16, 1924, in *Proceedings of the Legislative Council of the United Provinces* vol. 20 *December 15–20 1924* (Allahabad: Government Press, 1924), 130–1.
111 Ibid.
112 *Report of the Committee Appointed to Formulate a Scheme for the Separation of Judicial and Executive Functions in the United Provinces* (Agra, 1947), 1. LOC Microfiche 84/61273 (J).
113 The committee recommended removal of power of sections 107, 108, 109, and 110 which allowed the magistrate to take security from people for keeping the peace, from those suspected of distributing seditious material, or being vagrants, and of being habitual offenders. *Scheme for the Separation of Judicial and Executive Functions in the United Provinces*, 8.
114 Legislative committee members Pandit Brijnandan Prasad Misra asked with regards to a dispute in Pilibhit in 1924, "is it a fact that the local Hindus complained to the District Magistrate that their reports of the Muharram occurrences were not being registered by the police nor was any office making note of their complaints?." Proceedings April 3, *Proceedings of the Legislative Council of the United Provinces* vol. 24 *March 23–April 3*, 498–9.
115 No orders were available in the case of the 1924 riot in Jhansi, but Pandit Bhagwat Narayan Bhargava argued that he wanted to see "communication from the commissioner of Jhansi," Proceedings January 30, 1924, in *Proceedings of the Legislative Council of the United Provinces* vol. 16 *Jan 8–31 1924*, 84.

116 Translation of an order of the District Magistrate Moradabad, July 17, 1925. Appendix I in *Proceedings of the Legislative Council of the United Provinces* vol. 25 *Aug 19–24*, 374–6.
117 Proceedings April 4, 1924, *Proceedings of the Legislative Council of the United Provinces* vol. 18 *March 17-April 4 1924*, 516–22.
118 Honorable Raja Sir Muhammad Ali Muhammad Khan, the Raja Sahib of Mahmudabad, December 15, 1924, in *Proceedings of the Legislative Council of the United Provinces* vol. 20 *December 15–20 1924*, 18–19.
119 L. S. White, Deputy Secretary to Government United Provinces, Judicial Department, to All Commissioners of Divisions United Provinces, Allahabad, May 25, 1923. *Proceedings of the Legislative Council of the United Provinces* vol. 19 *Sept 5–11 1924*, 38.
120 Mr. A. M. Samiullah submitted a memo describing an outcome of the Calcutta Unity Conference where it was agreed that Muslims could sacrifice cows on their own lands and Hindus could play music outside mosques. Memo for Simon Commission IOR Q/13/1/3/E-Ben-674.
121 Memorandum Maulvi Nurul Huq IOR Q/13/1/3/ E-Ben-647.
122 In one such example from the Punjab, the author wrote:

> I cannot live without saying that I desire justice, and to those who say "live and let live," I am not asking for any illegitimate ri'ayat. If appealing for justice from the passions of the Hindu jati is like playing a flute in front of a cow then to what extent must we bear this? To what extent shall we become like stone, and to what extent shall we be the prey of the Hindu's sacred cow? . . . In Zila Karnal the seat is going to a Sanghatan Surma. Therefore we are showing this truth that in District Karnal the Hindu influence is so supported that the deputy commissioner and session judge, even not being Hindu, [support] the Hindu Raj . . . [The British Government and the Punjab High Court support the general murder/killing of the Muslim people].

> Usmani Panipati, Izharul Islam, *Fughan-i Muslim, Anjuman-i Islamiyya Panipat Tract Number 15* (Delhi: Silsilah Anjuman-i Islamiyya Panipat, 1933) British Library, South Asian Manuscripts, PIB 88/1.

123 Total area of the tehsil Bulandshahr was 1,915 sq. miles. Comparative Area Statement, T. Stoker, *Final Report on the Settlement of Land Revenue in the Bulandshahr District* (Allahabad, 1891), 2:36.
124 Rahman, *Locale, Everyday Islam, and Modernity*, 169.
125 Table showing the effects of new assessments on chief families who possess any considerable landed property in the district in Stoker, *Final Report on the Settlement of Land Revenue in the Bulandshahr District*, 1:25.
126 Rahman, *Locale, Everyday Islam, and Modernity*, 181–205.
127 William Wilson Hunter, *Imperial Gazetteer of India*, vol. 1 (London: Trubner and Co., 1881), 268.
128 *General Report on the Settlement of the Bulandshahr District, North Western Provinces* (Allahabad, 1877), 44.

129 H. R. Nevill, *Bulandshahr: A Gazetteer, Being Vol. V of District Gazetteers of the United Provinces of Agra and Oudh* (Allahabad: Superintendent Govt. Press, 1903), 192.
130 The provision of funding for such sites is described in the *Report of the Working of the Local and District Boards North West Provinces and Oudh 1891* (Allahabad: Government Press, 1891).
131 The Case for the Appellants, 5. *In the Privy Council No. 25 of 1923 Between Saiyed Manzur Hasan, Saied Hasan Ahmad, Sayed Muhammad Hussain and Saiyed Asghar Husain (Appellants) and Saiyed Muhammad Zaman and Ors. (Defendants)* Decided November 13, 1924. Privy Council Cases With Judgments, BL PP 1316 [Hereafter *Manzur Hasan v. Muhammad Zaman* JCPC Case Papers].
132 Evidence of Saiyid Hasan Ahmad September 4, 1918, Part I, 14. *Manzur Hasan v. Muhammad Zaman* JCPC Case Papers.
133 Routes of the Ashura processions winding past significant buildings and religious artefacts defined a religious spatial order and power relations in the city of Hyderabad during the nineteenth century. See Alison Shah, *Constructing a Capital on the Edge of Empire*, 174.
134 Petition of Plaint in the Court of the Second Additional Subordinate Judge of Aligarh May , 1918, in Part I, 2. *Manzur Hasan v. Muhammad Zaman* JCPC Case Papers.
135 *Report of the Working of the Local and District Boards NWP and Oudh 1906-07* (Allahabad: Government Press, 1907), 5; *Report of the Working of the Local and District Boards NWP and Oudh 1907-08* (Allahabad: Government Press, 1908), 7; The reports of the district boards note the thousands of plague-related deaths in from 1899 to 1916. Malaria outbreaks also occurred, affecting over 4 million people a year occurred in 1908–1910.
136 *Report of the Working of District Boards NWP and Oudh 1910-11*, 4.
137 Rahman, *Locale, Everyday Islam, and Modernity*, 186–9.
138 Case on Behalf of the Respondents, Part I, 3. *Manzur Hasan v. Muhammad Zaman* JCPC Case Papers.
139 The term used is 5 biswas mahals; a biswas is a share, but the term is also used to refer to a standard form of 5/20 of a bigha. Standard measure for a bigha is 3,025 yards, 5/8 of an acre. *A Glossary of Judicial and Revenue Terms* (London: W. H. Allen, 1855).
140 Deposition of Saiyed Hasan Ahmed Zamindar, September 4, 1918 in Part I, 14. *Manzur Hasan v. Muhammad Zaman* JCPC Case Papers.
141 Extract from the Khasra of the Abadi of the Mauza Aurangabad, pargana Baran, Tehsil and District Bulandshahr Prepared in 1268 Fasli/1861, Part III Exhibits, 56–7. *Manzur Hasan v. Muhammad Zaman* JCPC Case Papers.
142 Written statement on behalf of Sayyid Muhammad Zaman, Saiyid Abdul Aziz, Munchi Muhammad Zaman Khan, and Saiyid Abdus Sami, July 12, 1918, in Part I, 6–7. *Manzur Hasan v. Muhammad Zaman* JCPC Case Papers.
143 Ibid.

144 See for instance reference to the management of unmetalled roads by landowners in Bulandshahr as well as Dera Dun, Saharnpur, and other districts in *Report on the Working of District Boards in the United Provinces and Agra* (Allahabad, 1912), 10.
145 Statement Sayyid Muhammad Zaman and others.
146 *Hedaya*, vol. 1(Lucknow: Mustafa Press), 624–5 quoted in a handbook of Hanafi law relating to mosques prepared for reference by jurists. Janab Maulana Maulvi Hafiz Muhammad Abdullah, *Qanun-i Masjid* (Calcutta: Matbah Sarah Hind, 1917), 2–3.
147 *Bahrur Raek* (Cairo) 2:36 quoted in *Qanun-i Masajid*, 3–4.
148 Deposition of Mubarak Husain, Headmaster Islamia School at Khurja, September 18, 1918 in Part I, 33. *Manzur Hasan v. Muhammad Zaman* JCPC Case Papers.
149 Case on Behalf of the Respondents, in Part I, 7. *Manzur Hasan v. Muhammad Zaman* JCPC Case Papers.
150 C. A. Bayly, "A Pre-History of Communalism? Religious Conflict in India 1700-1860," *Modern Asian Studies*, 19, no. 2 (1985): 177–203.
151 Evidence of Kishori Lal in the Court of the Second Subordinate Judge at Aligarh September 5, 1918 in Part I, 24–5. *Manzur Hasan v. Muhammad Zaman* JCPC Case Papers.
152 Evidence of Kishori Lal September 5, 1918 in Part I, 24–5. *Manzur Hasan v. Muhammad Zaman* JCPC Case Papers.
153 H. R. Roe C.I.D. Special Branch, "Preface," in *Guide to Muhammadan and Hindu Festivals and Fasts in the United Provinces* (Allahabad: Government Press, 1924), i.
154 Order of the Sub-divisional Magistrate May 29, 1917 in Part III, 55. *Manzur Hasan v. Muhammad Zaman* JCPC Case Papers.
155 Justin Jones, *Shi'a Islam in Colonial India* (Cambridge: Cambridge University Press, 2011), 73–4.
156 Justin Jones, "The Shi'a Muslims of the United Provinces of India, c 1890-1940," PhD Dissertation, Cambridge University, 2007, 113–14.
157 *Judgment of the Lords of the Judicial Committee of the Privy Council on the Appeal of Saiyid Manzur Hasan and others (Appeal No. 25 of 1923) v Saiyid Muhammad Zaman and others (Allahabad) decided November 13, 1924.* The Judicial Committee of the Privy Council Decisions [1924] UKPC 83.
158 William Gould, *Religion and Conflict in Modern South Asia* (Cambridge: Cambridge University Press, 2012), 135.
159 Proceedings October 27, 1923, *Proceedings of the Legislative Council of the United Provinces* vol. 14 *October 1923* (Allahabad: Superintendent Press United Provinces, 1923), 174.
160 *Judgment November 13, 1924* [1924] UKPC 83, 4.
161 Julia Stephens's work on this subject of the exclusion of indigenous values in legal reasoning by colonial jurists is foundational to understanding why the JCPC was unable to accommodate such ideas.

Chapter 4

1 A few defining studies have highlighted the political importance of the mobilization for return of this site to Muslims in the 1930s. The most focused attention to the politics of Shahidganj is offered in David Gilmartin, "The Shahidganj Mosque Incident: A Prelude to Pakistan," in *Islam, Politics and Social Movements*, ed. Edmund Burke and Ira Lapidus (Berkeley: UC Press, 1988). More recently Tanweer Fazal explores the legal discourse which caste the mosque as a juristic person Tanveer Fazal, "The Mosque as Juristic Person: Law, Public Order and Inter-religious Disputes in India," *South Asian History and Culture*, 10, no. 2 (2019): 199–211. Naveeda Khan considers the impact of personifying a mosque on popular Muslim discourse, Naveeda Khan, "The Martyrdom of Mosques: Imagery and Iconoclasm in Modern Pakistan," in *Enchantments of Modernity*, ed. Saurabh Dube (New Delhi: Routledge, 2009), 372–401 and Naveeda Khan, *On Muslim Becoming; Aspiration and Skepticism in Pakistan* (Durham: Duke University Press, 2012). My first intervention in this subject and an early version of this chapter, a commentary on the nature of Sikh custodianship of the site was published as Sana Haroon, "Custodianship of Shahidganj in Colonial Lahore: Land, Land Use and the Formation of Religious Community, 1850–1936," *Indian Economic and Social History Review*, 54, no. 2 (2017): 183–220.
2 Robkar of Commissioner Lahore Division, April 9, 1856, vol. 4, 24–5. *In the Privy Council, On Appeal from the Court of Appeal of the High Court of Judicature at Lahore, The Mosque Known as Shahidganj and others (Appellants) and Shiromani Gurdwara Parbandhak Committee Amritsar (Respondents)*, JCPC Suit No. 91 of 1938, 1940, decided May 2, 1940. Privy Council Cases with Judgments, BL PP 1316 [hereafter *Shahidganj v. SGPC* JCPC Case Papers].
3 Application of Bhai Ganda Singh, March 7, 1870, vol. 4, 26–7. *Shahidganj v. SGPC* JCPC Case Papers.
4 Peter Robb, *Ancient Rights and Future Comforts* (Richmond: Curzon Press, 1997), 40–6.
5 James McCrone Douie, *Punjab Land Administration Manual* (Lahore: Superintendent Government Printing, 1931), 100–7.
6 In addition to exemplifying the principles of colonial governance through the union of executive and judicial functions, the "Punjab school of administration" had a unique feature in that administrators saw themselves as the gatekeepers of India and believed their work included a military mission. Shalini Sharma, *Radical Politics in Colonial Punjab: Governance and Sedition* (New York: Routledge, 2010), 14–19.
7 *General Report on the Administration of the Punjab for the Years 1849-1850 and 1850-51* (London: Court of Directors for the East India Company, 1854), 71–2.

8 Robb, *Ancient Rights and Future Comforts*, 78–82.
9 Edney, *Mapping an Empire*, 174.
10 *General Report on the Administration of the Punjab Territories 1851-2 and 1852-3* (Calcutta: Calcutta Gazette, 1854), 105–6.
11 *Imperial Gazetteer of India Provincial Series: Punjab* vol. 1 *The Province* (Calcutta: Superintendent Government Printing, 1908), 147–8.
12 L. Beni Prasad, *The Punjab Land Revenue Act XVII of 1887 as Amended and up to Date with Notes, Circulars, Rules and Notifications* (Lahore: Artistic Printing Works, 1913), 39–40.
13 Richard Saumarez Smith, "Rule-by-Records and Rule-by-Reports: Complementary Aspects of British Imperial Rule of Law," *Contributions to Indian Sociology*, 19, no. 1 (1985): 153–76; 154.
14 *Report of the Department of Land Records and Agriculture Punjab* (Lahore: Civil and Military Press, 1899).
15 Prashad, *The Punjab Land Revenue Act of 1887*, 42–4.
16 Douie, *Punjab Land Administration Manual 1931*, 152.
17 A person with another claim to land could file a declaratory suit which would lead to an internal reinvestigation of title, record, and rights and the determination of the prevailing rights over land. Paragraph 158 of the Punjab Land Revenue Act 1887, Prasad, *The Punjab Land Revenue Act*, 99.
18 *Rules under the Land Revenue and Tenancy Acts, 1887* (Lahore: Mufid-i Am Press, 1899), 131.
19 This pattern is described by Anne Murphy in her study of Sikh organization in colonial Punjab. Anne Murphy, *The Materiality of the Past: History and Representation in the Sikh Tradition* (Oxford: Oxford University Press, 2013), 166.
20 Extract from Statement of Charitable Grants Enjoyed by Certain Bullas, Granthis, Sadhus Etc., Under the Late Government, n.d but probably 1850, vol. 4, 134–7. *Shahidganj v. SGPC* JCPC Case Papers. This statement is also listed in the holdings of the Punjab Archives in Lahore but had been removed from the bundle in which it was contained and could not be found after an extensive search in 2015. The fact of the preservation of this administrative document in this JCPC case file highlighted to me the usefulness of the legal archive for work on social and administrative history.
21 *General Report on the Administration of the Punjab 1849-50 and 1850-51*, 85.
22 Arjun Appadurai describes the relationship of temples to kingship in "Kings, Sects and Temples in South India 1350-1700 AD," *Indian Economic and Social History Review*, 14, no. 1 (1977): 47–73.
23 Anne Murphy has echoed Arjun Appadurai's identification of the political importance of the religious grant in Ranjit Singh's state, noting that Ranjit Singh reconfirmed grants made by previous rulers and conferred his own. *The Materiality of the Past*, 163–4.
24 Statement of Bhai Jiwan Singh May 2, 1850 translation and copy of statement made before Mr. John Lawrence and description of sanad, vol. 4, 2–7. *Shahidganj v. SGPC* JCPC Case Papers.

25 Ibid.
26 Statement of Charitable Grants.
27 Robkar issued by the Court of the Financial Commissioner Punjab, July 24, 1855, vol. 4, 16–17, *Shahidganj v. SGPC* JCPC Case Papers.

> I most sinful person Nur Ahmad, son of Allah Jowaya, son of Sheikh Din Muhammad, son of Shaikh Muhammad Roshan, son of Shaikh Karamullah, son of Shaikh Hassan Muhammad, one of the descendants of Shaikh Kaku Chishti, custodians of the mosque of Mirza Qurban Beg, invites testimony and wants to establish his right by submitting to the great men of the faith, the doctors of the firm Muhammadan Law, and all the Muslims as follows: During his lifetime Mirza Qurban Beg made a gift in respect of a mosque founded by him, together with a well-built of pucca masonry, and thirteen bighas of cultivable land in favor of my ancestor ... everyone who possesses any information and knowledge in this respect is requested to put his seal on this paper.

Petition dated 1270/14 December 1853, vol. 1, 4–7. *Shahidganj v. SGPC* JCPC Case Papers.
29 Deed of Gift Executed by Mirza Falak Beg Khan for three kanals and fifteen marlas of a site attached to a mosque 1134 AH/22 September 1722, vol. 1, 60–2. *Shahidganj v. SGPC* JCPC Case Papers.
30 Claim to *mu'afi* lands in Pargana Saurian. Letter in Persian attached to the file of a case relating to enquiry into the Jagir of Rs 1,680 per annum, enjoyed by Bhai Jiwan Singh, son of Jagga Singh, resident of Lahore, May 8, 1850, vol. 4, 7–8. *Shahidganj v. SGPC* JCPC Case Papers.
31 By 1868, the size of the endowment was further reduced, but it is unclear how much by 1929, the entirety of the endowment was reduced to the two large contiguous portions of land, one to the north and the other to the south of Shahidganj road, shown in the plan in Figure 5. The pedigree table prepared at the settlement of 1892 notes Asa Singh as a proprietor of Naulakha. In 1896, the officer called the Darogha Nazul noted action against Harnam Singh and Hari Singh as proprietors of Naulakha. Rights of custodianship were first claimed jointly by Harnam Singh and his brother Hari Singh. During the Sikh Tribunal, Harnam Singh acted singly as custodian by the agreement of both brothers. Statement of Bhai Jiwan Singh in the form of questions and answers, May 2, 1850, D 26, pp. 2–7 *The Mosque Known as Shahidganj v. SGPC* JCPC Case Papers.
32 Mutakhib papers related to Mauza Naulakha Prepared at Settlement of 1856, vol. 4, 22–3, *The Mosque Known as Shahidganj v. SGPC* JCPC Case Papers.
33 Whitehead, *Report on the Administration of Delhi Crown Lands* (Delhi: Oxford Printing Works, 1933).
34 *General Report on the Administration of the Punjab Territories 1851-2 and 1852-3* (Calcutta: Calcutta Gazette, 1854), 139–40.
35 Extract from Record of Rights Drawn in 1868 vol. 4, 32–3, *The Mosque Known as Shahidganj v. SGPC* JCPC Case Papers.

36 *Report on the Administration of the Punjab, 1849-1850 and 1850-1851*, 285.
37 Ibid., 72.
38 Deed of Gift Executed by Mirza Falak Beg Khan for 3 kanals and 15 marlas of a site attached to a mosque, 9 Zilhaj 1134 AH/22 September 1722, vol. 1, 60–2. *The Mosque Known as Shahidganj v. SGPC* JCPC Case Papers.
39 Deed Executed by Nur Ahmad.
40 Robkar of Mirza Kalab Abad Khan Extra-Assistant Commissioner Doab Bari, December 11, 1853, vol. 4, 11–12. *Shahidganj v. SGPC* JCPC Case Papers.
41 Robb, *Ancient Rights and Future Comforts*, 82, 76.
42 The principle of adverse possession created a strange paradox. Laws governing trusts enabled worshippers to bring charges of mismanagement against the trustees of the endowments without any time limit, to sue for the return of lands and emoluments, a story which emerges in its entirety in Chapter 5. Yet a stranger who took possession of endowment properties had only to maintain unchallenged occupancy of the site for the required twelve years to establish unobjectionable proprietorship. K. Rustomji, *The Law of Limitation and Adverse Possession* (Lahore: Empire Law Publishing, 1922), 77.
43 Robkar Issued by the Court of Robert Henry Davis February 25, 1854, vol. 4, 15–16. *Shahidganj v. SGPC* JCPC Case Papers.
44 Statement of Asa Singh June 8, 1885 given in another suit *Musammat Khem Jaur v. Asa Singh*, vol. 4. 51–6. *The Mosque Known as Shahidganj v. SGPC* JCPC Case Papers.
45 Report of the Extra Assistant Commissioner Lahore July 11, 1883, vol. 4, 44–6. *The Mosque Known as Shahidganj v. SGPC* JCPC Case Papers.
46 "Will the Shahidganj Mosque Be Restored to Muslims"? *Daily Paisa Akhbar*, April 15, 1919 in vol. 3, 16–17. *Shahidganj v. SGPC* JCPC Case Papers.
47 *Report on the Administration of the Punjab for the Years 1849-1850 and 1850-1851*, 106.
48 "The term of limitation is twelve-year; and complete occupancy for that period confers a valid title," ibid, 107.
49 Report of the Extra Assistant Commissioner Lahore July 11, 1883, vol. 4, 44.
50 Rai Bahadur Kannhyalal, *Tarikh-i Lahore* (1282/1865; repr., Lahore: Sang-i Meel, 2001), 111.
51 Robkar issued by District Commissioner Lahore November 14, 1855, vol. 4, 18–19.
52 I saw posters inviting people to a commemoration of the Eid-i Milad ul Nabi plastered at the site in July 2015. Posters and other photographs from events held here since are posted to Facebook and suggest that at the time of completion of this text in November 2020, the revival of the memory of Hazrat Shah Kaku has progressed. https://www.facebook.com/SHAHKAKUCHISHTI/.
53 Testimony of Asa Singh in 1885 *Musammat Khem Jaur v. Asa Singh*, vol. 4, 51. *The Mosque Known as Shahidganj v. SGPC* JCPC Case Papers.

54 They were unable to make much use of the laws relating to Sufi waqfs which tended to be framed as private trusts and so the story of the disciples of Hazrat Shah Kaku at Shahidganj will remain in the shadows until such a time that more historical evidence emerges. Judgment of the Sikh Gurdwara Tribunal January 20, 1930, vol. 4, 121. *The Mosque Known as Shahidganj v. SGPC* JCPC Case Papers.
55 I will give attention to shared uses of mosque sites once again in Chapter 5, offering deeper reflection on the nature of religious cohabitation and the disentangling of these interests in sacred spaces, but here the story returns to administrative processes under which enabled the mismanagement and adverse possession of endowment land.
56 Translation of a copy of a registered will, November 1, 1879 vol. 4, 41–3. *The Mosque Known as Shahidganj v. SGPC* JCPC Case Papers.
57 Mohammad Sultan Contractor was a well-known land developer in early colonial Lahore. William Glover tells us that he bought an historic Mughal Serai near the railway station and dismantled it for parts. William Glover, "Making Lahore Modern: Urban Form and Social Practice in Colonial Punjab, 1849-1920," PhD Dissertation U. C. Berkeley, 1999, 48.
58 Judgment of the Sikh Gurdwara Tribunal, January 20, 1930, relating to petitions 1317 and 1318 of Nasir Ali and two others, vol. 4, 82–124. *The Mosque Known as Shahidganj v. SGPC* JCPC Case Papers.
59 Statement of Asa Singh Defendant in case of *Musammat Khem Kaur v Asa Singh* in vol. 4, 51. *The Mosque Known as Shahidganj v. SGPC* JCPC Case Papers.
60 Order of the Sikh Gurdwara Tribunal, January 20, 1930 relating to petition 1275 of Balkishen in vol. 4, 117. *The Mosque Known as Shahidganj v. SGPC* JCPC Case Papers.
61 Order of the Sikh Gurdwara Tribunal, January 20, 1930, relating to petition 1277 of Kishen Chand Darianwala, vol. 4, 117–18.
62 Gian Singh's father had mortgaged one shop from Karam "90 years earlier," in the 1870s. In 1897 he bought the additional shops from Nikka Singh and Jita Singh, knocked them down and built another building in their place. Evidence of Sardar Gian Singh April 6, 1936, vol. 1, 79–80. *The Mosque Known as Shahidganj v. SGPC* JCPC Case Papers.
63 Ganda Singh willed this property to Attar Singh. Will Executed by Ganda Singh, November 1, 1879, vol. 4, 4–42. *The Mosque Known as Shahidganj v. SGPC* JCPC Case Papers.
64 Prasad, *The Punjab Land Revenue Act of 1887*, 42–3.
65 SDA NWP 38 [1850], quoted in William Hay MacNaughten, *Principles and Precedents of Moohummudan Law* (Madras: Higginbotham and Co., 1897), 483.
66 *Syud Muhammad Moosa v. The Collector of Delhi* [1853] SDA NWP 8 679.
67 *Allahoudee Khan v. Dhurmraj* [1850] SDA 5 NWP 38-39.
68 *Nilmoni Singh v. Jaganbandhu Roy* [1896] ILR 23 Cal 536.
69 *Chidambaram Chetti v. Minammal* [1898] ILR 23 Mad 439.

70 *Subbaramayar v. Nigamadullah Sahib* [1895] ILR 18 Mad 342.
71 Peter Robb, "The Case of Gau Mata: British Policy and Religious Change in India, 1880-1916," *Modern Asian Studies*, 20, no. 2 (1986): 285–319.
72 The Bombay district rules for survey were supplemented by a chapter on city survey in the 1914 edition, describing the development of such challenges. *The Bombay Settlement and Survey Manual* (Bombay: Government Central Press, 1914), 237–9.
73 See Jyoti Hosagrahar on the Delhi nazul land survey of 1908–10, which was undertaken to regularize categories of land use and ownership, Hosagrahar, *Indigenous Modernities*, 137–9.
74 Patrick Geddes, *Patrick Geddes: Spokesman for Man and Environment* (New Brunswick: Rutgers University Press, 1972), 390.
75 Extract from a Part of the Khasra Measurement Papers for 1907–1908, vol. 3, 10–15. *Shahidganj v. SGPC* JCPC Case Papers.
76 Evidence of Maulana Ghulam Murshid, March 24, 1936, vol. 3, 38–40. *The Mosque Known as Shahidganj v. SGPC* JCPC Case Papers.
77 Extract from the quadrennial Jambandi papers relating to Mauza Madu Khalil for the years 1933–34 P.W.8/B. pp. 38–9 in *The Mosque Known as Shahidganj v. SGPC* JCPC Case Papers.
78 Extract from Patwari's Khewat Papers Town of Bijnor Mahal Sufed 1931–32, vol. 3, 37. *Shahidganj v. SGPC* JCPC Case Papers.
79 Appendix VIII: Amendments in *The Berar Land Records and Survey Manual*, vol. 2 (Nagpur: Government Printing, 1932), 166. The amendments introduced a column for "ante-alienation tenant," "tenant of antiquity" or "other tenant" and provided a sample entry for a temple entered "Shri Devi temple, Asole, through managers . . ." in the "name of tenant column."
80 Qari Abdul Sattar khadim of the mosque narrated its history in 2013. He grew up in the neighborhood, had studied at the mosque, had been affiliated with the mosque for forty to fifty years at the time of my visit.
81 "Budget Amadni Masjid Shaheed," Anjuman Islamia, *Budget Babat Saal 1943-1944* (Lahore: Haji Ghulam Nabi, 1944), 11.
82 Alternately *nuzzool, nazool, nuzzul*, meaning "descent; property which falls to the state from default of heirs, an escheat." H. H. Wilson, *A Glossary of Judicial and Revenue Term and of Useful Words Occurring in Official Documents of British India* (London: W. H. Allen, 1855), 381.
83 *Orders of the Government United Provinces of Agra and Oudh* (Allahabad: Government Press, 1902), 87.
84 Oldenburg, *The Making of Colonial Lucknow*, 77–8.
85 The administration at Delhi, while tasked with revenue management functions, had to acknowledge the civic functions of nazul lands in the presence of a still incumbent Mughal emperor. The Assistant at the Delhi Residency, the primary office of the East India Company in Delhi, reported in 1822 that: "an attempt was made by a near female relative of the Queen's to sell the shops which had been built under one of the great mosques. I had to eject the purchaser, and it is most strange that the King actually

sanctioned the sale." H. Middleton to George Swinton, December 5, 1822 on Nazul, Taiul Waqf Lands at Delhi Punjab Archives, Records of the Delhi Residency File 66.
86   Ibid.
87   Ahmed, *Monuments, Memory, Contestation*, 69–80.
88   *Mahommedan Society of Delhi on the Occasion of the Imperial Assemblage at Delhi*, IOR/MSS/EUR/ C643.
89   Ibid.
90   Whitehead, "Appendix 1," *Report on the Administration of Delhi Crown Lands*.
91   Sagat Singh, *Freedom Movement in Delhi* (New Delhi: Association Publishing House, 1972), 11–12; Oswald Wood and R. Maconachie, *Final Report on the Settlement of the Revenues of the Delhi District* (Lahore: Victoria Press, 1882), 277. The Fatehpuri mosque was purchased back for Rs 117,833.
92   Gardezi, *Badshahi Masjid*, 15. See also Nabi Khan, *Development of Mosque Architecture in Pakistan*, 129.
93   Listed in the annual reports of the Anjuman-i Islamia Lahore including *Anjuman-i islamia Lahore Punjab Ka Shish Mahi Risalah October-December 1925* (Lahore: Cooperative Printing Press, 1926).
94   Gilmartin, "The Shahidganj Mosque Incident," 157–9. Khan, "The Martyrdom of Mosques" and *On Muslim Becoming*.
95   *Qanun-i Masajid*, paragraphs 68–76.
96   Raza, *Al Tahrir*, 2.
97   Court of Directors to the Governor General in Council at Fort William in Bengal, April 26, 1820. IOR F/4/1306/51857.
98   "Statement of Number and Designation of Buildings as Borne upon by the Chief Engineer's Eeport 1846," Sindh Archives, Revenue Department Records file 3636.
99   Robinson, *Separatism among Indian Muslims*, 213–15.
100 Maulana Abul Kalam Azad made reference to the Ka'aba as "Khuda ka ghar" and used his argument relating to the Ka'aba to claim Muslim rights in mosques. *Khutbat-i Siyasiyya aur Masajid-i Islamia* (Meerut: Mushtaq Ahmad, 1921), 23. Kannhyalal reported that the 'ulama of the late Mughal period had opposed the governor's urban planning efforts relating to a mosque and issued a fatwa saying "the land (*zameen*) underlying the masjid is God's country (*mulk*)." Kannhyalal, *Tarikh-i Lahore*, 149.
101 Sayyid Amir Ali, *Tagore Law Lectures, 1884: The Law Relating to Gifts, Trusts, and Testamentary Depositions among Mahommedans* (Calcutta: Tacker Spink and Co., 1885), 427.
102 Masjid at Buriya Punjab Archives, Ambala Agency Records, Book 79/37-138.
103 G. R. Clerk to William Fraser, May 1835, 4, ibid.
104 These mosques had their counterparts in three temples built by the Hindus of the Maharajah's army in the same area. Demolition of Mosques and

Temples by the Bharatpur Darbar IOR R/1/1/1570, seen in the collection held at the National Documentation Center Islamabad.
105 "The World Has Not Yet Forgotten the Machhli Bazaar Tragedy at Cawnpore," *The Albarid of Cawnpore*, May 18, 1924, ibid.
106 K. B. Wali Mahomed Hassanalli General Secretary Sind Mahomedan Association Karachi, to the Assistant Commissioner Sind, October 17, 1926. Sindh Archives 1160/General Series, File 570C.
107 Maulana Zafiruddin Purah Nodaihavi, *Islam Ka Nizam-i Masajid* (Lahore: Nadwatul Musannifin, 1961).
108 Ibid., 183.
109 Mufti Muhammad Shafi, *Islam Ka Nizam-i Arazi* (Karachi: Matba-yi Darul Ulum, 1979), 160–5.
110 Muhammad Iqbal, *Masjid-i Qurtaba* c. 1932 tr. Francis Pritchett, http://www.columbia.edu/itc/mealac/pritchett/00urdu/iqbal/masjid_index.html#index.
111 Ashiq Husain Batalvi, *Iqbal Kay Akhri Do Saal* (Karachi: Iqbal Academy, 1961), 584–5.
112 Ibid., 586–7.
113 Ibid., 596–7.
114 Ibid., 598.
115 Newal Osman takes a close look at the tensions between the new Unionist members and the Muslim League and the old guard which included Iqbal, Ghulam Rasool, and Barkat Ali, which foregrounded Barkat Ali's preparation of the Muslim Mosque Protection Bill. He does not attend to the nature of "the law" under which the "site had been declared a Sikh property," and incorrectly dates this to 1935 and interprets it as being enabled by the Sikh Gurdwara Act. Newal Osman, "Dancing with the Enemy," in *Muslims Against the Muslim League*, ed. Ali Usman Qasimi and Megan Eaton Robb (Cambridge: Cambridge University Press, 2017), 316–17.
116 Judgment of the Lords of the Judicial Committee of the Privy Council on the Appeal of *The Mosque known as Masjid Shahid Ganj, and Others v Shiromani Gurdwara Parbandhak Committee, Amritsar and Another*. The Judicial Committee of the Privy Council Decisions, [1940] UKPC 1940 21.
117 While I do not detail this story here, a long and important effort by Sikhs to claim rights in their endowments led to the constitution of the Tribunal and provided the context for its award. See in particular Murphy, *The Materiality of the Past*; Tan Tai Yong, *Garrison State: Military, Government and Society in Colonial Punjab, 1849-1947* (New Delhi; Sage, 2005). Also see my commentary on the nature of Sikh custodianship of the site in Haroon, "Custodianship of Shahidganj in Colonial Lahore."
118 Naveeda Khan also argues that the significance of the representation of the mosque as a plaintiff was to call to mind the travesty of its martyrdom and that this line of legal reasoning became more powerful in later years in Pakistan. Naveeda Khan, "The Martyrdom of Mosques: Imagery and

Iconoclasm in Modern Pakistan," in *Enchantments of Modernity*, ed. Saurabh Dube (New Delhi: Routledge, 2009), 372–401.
119 Case on Behalf of the Appellants, Case for Appellants p. 2 in *The Mosque Known as Shahidganj v. SGPC* JCPC Case Papers.
120 Birla, *Stages of Capital*, 80–2.
121 Naveeda Khan draws attention to the significance of the precedent in Hindu law relating to temples for the Shahidganj case with a view to highlighting the discursive consequences for recalling image to mind. "The Martyrdom of Mosques," 393–5.
122 J. M. Pringle Case on Behalf of Appellants, 16. *The Mosque Known as Shahidganj v. SGPC* JCPC Case Papers.
123 JCPC Judgment, [1940] UKPC 1940, 21.
124 Pringle Case on Behalf of Appellants, 16.
125 Observations of the Chief Justice of the Lahore High Court, in Pringle Case on Behalf of the Appellants, 13.
126 Pringle, Case on behalf of the Appellants, 18.
127 Kannhyalal, *Tarikh-i Lahore*, 284–5; Nur Ahmad Chishti, *Tahqiqat-i Chishti* (1884), 104–5, quoted in Haji Rahim Bakhsh, *Masjid Shahidganj, Masjid Shah Chiragh aur Mazar-i Hazrat Shah Kaku* (Lahore: Muhammad Abdul Jameel Qureshi, 1935), 42–4.
128 Announcement in the *Civil and Military Gazette*, reproduced in *Anjuman-i Islamia Lahore Punjab Ka Risalah 1934-1935* (Lahore: Cooperative Printing Press, 1935), 2–4.
129 The recognition of communal claims to sites through the elevation of myth to the status of historical evidence was termed "the political abuse of history," in Sarvepalli Gopal, Romila Thapar, Bipan Chandra and others, "The Political Abuse of History: Babri Masjid-Rama Janmabhumi Dispute," *Social Scientist*, 18, no. 1/2 (1990): 76–81. See Van der Veer on the contestation of history in the Babri Mosque case in Peter Van der Veer, "Ayodhya and Somnath: Eternal Shrines, Contested Histories," *Social Research*, 59, no. 1 (1992): 91, 94. More recently Tanweer Fazal has turned her attention to the principle of the juristic personhood of a building and its implications in the Babri Mosque matter in postcolonial India. Fazal, "The Mosque as Juristic Person," 199–211.
130 Sheriff Kaunain and Purva Vishwanath, "Issues in Ayodhya Title Suit," *Indian Express*, November 6, 2019. http://hdl.handle.net/123456789/425.
131 Khan, *On Muslim Becoming*, 21–54 esp. the story of Masjid Noor, 30–2.

Chapter 5

1 "Pukhta" or pucca rights were full management rights recognized by the local tauqadars, free of demands of shikar, nazrana, forced labor, fine, as well as revenue collection. See Sanad Granted to Khuda Baksh Exhibit CC, *In the Privy Council, On Appeal from the High Court of Judicature at Allahabad,*

between *Syed Mazhar Hussain and others Appellants and Rao Bahadur Adiya Saran Singh Respondents*, 150 in JCPC Appeal No. 59 of 1944, decided July 24, 1947. Privy Council Cases with Judgments, BL PP 1316 [hereafter *Mazhar Hussain v. Adiya Singh* JCPC Case Papers].

2 Almas Khan was notorious among Europeans for his calculated leases of indigo land in the annexed Oudh state. Eric Stokes, *The Peasant and the Raj* (Cambridge: Cambridge University Press, 1978), 66, 68.

3 Report of the Committee on Waqf Property n.d. Exhibit 38 p. 349–51 in *Mazhar Hussain v. Adiya Singh* JCPC Case Papers.

4 Judgment of the Lords of the Judicial Committee of the Privy Council on the Appeal of Saiyed Mazhar Husain and Others v. Rao Bahadur Adiya Saran Singh. The Judicial Committee of the Privy Council Decisions [1947] UKPC 61, 2.

5 Plaint Mirza Mohammed Ali Khan v Iqbal Bahadur, November 10, 1873 and Plaint Kulsum Begum and another v. Iqbal Bahadur and another, February 3, 1875, Part 2, 196–8, 207–12. *Mazhar Hussain v. Adiya Singh* JCPC Case Papers.

6 Judgment of the Sadar Diwani Adalat, Agra 1861, Part 2, 187. *Mazhar Hussain v. Adiya Singh* JCPC Case Papers.

7 Judgment of the Subordinate Judge Cawnpore, July 31, 1875, Part 2, 272–3. *Mazhar Hussain v. Adiya Singh* JCPC Case Papers.

8 Revenue Agreement by Iqbal Lal Bahadur, October 16, 1875, Part 2, 232. *Mazhar Hussain v. Adiya Singh* JCPC Case Papers.

9 Sanad conferring title of Rao on Iqbal Bahadur, November 15, 1858, Part 2, 176. *Mazhar Hussain v. Adiya Singh* JCPC Case Papers.

10 Written statement of Adya Singh, April 29, 1930, Part 2, 332–6. *Mazhar Hussain v. Adiya Singh* JCPC Case Papers.

11 Wajibul Arz of Mauza Jafarpur for 1875–1876, Part 2, 246. *Mazhar Hussain v. Adiya Singh* JCPC Case Papers.

12 Ashiq Hussain and Hasan Askari were named as managers of the imambargah and the mosque by Mewa Lal, in his capacity as custodian, in an unrelated case of sectarian violence in 1895. See Deposition of Mewa Lal, August 25, 1895, Part 2, 306. *Mazhar Hussain v. Adiya Singh* JCPC Case Papers.

13 Chart of Miscellaneous Payments Made to Baqals and Others Moharram 1303 Hijri to Moharam 1304 Hijri (1885–1887), Part 2, 286. *Mazhar Hussain v. Adiya Singh* JCPC Case Papers.

14 There was a considerably larger population of Shi'as in the neighboring town, but no evidence was presented in the case which demonstrated that any of them regularly attended worship at the imambargah of Haider Baksh.

15 Judgment of District Judge of Cawnpore D. C. Hunter, October 4, 1934, Part 1, 101. *Mazhar Hussain v. Adiya Singh* JCPC Case Papers.

16 Evidence of Munna Lal age 70 occupation shop of clothes, August 2, 1934, Part 1, 65–6. *Mazhar Hussain v. Adiya Singh* JCPC Case Papers.

17 Evidence of Lachman Prasad age 65 occupation Sonar, August 2, 1934, Part 1, 68–9. *Mazhar Hussain v. Adiya Singh* JCPC Case Papers.

18 Evidence of Farzand Ali age 81 occupation taluqadari, August 1, 1933. Part 1, 23–5. *Mazhar Hussain v. Adiya Singh* JCPC Case Papers.
19 See especially Teena Purohit, *The Aga Khan Case*, 1–1, and Amy Caitlin-Jairazbhoy, "Sacred Songs of Khoja Muslims: Sounded and Embodied Litugy and Devotion," *Ethnomusicology*, 48, no. 2 (2004): 251–70.
20 Robert Hayden, "Antagonistic Tolerance: Competitive Sharing of Religious Sites in South Asia and the Balkans," *Current Anthropology*, 43, no. 2 (2002): 209–10.
21 Masahiko Togawa, "Syncretism Revisited," *Numen*, 55, no. 1 (2008): 27–43.
22 Section 539 of the 1882 code of Civil Procedure, later incorporated as section 92 of the Civil Procedure Code of 1908 governing Public Charities.
23 Judgment of the Subordinate Judge Cawnpore in Suit No. 94 of 1889 delivered, August 22, 1889, Part 2, 304. *Mazhar Hussain v. Adiya Singh* JCPC Case Papers.
24 Ibid.
25 Barbara Metcalf calls attention to Nasrat Hussain's work in the courts as an "a telling comment to describe the pervasive adversarial legal culture produced by land policies in British India" in her important and brief biographical comments on Nasrat Husain, *Hussain Ahmad Madani: The Jihad for Islam and India's Freedom* (London: Oneworld Publications, 2009), 25, 30, 35.
26 Maulvi Nasrat Husain "owned a comfortable little estate in Fatehpur District," Robinson, *Separatism Among Indian Muslims*, 264.
27 Letter Legal Remembrancer to Government U. P. to Maulvi Nasrat Husain and Another, July 10, 1911, Part 2, 321. *Mazhar Hussain v. Adiya Singh* JCPC Case Papers.
28 Dasturdehi of Mauza Charli 1911–12, Part 2, 322. *Mazhar Hussain v. Adiya Singh* JCPC Case Papers.
29 Rubkar of Collector of Fatehpur, March 11, 1911, Part 1, 317. *Mazhar Hussain v. Adiya Singh* JCPC Case Papers.
30 Letter Collector to Legal Remembrancer, August 10, 1923, Part 2, 330. *Mazhar Hussain v. Adiya Singh* JCPC Case Papers.
31 While this term has often been used to indicate the formation of religious identity in opposition to or in a desire to achieve parity with other religious groups, I do not engage this meaning in my argument. It is only the implied unanimity of the communal formation which is of interest here.
32 Application of Rao Iqbal Bahadur, March 27, 1911, Part 2, 319–20. *Mazhar Hussain v. Adiya Singh* JCPC Case Papers.
33 See particularly Francis Robinson's arguments linking Muslim culture to politics in *Muslim Separatism*.
34 See particularly Ayesha Jalal's arguments pertaining to the development of a Muslim communitarian identity over the period of legislative change and creation of representative government in India. Ayesha Jalal, *The Sole Spokesman* (Cambridge: Cambridge University Press, 2004).
35 Later substituted by the office of the legal remembrancer. *Administration of the North-Western Provinces and Oudh, April 1882-November 1887* (Allahabad: Government Press, 1887), 104.

36 Muhammad Aslam Saifi, "Resolution re. the Application of the Mussalman Waqf Act 1923, to the United Provinces," February 27, 1924. *Proceedings of the Legislative Council of the United Provinces,* vol. 17 (Allahabad: Superintendent Press United Provinces, 1924), 102.
37 Purohit, *The Aga Khan Case,* 35–7.
38 Murphy, *The Materiality of the Past,* 214–17.
39 Saifi, "Resolution re. the Application of the Mussalman Waqf Act," 337.
40 Anne Murphy, "Defining the Religious and the Political," *Sikh Formations: Religion, Culture, Theory,* 9, no. 1 (2013): 51–62; Murphy, *The Materiality of the Past,* 214–17.
41 Malavika Kasturi, "'All Gifting Is Sacred': The Sanatana Dharma Sabha Movement, the Reform of *Dana* and Civil Society in Late Colonial India," *IESHR,* 47, no. 1 (2010): 107–39.
42 The Government of India issued a press communique before the 1914 Religious Endowments Conference stating that the major policy question was whether the government of India should change its policy of noninterference. Birla, *Stages of Capital,* 132.
43 Statement presented by H. S. Crosthwaite in the United Provinces Legislative Assembly, October 24, 1923, in *Proceedings of the Legislative Council of the United Provinces,* vol. 15 (Allahabad: Superintendent Press United Provinces, 1923), 7–9.
44 *Report of the Muslim Public and Charitable Waqfs Committee United Provinces* (Allahabad: Superintendent Printing, 1933), 12.
45 *Proceedings of the Legislative Council of the United Provinces,* vol. 19 *September 5–11, 1924* (Allahabad: Superintendent Press United Provinces, 1924), 337.
46 *Report of the Muslim Public and Charitable Waqfs Committee,* 12.
47 Hafiz Hidayat Husain, Resolution, *Proceedings of the Legislative Council of the United Provinces,* vol. 17, 114.
48 Zubair Abbasi, "Colonial State and Muslim Institutions," in *Charities in the Non-Western World,* ed. Rajeswary Brown and Justin Pierce (New York: Routledge, 2013), 326.
49 Masud uz Zaman Khan, "Resolution re. the Application of the Musalman Waqf Act, 1923 Feb 26, 1924," in *United Provinces Legislative Council Proceedings,* vol. 17, *Feb 26–March 15 1924* (Allahabad: Superintendent Press United Provinces, 1924), 118.
50 Ibid., 111–13.
51 The Benghal Legislative Council also adopted this legislation and went much further than the United Provinces in putting regulatory frameworks in place. See Abbasi's interesting discussion of the debates surrounding this bill, "Muslim Institutions," 324–7.
52 Question posed by Shafa'at Ahmad Khan, February 23, 1926 (first raised December 25, 1925) *Proceedings of the Legislative Council of the United Provinces* vol. 27, *Jan 19–Feb 25 1926* (Allahabad: Superintendent Press United Provinces, 1926), 367–70.

53 Question posed by Shafa'at Ahmad Khan on Muslim waqfs, their accounts and *mutawallis* on February 25, 1926, and answered by Rai Rajeshwar Bali. Ibid., 496–7.
54 Hon'ble Lt Nawab Muhammad Ahmad Sa'id Khan, December 22, 1925, in *Proceedings of the Legislative Council of the United Provinces* vol. 26 *Dec 14–23*, 603–4.
55 United Provinces Muslim Waqf Act 1936, Bengal Waqf Act, 1924, 1934; Bihar and Orissa Mussalman Waqf Amendment Act, 1926; Musalman Waqf (Bombay Amendment Act, 1935). For an interesting discussion of the debates surrounding this bill. See Abbasi, "Muslim Institutions," 324–7.
56 Masud uz Zaman "Resolution re. the application of the Musalman Waqf Act 1923, 26 Feb 1924," 120.
57 See particularly Nawab Muhammad Yusuf's arguments on the subject on the resolution tabled by Shafa'at Ahmad Khan on the application of the Mussalman Waqf Act of 1923, September 9, 1924. A small but vocal group came together to dispute the wording of the act which could be seen to apply to private waqfs as well as public ones. Facing a lack of consensus in favor of the waqf act, although the vast majority supported its passage, the president of the legislative council constituted a select committee of UP council members who held "expert views on the subject" of waqfs. *Proceedings of the Legislative Council of the United Provinces*, vol. 19, *Sept 5–11, 1924* (Allahabad: Superintendent Press United Provinces, 1924), 327–41.
58 Hafiz Hidayat Husain on "Resolution re. Musalman Waqfs, 19 December 1924," in *United Provinces Legislative Council Proceedings*, vol. 20, *1924* (Allahabad: Superintendent Press United Provinces, 1924), 433–8.
59 This was one of the clauses in Abdul Qasim's bill prepared for the Imperial Legislative Council but was not approved by the Imperial Legislative Council.
60 Two years after his first introduction of the resolution, with few applications under the Waqf Act, Hidayat Husain brought a more detailed proposal before the Legislative Assembly, Hidayat Husain, "Resolution re. Muslim Public and Charitable Waqfs June 29, 1927," *Proceedings of the Legislative Council of the United Provinces* vol. 34 *June 20–30, 1927* (Allahabad: Superintendent Press United Provinces, 1927), 707–17, esp. 710–11.
61 Clause 48 of the Hidayat Muslim Waqf Bill tabled December 3, 1936, *Proceedings of the Legislative Council of the United Provinces* vol. 73 *3–10 November and 1–4 December 1936* (Allahabad: Superintendent Press United Provinces, 1937), 595–6.
62 Clauses 5–7 of the Hidayat Muslim Waqf Bill tabled December 2, 1936: Membership of the Sunni Central Board: five elected in manner prescribed by Sunni members of the local legislature, five by district waqf committees, three coopted by the above nine members who are 'ulama. Membership of the Shi'a Central Board: five elected by Shi'a members of local legislature, one by executive committee of AISC, one by Board of Trustees of Shi'a College Lucknow, three 'ulama cooped by the above. *Proceedings of the Legislative*

Council of the United Provinces vol. 73 *3–10 November and 1–4 December 1936* (Allahabad: Superintendent Press United Provinces, 1937), 546–7, 555–9, 557.

63 Clause 4 of the Hidayat Muslim Waqf Bill tabled December 2, 1936, *Proceedings of the Legislative Council of the United Provinces*, vol. 73, 540–6.

64 In Bombay, a large number of powerful Dawoodi Bohras strongly opposed the passage of the legislation altogether as Bohra community life and religious practice were centered in properties classed as waqfs under the management of custodians who operated under the moral and spiritual authority of a leader. They saw both the 1923 waqf act and the notion of the constitution of a central waqf board to undermine the systems of authority which were central to their practice. Sh. T. Lokhandwalla, "The Bohra: A Muslim Community of Gujarat," *Studia Islamica*, 3 (1955): 117–35.

65 Jamal Malik, "Waqf in Pakistan," 64.

66 Peter Miller proposes an approach to governmentality which approaches governance as activities in which socially legitimated authorities interfere in the lives of individuals in sites as diverse as the school, the home, the workplace, the courtroom and the dole queue. Peter Miller and Nikolas Rose, *Governing the Present: Administering Economic, Social and Personal Life* (Cambridge: Polity Press, 2008), 1–2.

67 I take the term "rationalities of government" from work on Foucault's theories of governance, primary that of Peter Miller cited earlier, but with attention to conceptualization of rationalities of state in work on colonial South Asia, particularly that of Julia Stephen, *Governing Islam*, in which she argues that the rationalism of the modern secular state was posited in stark contrast to the irrational nature of religion. See also Sturman, *The Government of Social Life in Colonial India*; Sturman suggests that that the governance of social life was explicitly conceptualized as rational, but more importantly demonstrates the ways in which it was not, through the preservation of hereditary and non-secular power relations.

68 The Loharu state and the title of the Nawab had been created after the conclusion of the Maratha wars, under the auspices of the colonial state. Ziauddin was one of three Indians, along with Sir Syed Ahmed Khan, who was a member of the Archaeological Society of Delhi. Sayyid Ahmed Khan was writing the second draft of his architectural survey, *Asar-us Sanadid* at the time that the meetings of the Delhi society took place. Christian Troll, "A Note on the Early Topographical Work of Sayyid Ahmad Khan," 135–46.

69 See Kozlowki's treatment of this case in *Muslim Endowments and Society in British India*, 133, 174. The Board of Revenue at Hooghly had received and heard a petition that the hereditary *mutawallis* of an *imambargah* at Hooghly were unfit for the position and in 1836 they appointed a man of "high character for integrity, information and intelligence" who was "eminently calculated to fill such a post" in their place. The case was revived in court several times, forcing detailed articulation of the rights and limitations of the government in intervention in matters of *waqf* management. Also see Bengal

Board of Revenue, *Papers Regarding the Hooghly Imambargah 1815-1910* (Calcutta: Bengal Secretariat Book Depot, 1914), 29–35, 250, 369. https://hdl.handle.net/2027/mdp.39015084500282.

70 Letter of Brereton, Deputy Commissioner Lahore to Clarke, Chief Commissioner and Superintendent Lahore Division, May 24, 1856, reproduced in Talha Jalal, *Memoirs of the Badshahi Mosque* (Karachi: Oxford University Press, 2013), 124–5.

71 Clarke as Officiating Commander and Superintendent Lahore Division to Temple, Secretary to the Chief Commissioner Punjab, June 13, 1856, in Jalal, *Memoirs*, 101.

72 This committee was similar to the Sikh SGPC but had a very different relationship to community, an argument which I first presented in Sana Haroon, "Land, Land Use and the Formation of Religious Community at the Lahore Shahidganj 1850-1940," *IESHR*, 54, no. 2 (2017): 1–38.

73 Letter of Brereton, Deputy Commissioner Lahore to Clarke, Chief Commissioner and Superintendent Lahore Division, May 24, 1856, reproduced in Jalal, *Memoirs of the Badshahi Mosque*, 124–5.

74 Gilmartin, "The Shahidganj Mosque Incident," 157.

75 "Anjuman aur us kay maqasid," addendum to Anjuman-i Islamia, *Anjuman-i Islamia Lahore Punjab Ka Sah Mahi Risalah October-December 1925* (Lahore: Cooperative Printing Press, 1927). Also included in all reports after 1935.

76 Ibid.

77 Ibid., 45–6. For more on the Anjuman-i Islamia and its Sikh counterparts in early twentieth century Lahore, see Haroon, "Custodianship of Shahidganj."

78 Justin Jones, "Shi'a Muslims of the United Provinces of India c. 1890-1940," PhD Dissertation, University of Cambridge, 2007, 47–9.

79 Ibid., 57.

80 Ibid., 47–9.

81 Deposition of Nasir Ali, Girdawar of Waqf Section of the AISC, August 4, 1933, Part 1, 38. *Mazhar Hussain v. Adiya Singh* JCPC Case Papers.

82 Birla, *Stages of Capital*, 128–38.

83 Anne Murphy, *The Materiality of the Past*, 214–17; Yong, *Garrison State*, 200–13.

84 Hafiz Hidayat Husain, "Resolution Re. Public and Charitable Waqfs," June 28, 1927 in *Proceedings of the Legislative Council of the United Provinces 1927* vol. 17, 707–11.

85 Evidence of Hafiz Hidayat Husain, July 31, 1934, Part 1, 55 in *Mazhar Hussain v. Adiya Singh* JCPC Case Papers.

86 The report contained two descriptions of the mosque, possibly owing to poor editing of a multi-authored work. Report of Committee on Waqf Property, Kora Jahanabad, n.d., Part 2, 349 in *Mazhar Hussain v. Adiya Singh* JCPC Case Papers.

87 See Ayesha Jalal on this history of anjumans providing social services and calling general Muslim attention to matters such as the Turkish Caliphate, educational preferences, and "a range of issues, some purely religious,

others political and economic, a few utterly fatuous and ephemeral to bring individuals in line with community," *Self and Sovereignty: Individual and Community in South Asian Islam Since 1850* (New York: Routledge, 2000), 209, 248. See Robert Ivermee's consideration of the resonance of the ideals of the Anjuman-i Punjab and Anjuman-i Islam Lahore with the interests of a variety of "Muslim parties" in "Shari'at and Muslim Community in Colonial Punjab, 1865-1885," *Modern Asian Studies*, 48, no. 4 (2014): 1058–95. Nandini Gooptu attends to the inspirational value of mosque protection movements led by anjumans in the early twentieth century in *Politics of the Urban Poor*, 270–6, 295. A recent study which proposes that the work of Anjumans also served elite and more restricted interests is Maria Magdalena Fuchs' dissertation "Islamic Modernism in Colonial Punjab: The Anjuman-i Himayat-i Islam, 1884-1923," PhD Dissertation, Princeton University, 2019.

88 Deposition of Kalbe Abbas July 31, 1933, Part 1, 18. *Mazhar Hussain v. Adiya Singh* JCPC Case Papers.

89 Letter from J. R. W. Bennett Legal Remembrancer Government of the U.P. to Syed Kalbe Abbas, Syed Mazhar Husain, Yusuf Ali Naqvi, April 5, 1932, Part 2, 340. *Mazhar Hussain v. Adiya Singh* JCPC Case Papers.

90 There is much more to be said on this subject. This was partly an outcrop of communal efforts to appoint friendly magistrates and other local government officers across the region, discussed in Chapter 3. Government, politicians, and communal organizations worked together in ways that reassured Muslims in the important essay by Anil Seal and Ayesha Jalal, "Alternative to Partition: Muslim Politics Between the Wars," *Modern Asian Studies*, 15, no. 3 (1981): 415–54. More recently we are reminded to think about the early period of the introduction of dyarchy as a meeting of the imperial rationalities of government and a nationalist ideal of friendly and good government, "the subtle and indescribable attributes of democratic art" in Stephen Legg, "Dyarchy: Democracy, Autocracy, and the Scalar Sovereignty of Interwar India," *Comparative Studies of South Asia, Africa and the Middle East*, 36, no. 1 (2016): 44–65.

91 Evidence of S. Mazhar Husain July 30, 1934, Part 2, 206–8. *Mazhar Hussain v. Adiya Singh* JCPC Case Papers.

92 Evidence of Yusuf Ali, July 31, 1933, Part 2, 20–2. *Mazhar Hussain v. Adiya Singh* JCPC Case Papers.

93 JCPC Judgment [1947] UKPC 61, 2: 7. © The British Library Board PP 1316.

94 Hunter District Judge, Judgment 1934, Part 1, 88. *Mazhar Hussain v. Adiya Singh* JCPC Case Papers.

95 Judgment of Hunter District Judge 1934, upheld in JCPC Judgment [1947] UKPC 61, 2: 6–11.

96 JCPC Judgment [1947] UKPC 61, 2.

97 On the construction of adversarial Sunni and Shi'a political identities and ritual practices, see Justin Jones, *Shi'a Islam in Colonial India*, 147–85; 186–220. There are numerous choices for exploring the course of the development

of Hindu and Muslim difference, too many to list here. A useful starting point, particularly for exploring the "ritual communication of identity" is Peter Van der Veer, *Religious Nationalism* (Berkeley: University of California Press, 1994), 78–106.

Afterword

1 This body of work is too large to account here, and I myself have relied on the surveys and assessments of the contributions of associations in the work of the following scholars in addition to specific books and articles referenced in various sections of this book. Ayesha Jalal, *Self and Sovereignty* (New York: Routledge, 2001); David Gilmartin, *Empire and Islam* (Berkeley: UC Press, 1988); Humeira Iqtidar, *Secularizing Islam* (Chicago: University of Chicago Press, 2011); Muhammad Qasim Zaman, *The 'Ulama in Contemporary Islam* (Princeton: Princeton University Press, 2010); M. Raisur Rehman, *Locale Everyday Islam and Modernity* (Delhi: Oxford University Press, 2015); Ali Usman Qasimi, *Questioning the Authority of the Past* (Karachi: Oxford University Press, 2012); For more on the popular revivalist movement of the Ahl-i Sunnat Wal Jamaat under the leadership of Ahmad Riza Barelwi, see Usha Sanyal, *Devotional Islam and Politics in British India: Ahmed Riza Khan Barelwi and His Movement 1870-1920* (New York: Oxford University Press, 1999). Barbara Metcalf, *Islamic Revival in British India*; Van der Veer, *Religious Nationalisms*; Gooptu, *Politics of the Urban Poor*.
2 Ali Riaz, *Faithful Education: Madrassas in South Asia* (New Brunswick: Rutgers University Press, 2008). See the important corrective to assumptions about the consequence of mosque schools in postcolonial South Asia in Tahir Andrabi, Jushnu Das, Asim Khawaja, and Tristan Zajonc, *Religious School Enrollment in Pakistan: A Look at the Data* (Washington D.C.: World Bank, 2013), 27.
3 Sunil Kumar, *Demolishing Myths or Mosques and Temples?* (Gurgaon: The Three Essays Collective, 2008). Kumar considers mosque and temple conflict to be inspired by popular historical discourse in contemporary India and considers the implications of competing claims to layered sites which contain remains of temples under the more recently built mosques.
4 Faisal Devji, "Red Mosque," in *Under the Drones: Modern Lives in Afghanistan-Pakistan*, ed. Robert Crews and Shahzad Bashir (Cambridge: Harvard University Press, 2012), 153–61.
5 See the history of waqf regulation in Andhra, composed by the officer of welfare schemes: Khwaja Mohammad Moinuddin, *Andhra Pardesh Vaqf Bord: Chand Haqaiq* (Andhra Pradesh: Waqf Board, 1967); Umber Bin Ibad's excellent study includes extensive commentary on the regulation and marginalization of 'folk Islam' at Sufi shrines under the West Pakistan Waqf Properties Ordinance of 1959. See Umber Bin Ibad, *Sufi Shrines and*

the Pakistani State: The End of Religious Pluralism (New York: Bloomsbury Academic, 2019).
6 Khan, *On Muslim Becoming: Aspiration and Skepticism in Pakistan.*
7 Sufia Uddin, *Constructing Bangladesh: Religion, Ethnicity, and Language in an Islamic Nation* (Charlotte: University of North Carolina Press, 2006).

Bibliography

Secondary Sources

Abbasi, Zubair. "Colonial State and Muslim Institutions." In *Charities in the Non-Western World*, edited by Rajeswary Brown and Justin Pierce, 311–32. New York: Routledge, 2013.
Adcock, Cassie. *The Limits of Secularism*. New York: Oxford University Press, 2013.
Ahmad, Aziz. *Islamic Modernism in India and Pakistan 1857–1964*. London: Oxford University Press, 1967.
Ahmad, Imtiaz. "The Mughal Governors of Bihar and Their Public Works." *Proceedings of the Indian History Congress*, 59 (1988): 383–92.
Ahmad, Mohiuddin. *Saiyid Ahmad Shahid: His Life and Mission*. Lucknow: Academy of Islamic Research and Publications, 1980.
Ahmed, Hilal. *Muslim Political Discourse in Postcolonial India: Monuments, Memory, Contestation*. London: Routledge, 2015.
Ahmed, Qeyamuddin. *The Wahhabi Movement in India*. Calcutta, 1966.
Alvi, Sajida. "Religion and State during the Reign of Mughal Emperor Jahāngīr (1605–27): Nonjuristical Perspectives." *Studia Islamica*, 69 (1989): 95–119.
Anderson, Michael. "Islamic Law and the Colonial Encounter in British India." In *Institutions and Ideologies: A SOAS South Asia Reader*, edited by David Arnold and Peter Robb. London: Routledge, 1993.
Ansari, Humayun. "Maulana Barkatullah Bhopali's Transnationalism: Pan-Islamism, Colonialism, and Radical Politics." In *Transnational Islam in Interwar Europe*, edited by Götz Nordbruch, Umar Ryad, 181–209. London: Palgrave Macmillan, 2014.
Appadurai, Arjun. "Kings, Sects and Temples in South India 1350–1700 AD." *Indian Economic and Social History Review*, 14, no. 1 (1977): 47–73.
Arnold, David. "On the Road: A Social Iteration of India." *Contemporary South Asia*, 22, no. 1 (2015): 8–20.
Arnold, David. "The Police and Colonial Control in South India." *Social Scientist*, 4, no. 12 (1976): 3–16.
Arnold, David. "The Problem of Traffic." *Modern Asian Studies*, 46, no. 1 (2012): 119–41.
Asani, Ali. "From Satpanthi to Ismaili Muslim: The Articulation of Ismaili Khoja Identity in South Asia." In *A Modern History of the Ismailis*, edited by Farhad Daftari, 95–117. London: I.B. Tauris, 2011.
Asher, Catherine. "Mapping Hindu-Muslim Identities through the Architecture of Shahjahanabad and Jaipur." In *Beyond Turk and Hindu: Rethinking Religious*

Identities in Islamicate South Asia, edited by David Gilmartin and Bruce Lawrence, 121–49. Gainesville: University Press of Florida, 2000.

Bayly, C. A. "A Pre-History of Communalism? Religious Conflict in India 1700–1860." *Modern Asian Studies*, 19, no. 2 (1985): 177–203.

Beverley, Eric Lewis. "Property, Authority, and Personal Law: Waqf in Colonial South Asia." *South Asia Research*, 31 (2011): 155–82.

Blake, Stephen. *Shahjahanabad: The Sovereign City in Mughal India 1639–1739*. Cambridge: Cambridge University Press, 1991.

Caitlin-Jairazbhoy, Amy. "Sacred Songs of Khoja Muslims: Sounded and Embodied Liturgy and Devotion." *Ethnomusicology*, 48, no. 2 (2004): 251–70.

Chan, Aye. "Development of a Muslim Enclave in Arakan State of Burma." *SOAS Bulletin of Burmese Studies*, 3, no. 2 (2005): 396–420.

Chatterjee, Nandini. *The Making of Indian Secularism: Empire, Law and Christianity*. London: Palgrave Macmillan, 2011.

Chaudhary, Latika. "Determinants of Primary Schooling in British India." *The Journal of Economic History*, 69, no. 1 (2009): 269–302.

Chaudhry, Faisal. "Rethinking the Nineteenth-Century Domestication of the Shari'a: Marriage and Family in the Imaginary of Classical Legal Thought and the Genealogy of (Muslim) Personal Law in Late Colonial India." *Law and History Review*, 35, no. 4 (2017): 841–79.

Devji, Faisal. "Apologetic Modernity." *Modern Intellectual History*, 4, no. 1 (2001): 67–76.

Devji, Faisal. "The Red Mosque." In *Under the Drones: Modern Lives in Afghanistan-Pakistan* Borderland, edited by Shahzad Bashir and Robert Crews, 153–61. Cambridge: Harvard University Press, 2012.

Dewey, C. J. "The Education of a Ruling Caste: The Indian Civil Service in the Era of Competitive Examination." *The English Historical Review*, 88, no. 347 (1973): 262–85.

Dirks, Nicholas. "The Policing of Tradition: Colonialism and Anthropology in South India." *Comparative Studies in History and Society*, 39, no. 1 (1997): 182–212.

Eaton, Richard. *The Rise of Islam and the Bengal Frontier 1204–1760*. Berkeley: UC Press, 1996.

Edney, Matthew. *Mapping an Empire*. Chicago and London: University of Chicago Press, 1997.

Eickelman, Dale. and Armando Salvatore. "The Public Sphere and Muslim Identities." *European Journal of Sociology*, 43, no. 1 (2002): 92–115.

Fazal, Tanveer. "The Mosque as Juristic Person: Law, Public Order and Inter-Religious Disputes in India." *South Asian History and Culture*, 10, no. 2 (2019): 199–211.

Freitag, Sandria. "Ambiguous Public Arenas and Coherent Personal Practice: Kanpur Muslims 1913–1931." In *Shari'at and Ambiguity in South Asian Islam*, edited by Katherine Ewing, 143–64. Berkeley: University of California Press, 1990.

Freitag, Sandria. *Collective Action and Community: Public Arenas and the Emergence of Communalism in North India*. Berkeley: University of California Press, 1989.

Freitag, Sandria. *Culture and Power in Banaras: Community, Performance and Environment*. Berkeley: University of California Press, 1992.

Freitag, Sandria. "Exploring Aspects of the Public." *South Asia: Journal of South Asian Studies*, 38, no. 3 (2015): 512–23.

Fuchs, Maria Magdalena. "Islamic Modernism in Colonial Punjab: The Anjuman-i Himayat-i Islam, 1884–1923." PhD Diss., Princeton University, 2019.

Geddes, Patrick. *Patrick Geddes: Spokesman for Man and Environment*. New Brunswick: Rutgers University Press, 1972.

Gilmartin, David. *Empire and Islam*. Berkeley: UC Press, 1988.

Gilmartin, David. "The Shahidganj Mosque Incident: A Prelude to Pakistan." In *Islam, Politics and Social Movements*, edited by Edmund Burke and Ira Lapidus, 146–68. Berkeley: UC Press, 1988.

Giunchi, Eliza. "The Reinvention of Shari'a Under the British Raj: In Search of Authenticity and Certainty." *The Journal of Asian Studies*, 59, no. 4 (2010): 1119–42.

Glover, William. *Making Lahore Modern*. Minnesota: University of Minnesota Press, 2008.

Gooptu, Nandini. *The Politics of the Urban Poor in Early Twentieth Century India*. Cambridge: Cambridge University Press, 2001.

Gould, William. *Religion and Conflict in Modern South Asia*. Cambridge: Cambridge University Press, 2012.

Grabar, Oleg. "Cities and Citizens: The Growth and Culture of Urban Islam," *Islamic Art and Beyond: Constructing the Study of Islamic Art*, vol. 3, 155–74. Burlington: Ashgate Publishing, 2006.

Green, Nile. *Bombay Islam: The Religious Economy of the Western Indian Ocean 1840–1915*. Cambridge: Cambridge University Press, 2011.

Green, Nile. *Terrains of Exchange: Religious Economies of Global Islam*. New York: Oxford University Press, 2015.

Guenther, Alan M. "Hanafi *fiqh* in Mughal India: The *Fatawa-i Alamgiriyya*." In *India's Islamic Traditions 711-1750*, edited by Richard Eaton, 209–29. Oxford: Oxford University Press, 2003.

Guha-Thakurta, Tapati. *Monuments, Objects, Histories: Institutions of Art in Colonial and Postcolonial India*. New York: Columbia University Press, 2004.

Haque, Ziaul. "Muslim Religious Education in India and Pakistan." *Islamic Studies*, 14, no. 4 (1975): 271–92.

Haroon, Sana. "Contextualizing the Deobandi Approach to Congregation and Management of Mosques in Colonial North India." *Journal of Islamic Studies*, 28, no. 1 (2017): 68–93.

Haroon, Sana. "Land, Land Use and the Formation of Religious Community at the Lahore Shahidganj 1850–1940." *Indian Economic and Social History Review*, 54, no. 2 (2017): 1–38.

Hay, Douglas. "Legislation, Magistrates and Judges: High Law and Low Law in England and the Empire." In *The British and their Laws in the Eighteenth Century*, edited by David Lemmings, 59–80. London: Boydell Press, 2005.

Hayden, Robert. "Antagonistic Tolerance: Competitive Sharing of Religious Sites in South Asia and the Balkans." *Current Anthropology*, 43, no. 2 (2002): 205–51.

Haynes, Douglas. "From Tribute to Philanthropy: The Politics of Gift Giving in a Western Indian City." *The Journal of Asian Studies*, 46, no. 2 (1987): 339–60.

Haynes, Douglas. *Rhetoric and Ritual in Colonial India: The Shaping of a Public Culture in Surat City*. Berkeley: University of California Press, 1991.

Hays, Douglas and Paul Craven. *Masters, Servants, and Magistrates in Britain and the Empire, 1562–1955*. Chapel Hill: UNC Press, 2004.

Hosagrahar, Jyoti. "Mansions to Margins." *Journal of the Society of Architectural Historians*, 60, no. 1 (2001): 26–45.

Ibad, Umber Bin. *Sufi Shrines and the Pakistani State: The End of Religious Pluralism*. New York: Bloomsbury Academic, 2019.

Ingram, Brannon. *Revival from Below*. Berkeley: University of California Press, 2018.

Iqtidar, Humeira. *Secularizing Islamists: Jama'at-e-Islami and Jama'at-ud-Da'awa in Urban Pakistan*. Chicago: University of Chicago Press, 2011.

Irvine, William. "A History of the Bangash Nawabs of Farrukhabad, 1713–1857." *Journal of the Royal Asiatic Society*, 18, no. 1 (1879): 49–170.

Ivermee, Robert. *Secularism, Islam and Education in India 1830–1910*. London: Routledge, 2015.

Jalal, Ayesha. "Alternative to Partition: Muslim Politics Between the Wars." *Modern Asian Studies*, 15, no. 3 (1981): 415–54.

Jalal, Ayesha. *Self and Sovereignty: Individual and Community in South Asian Islam Since 1850*. New York: Routledge, 2000.

Jalal, Ayesha. *The Sole Spokesman*. Cambridge: Cambridge University Press, 2004.

Jalal, Talha. *Memoirs of the Badshahi Mosque*. Karachi: Oxford University Press, 2013.

Jones, Justin. "Shi'a Muslims of the United Provinces of India c. 1890–1940." PhD Diss., University of Cambridge, 2007.

Jones, Justin. *Shi'a Islam in Colonial India*. Cambridge: Cambridge University Press, 2011.

Jones, Justin. "Urban Mythologies and Urbane Islam: Refining the Past and Present in Colonial-Era Lucknow." *South Asia Multidisciplinary Academic Journal*, 11 (2015): 1–19.

Jones, Reece. "Sacred Cows and Thumping Drums: Claiming Territory as Zones of Tradition in British India." *Royal Geographical Society*, 39, no. 1 (2007): 55–65.

Jones, Rodney. *Urban Politics in India*. Berkeley: University of California Press, 1974.

Kaicker, Abishek. "Unquiet City." PhD Diss., Columbia University, New York, 2014.

Kasturi, Malavika. "'All Gifting Is Sacred': The Sanatana Dharma Sabha Movement, the Reform of *Dana* and Civil Society in Late Colonial India." *Indian Economic and Social History Review*, 47, no. 1 (2010): 107–39.

Kasturi, Malavika. "'Asceticising' Monastic Families: Ascetic Genealogies, Property Feuds and Anglo-Hindu Law in Late Colonial India." *Modern Asian Studies*, 43, no. 5 (2009): 1039–83.

Kaunain, Sheriff and Purva Vishwanath. "Issues in Ayodhya Title Suit." *Indian Express*, 6 November 2019.

Keshani, Hussein. "Architecture and the Twelver Shi'i Tradition: The Great Imambara Complex of Lucknow." *Muqarnas*, 23 (2006): 219–50.

Khalfoui, Mouez. "Together but Separate: How Muslim Scholars Conceived of Religious Plurality in South Asia in the Seventeenth Century." *Bulletin of the School of Oriental and African Studies*, 74, no. 1 (2011): 87–96.

Khan, Ahmed Nabi. *Development of Mosque Architecture in Pakistan*. Islamabad: Lok Virsa, 1991.

Khan, Naveeda. "The Martyrdom of Mosques: Imagery and Iconoclasm in Modern Pakistan." In *Enchantments of Modernity*, edited by Saurabh Dube, 372–401. New Delhi: Routledge, 2009.

Khan, Naveeda. *On Muslim Becoming; Aspiration and Skepticism in Pakistan*. Durham: Duke University Press, 2012.

Khan, Shaharyar. *The Begums of Bhopal*. New Delhi: Viva Books, 2004.

Kishore, Raghav. "Urban 'Failures': Municipal Governance, Planning and Power in Colonial Delhi, 1863–1910." *Indian Economic and Social History Review*, 52, no. 4 (2015): 439–61.

Kolsky, Elizabeth. *Colonial Justice in British India*. Cambridge: Cambridge University Press, 2011.

Kozlowski, Gregory. "Community Building and Communal Control of Muslim Endowments (waqfs) in Modern South Asia." *Revue Du Monde Musalman et de la Méditerranée*, 79–80 (1996): 201–14.

Kozlowksi, Gregory. "Imperial Authority, Benefactions and Endowments in India." *Journal of the Economic and Social History of the Orient*, 38, no. 3 (1995): 355–70.

Kozlowski, Gregory. *Muslim Endowments and Society in British India*. Cambridge: Cambridge University Press, 1985.

Kugle, Scott. "Framed, Blamed, Renamed: The Recasting of Islamic Jurisprudence in Colonial South Asia." *Modern Asian Studies*, 35, no. 2 (2001): 257–313.

Kumar, Sunil. *Demolishing Myths or Mosques and Temples?* Gurgaon: The Three Essays Collective, 2008.

Latif, Syad Muhammad. *Lahore: Its History, Architectural Remains and Antiquities*. Lahore: New Imperial Press, 1892.

Legg, Stephen. "Dyarchy: Democracy, Autocracy, and the Scalar Sovereignty of Interwar India." *Comparative Studies of South Asia, Africa and the Middle East*, 36, no. 1 (2016): 44–65.

Legg, Stephen. "Governing Prostitution in Colonial Delhi: From Cantonment Regulations to International Hygiene (1864–1939)." *Social History*, 34, no. 4 (2009): 447–67.

Lelyveld, David. *Aligarh's First Generation: Muslim Solidarity in British India*. Princeton: Princeton University Press, 1978.
Lokhandwalla, Sh. T. "The Bohra: A Muslim Community of Gujarat." *Studia Islamica*, 3 (1955): 117–35.
Macpherson, K. "Chulias and Klings: Indigenous Trade Diasporas and European Penetration of the Indian Ocean Littoral." In *Trade and Politics in the Indian Ocean: Historical and Contemporary Perspectives*, edited by Giorgio Borsa, 33–46. New Delhi: Manohar Publications, 1990.
Malik, S. Jamal. "Waqf in Pakistan." *Die Welt des Islams*, New Series, Bd. 30,1/4 (1990): 63–97.
Markovits, Claude. *The Global World of Indian Merchants*. Cambridge: Cambridge University Press, 2000.
McChesney, R. D. "Earning a Living: Promoting Islamic Culture in the Sixteenth and Seventeenth Centuries." In *Afghanistan's Islam from Conversion to the Taliban*, edited by Nile Green, 89–104. Los Angeles: University of California Press, 2017.
Mehta, S. P. *Cawnpore Civic Problems: A Critical and Historical Review of City Government in Cawnpore*. Kanpur: Citizen Press, 1952.
Metcalf, Barbara. *Hussain Ahmad Madani: The Jihad for Islam and India's Freedom*. London: Oneworld Publications, 2009.
Metcalf, Barbara. *Islamic Revival in British India: Deoband 1860–1900*. Princeton: Princeton University Press, 1982.
Metcalf, Barbara. "The Madrasa at Deoband: A Model for Religious Education in Modern India." *Modern Asian Studies*, 12, no. 1 (1978): 111–34.
Metcalf, Thomas. *Imperial Connections: India in the Indian Ocean Arena*. Berkeley: UC Press, 2007.
Mian, Ali Altaf. "Mental Disability in Medieval Hanafi legalism." *Islamic Studies*, 51, no. 3 (2012): 247–62.
Miller, Peter and Nikolas Rose. *Governing the Present: Administering Economic, Social and Personal Life*. Cambridge: Polity Press, 2008.
Murphy, Anne. "Defining the Religious and the Political." *Sikh Formations: Religion, Culture, Theory*, 9, no. 1 (2013): 51–62.
Murphy, Anne. *The Materiality of the Past: History and Representation in the Sikh Tradition*. Oxford: Oxford University Press, 2013.
Muslim, Abdul Ghafur. "The Theory of Interest in Islamic Law and the Effects of Interpretation of This by the Hanafi School Up to the End of the Mughal Empire." PhD Diss., University of Glasgow, 1974.
Naim, C. M. "Syed Ahmad and His Two Books Called 'Asar-al-Sanadid'." *Modern Asian Studies*, 45, no. 3 (2011): 669–708.
New, Than Than. "Yangon: The Emergence of a New Spatial Order in Myanmar's Capital City." *Soujourn: Journal of Social Sciences in South East Asia*, 13, no. 1 (1998): 86–113.
Nizami, K. A. *Sayyid Ahmad Khan*. New Delhi: Ministry of Information and Broadcasting, 1974.

O'Connor, V. C. Scott. *The Silken East: A Record of Life and Travels in Burma*, vol. 1. London: Hutchinson and Co., 1904.
Oldenburg, Veena. *The Making of Colonial Lucknow: 1856–1877*. Princeton: Princeton University Press, 1984.
Osman, Newal. "Dancing with the Enemy." In *Muslims Against the Muslim League*, edited by Ali Usman Qasimi and Megan Eaton Robb, 311–37. Cambridge: Cambridge University Press, 2017.
Pearson, Harlan O. *Islamic Reform and Revival in Nineteenth-Century India: The Tariqah-i Muhammadiyah*. New Delhi, 2007.
Powers, David. "Orientalism, Colonialism and Legal History: The Attack on Family Endowments in Algeria and India." *Comparative Studies in Society and History*, 31, no. 1 (1989): 557.
Prasad, Vijay. "The Technology of Sanitation in Colonial Delhi." *Modern Asian Studies*, 35, no. 1 (2001): 113–55.
Purohit, Teena. *The Aga Khan Case*. Cambridge: Harvard University Press, 2012.
Qasimi, Ali Usma. *Questioning the Authority of the Past*. Karachi: Oxford University Press, 2012.
Qureshi, Naeem. *Pan-Islam in British Indian Politics: A Study of the Khilafat Movement 1918–1924*. London: Brill, 1999.
Rahman, M. Raisur. *Locale, Everyday Islam, Modernity: Qasbah Towns and Muslim Life in Colonial India*. Delhi: Oxford University Press, 2015.
Riaz, Ali. *Faithful Education: Madrassas in South Asia*. New Brunswick: Rutgers University Press, 2008.
Richards, John F., James R. Hagen, and Edward S. Haynes. "Changing Land Use in Bihar, Punjab and Haryana, 1850–1970." *Modern Asian Studies*, 19, no. 3 (1984): 699–732.
Riexinger, Martin. "Ibn Taymiyya's Worldview and the Challenge of Modernity: A Conflict among the Ahl-i Hadith in British India." In *Islamic Theology, Philosophy and Law: Debating Ibn Taymiyya and Ibn Qayyim al-Jawziyya*, edited by Birgit Kraizetz and Georges Tamer, 497–9. Berlin and Boston: Walter de Gruyter, 2013.
Robinson, Francis. "Technology and Religious Change: Islam and the Impact of Print in South Asia." *Modern Asian Studies*, 27, no. 1 (1993): 229–51.
Roy, Tirthankar. "Out of Tradition: Master Artisans and Economic Change in Colonial India." *Journal of Asian Studies*, 66, no. 4 (2007): 963–91.
Salafi, Muhammad Fazal-ur Rehman. *Maulana Abdul Aziz Rahimabadi: Hayat-o Khidmat*. Mumbai: Farooq Brothers, 2001.
Sanyal, Usha. *Devotional Islam and Politics in British India: Ahmed Riza Khan Barelwi and his Movement 1870–1920*. New York: Oxford University Press, 1999.
Schimmel, Anne Marie. *The Empire of the Great Mughals: History, Art Culture*, translated by Corinne Atwood. London: Reaktion Books, 2004.
Scott, J. Barton and Brannon Ingram. "What Is a Public? Notes from South Asia." *Journal of South Asian Studies*, 38, no. 3 (2015): 357–70.

Seekins, Donald M. *State and Society in Modern Rangoon*. London: Routledge, 2011.

Sengupta, Parna. *Pedagogy for Religion: Missionary Education and the Fashioning of Hindus and Muslims in Bengal*. Berkeley: UC Press, 2011.

Shah, Alison Mackenzie. "Constructing a Capital on the Edge of Empire: Urban Patronage and Politics in the Nizams' Hyderabad, 1750–1950." PhD Diss, University of Pennsylvania, 2005.

Shah, Maulana Akbar, Mohd Abbas Abdul Razak and Mohammed Farid Ali Al Fijawi. "Transformation of Myanmar Muslim Community: Singapore as a Role-Model." *Journal of Muslim Minority Affairs*, 39, no. 4 (2019): 493–512.

Shamsi, Abulkalam Qasmi. *Tazkirah 'ulama Bihar*. Sitamarhi: Shu'ba Nashar-o-Isha'at, 1995.

Sharan, Awadhendra. "Delhi's Belly." *The Indian Economic and Social History Review*, 48, no. 3 (2011): 425–62.

Sharma, Shalini. *Radical Politics in Colonial Punjab: Governance and Sedition*. New York: Routledge, 2010.

Shorto, Sylvia. "A Tomb of One's Own." In *Colonial Modernities: Buildings, Dwelling, Architecture in British India*, edited by Peter Scriver and Vikramaditya Prakash, 151–68. New York: Routledge, 2007.

Singh, Sagat. *Freedom Movement in Delhi*. New Delhi: Association Publishing House, 1972.

Singha, Radhika. *A Despotism of Law: Crime and Justice in Early Colonial India*. Oxford: Oxford University Press, 1998.

Singha, Randhika. "Punished by Surveillance: Policing Dangerousness in Colonial India." *Modern Asian Studies*, 49, no. 2 (2015): 241–69.

Sivaramakrishnan, K. "Environment, Law and Democracy in Colonial India." *The Journal of Asian Studies*, 70, no. 4 (2011): 905–28.

Smith, Richard Saumarez. "Rule-by-Records and Rule-by-Reports: Complementary Aspects of British Imperial Rule of Law." *Contributions to Indian Sociology*, 19, no. 1 (1985): 153–76.

Spate, O. H. K and L. W. Trueblood. "Rangoon: A Study in Urban Geography." *Geographical Review*, 32, no. 1 (1942): 56–73.

Srivastava, S. "Separation of Judiciary from Executive in India with Particular Reference to the State of Uttar Pradesh." *The Indian Journal of Political Science*, 25, no. 3–4 (1964): 339–46.

Stark, Ulrike. "An Indian Success Story: The House of Naval Kishore." In *The History of the Book in South Asia*, edited by Francesca Orsini, 164–224. New York: Routledge, 2016.

Stephens, Julia. *Governing Islam: Law, Empire and Secularism in India*. Cambridge: Cambridge University Press, 2018.

Sturman, Rachel. *The Government of Social Life in Colonial India: Liberalism, Religious Law and Women's Rights*. Cambridge: Cambridge University Press, 2012.

Subrahmanyam, Sanjay. "A Note of the Rise of Surat in the Sixteenth Century." *Journal of the Economic and Social History of the Orient*, 43, no. 1 (2000): 23–33.

Togawa, Masahiko. "Syncretism Revisited." *Numen*, 55, no. 1 (2008): 27–43.
Travers, Robert. *Ideology and Empire in Colonial India*. Cambridge: Cambridge University Press, 2007.
Troll, Christian. "A Note on the Early Topographical Work of Sayyid Ahmad Khan." *Journal of the Royal Asiatic Society of Great Britain and Ireland*, 2 (1972): 135–46.
Uddin, Sufia. *Constructing Bangladesh: Religion, Ethnicity, and Language in an Islamic Nation*. Charlotte: University of North Carolina Press, 2006.
Vahed, Goolam. "'Unhappily Torn by Dissension and Litigation': Durban's 'Memon' Mosque, 1880–1930." *Journal of Religion in Africa* 36, no. 1 (2006): 23–49.
Van der Veer, Peter. "Ayodhya and Somnath: Eternal Shrines, Contested Histories." *Social Research*, 59, no. 1 (1992): 85–109.
Varshney, Ashuthosh. *Ethnic Conflict and Civic Life: Hindus and Muslims in India*. New Haven: Yale University Press, 2002.
Waheeduzzaman, Abu Muhammad. "Land Resumption in Bengal, 1819–1846." PhD Diss., University of London SOAS, 1969.
Webb, Alexander Russell. *Yankee Muslim: The Asian Travels of Mohammed Alexander Russell Webb*. Edited by Brent Singleton. Reprinted by Wildside Press, Cabin John MD, 2007.
Yang, Anand. "Sacred Symbol and Sacred Space in Rural India: Community Mobilization in the 'anti-Cow Killing' Riot of 1893." *Comparative Studies in Society and History*, 22, no. 4 (1980): 576–96.
Yegar, Moshe. *Muslims of Burma: A Study of a Minority Group*. Wiesbaden: University of Heidelberg, 1972.
Zaman, Faridah. "Colonizing the Sacred: Allahabad and the Company State, 1797–1857." *Journal of Asian Studies*, 74, no. 2 (2015): 347–67.
Zaman, Muhammad Qasim. *Modern Islamic Thought in a Radical Age: Religious Authority and Internal Criticism*. New York: Cambridge University Press, 2012.
Zaman, Muhammad Qasim. "Nation Nationalism and the 'ulama: Hadith in Religio-Political Debates in Twentieth Century India." *Oriente Moderno*, 21, no. 82 (2002): 93–113.
Zaman, Muhammad Qasim. *The 'ulama in Contemporary Islam: Custodians of Change*. Princeton: Princeton University Press, 2010.

Primary Sources

Urdu and Persian and other published and manuscript sources

Abdullah, Janab Maulana Maulvi Hafiz Muhammad. *Qanun-i Masjid*. Calcutta: Matbah Sitarah-yi Hind, 1917.
Ahmad, Rasheed. *Riport Mutaliq Ijlas Bist-o Som*. Aligarh: Matbu'a Hamdi, 1910.
al-Qadri, Mufti Sayyid Abdul Fatah al-Hussaini. "Tuhfa-yi Muhammadiyyah." Calcutta, 1849. Karachi National Museum Archive N. 93.

Ali, Sayyid Amir. *Tagore Law Lectures, 1884: The Law Relating to Gifts, Trusts, and Testamentary Depositions among Mahommedans*. Calcutta: Tacker Spink and Co., 1885.
Anjuman Islamia. *Anjuman-i Islamia Lahore Punjab Ka Risalah 1934-1935*. Lahore: Cooperative Printing Press, 1935.
Anjuman Islamia. *Budget Babat Saal 1943–1944*. Lahore: Haji Ghulam Nabi, 1944.
Anjuman Islamia. *Budget Sah Mahi Jun-Aug 1924 to Oct-Dec 1935*. Lahore: Matba Karimi, 1935.
Azad, Abul Kalam. *Khutbat-i Siyasiya aur Masajid-i Islamia*. Meerut: Munshi Mushtaq Ahmad, 1921.
Aziz, Arif. *Masajid-i Bhopal*. Bhopal: Iqra Publishing House, 2003.
Bakhsh, Haji Rahim. *Masjid Shahidganj, Masjid Shah Chiragh aur Mazar-i Hazrat Shah Kaku*. Lahore: Muhammad Abdul Jameel Qureshi, 1935.
Baksh, Mistri Muhammad. *Masjid*. 1915.
Barelvi, Sayyid Altaf. *Life of Hafiz Rahmat Khan*. Translated by Muhammad Hamiduddin Khan. Karachi: Academy of Educational Research,1966.
Batalvi, Ashiq Husain. *Iqbal Ke Akhri Do Saal*. Lahore, 1961.
Djinguiz M. "Notes et Documents : L'Islam dans l'Inde." *Revue Du Monde Musulman*, 6 (1907): 85–118.
Farrukhabadi, Wali Allah. *Ahd-i Bangash ki Siyafi Ilmi aur Siqafati Tarikh*. Translated by Ayub Qadri. Karachi: Academy of Educational Research, 1965.
Fatawa Alamgiriyah. Translated by Amir Ali. 2 vols. Lucknow: Nawal Kishore Press, n.d.
Gardezi, Syed. *Badshahi Masjid*. Lahore: Insaf Press, 1962.
Iqbal, Muhammad. *Masjid-i Qurtaba* c. 1932. Translated by Francis Pritchett. http://www.columbia.edu/itc/mealac/pritchett/00urdu/iqbal/masjid_index.html.
Kannhyalal, Rai Bahadur. *Tarikh-i Lahore*. Lahore: Katoriya Press, 1886.
Kannhyalal, Rai Bahadur. *Tarikh-i Lahore*. Reprinted. Lahore: Sang-i Meel, 2001.
Karim Allah Muhammad (?). Untitled Manuscript on Illuminating Mosques c. 1266/1849. IOL South Asian Manuscripts Collection, Delhi Persian 1151k.
Khan, Ahmad Raza and Abul Ala Muhammad Amjad Ali. *Masjid-i Kanpur Kay Mutaliq aik Nihayat Zaruri Fatwa*. Bareilly: Abdul Wudud, 1914.
Khan, Ahmad Raza and Abul Ala Muhammad Amjad Ali. *Masjid-i Kanpur Kay Mutaliq aik Nihayat Zaruri Fatwa*. Bareilly: Abdul Wudud, 1914.
Khan, Muhammad Abdullah. *Masail-i Thalathin*. Shahjahanabad: Matbuʻa Mustafa Muhammad Hussain Khan, 1270/1853.
Madrasa Mohammedia Randeria High School, Golden Jubilee Souvenir: 1906–1956. Rangoon, n.d.
Moinuddin, Khwaja Mohammad. *Andhra Pardesh Vaqf Bord: Chand Haqaiq*. Andhra Pradesh: Waqf Board, 1967.
Nodaihavi, Maulana Zafiruddin Purah. *Islam Ka Nizam-i Masajid*. Lahore: Nadwatul Musannifin, 1961.
Raza Khan Sahib, Maulvi Muhammad Ibrahim. *Al-Tahrir al-Jayyad fi Haq al-Masajid*. Bengal: Matbua Ahl-i Sunnat wʻal Jamaat Bareily Waqai Astanah Aliya Rizviyya, 1315/1897.

Revue Du Monde Musulman Publiée Par La Mission Scientifique Du Maroc, vol. 6. Paris: Ernest Leroux, 1908.
Salafi, Muhammad Fazal-ur Rehman. *Maulana Abdul Aziz Rahimabadi: Hayat-o Khidmat*. Mumbai: Farooq Brothers, 2001.
Shafi, Mufti Muhammad. *Islam Ka Nizam-i Arazi*. Karachi: Matba-yi Darul Ulum, 1979.
Surati (Kaflaytvi), Abdul Hai. *Musalmanan-i Burma aur Talim*. Delhi: M. Mohammed Ibrahim, 1918.
Surati Kaflaytvi, Abdul Hai. *As-Sabil al-Aqwam: Sharh-i Musallam az Subut-i Urdu*. Deoband: Imtiaz Ahmad, n.d.

Official Reports and Publications

Punjab including Delhi

Douie, James McCrone. *Punjab Land Administration Manual 1931*. Lahore: Superintendent Government Printing, 1931.
Edwardes, Herbert Benjamin. *A Year on the Punjab Frontier: 1848–49*, vol. 2. London: Richard Bentley, 1851.
General Report on the Administration of the Punjab for the Years 1849–1850 and 1850–51. London: Court of Directors for the East India Company, 1854.
General Report on the Administration of the Punjab Territories 1849–50 to 1852-3 and 1902–03. Calcutta: Calcutta Gazette, 1904.
Imperial Gazetteer of India Provincial Series: Punjab vol. 1 *The Province*. Calcutta: Superintendent Government Printing, 1908.
Maconachie, R. *Final Report on the Settlement of the Revenues of the Delhi District*. Lahore: Victoria Press, 1882.
Prasad, L. Beni. *The Punjab Land Revenue Act XVII of 1887*. Lahore: Artistic Printing Works, 1913.
Punjab Land Administration Manual. Lahore: Superintendent Government Printing, 1931.
Report on the Administration of Delhi Crown Lands. Delhi: Oxford Printing Works, 1933.
Report of the Department of Land Records and Agriculture Punjab. Lahore: Civil and Military Press, 1899.
Rules Under the Land Revenue and Tenancy Acts, 1887. Lahore: Mufid-i Am Press, 1899.
The Punjab Record, vol. 27. Lahore: Civil and Military Gazette Press, 1893.

Bengal and Bihar

Bengal Board of Revenue. *Papers Regarding the Hooghly Imambargah 1815-1910*. Calcutta: Bengal Secretariat Book Depot, 1914.

Final Report on the Survey and Settlement operations in Darbhanga 1896-1903. Calcutta: Bengal Secretariat Press, 1904.
The Bengal Code in Two Volumes, vol. 2. Calcutta: Superintendent Government Printing, 1890.
The Berar Land Records and Survey Manual, vol. 2. Nagpur: Government Printing, 1932.

Burma

Annual Report for the Burma Educational Syndicate for the Year 1911-1912. Rangoon: Office of the Superintendent Govt. Printing, 1912.
Burma Reforms Committee. *Burma Reforms Committee Report and Appendices.* Rangoon: Superintendent Government Printing, 1921.
Census of India 1901. vol. 12 Part 1 Burma Report. Rangoon: Superintendent Government Printing, 1902.
Fryer, G. E. *Handbook of British Burma.* Maulmain: T. Whitman, 1867.
Rangoon Gazette Weekly Budget
Report on Public Instruction in Burma for the Year 1907-1908 to 1921-22. Rangoon, Office of the Superintendent Government Printing, 1918.
Report on the Administration of Burma 1917-18. Rangoon: Superintendent Government Printing, 1917.

United Provinces and Awadh

General Report on the Settlement of the Bulandshahr District, North Western Provinces. Allahabad, 1877.
Guide to Muhammadan and Hindu Festivals and Fasts in the United Provinces. Allahabad: Government Press, 1924.
Hamilton, W. R. *The Indian Penal Code with Commentary.* Calcutta: Thacker, Spink and Co., 1895.
Nevill, H. R. *Bulandshahr: A Gazetteer: Vol. 5 of District Gazetteers of the United Provinces of Agra and Oudh.* Allahabad: Superintendent Govt. Press, 1903.
Orders of the Government United Provinces of Agra and Oudh. Allahabad: Government Press, 1902.
Proceedings of the Legislative Council of the United Provinces, 1923 to 1935. Allahabad: Government Press, 1936.
Report on the Administration of the North-Western Provinces and Oudh, 1882 to 1887. Allahabad: Government Press, 1887.
Report on the Administration of Police of the United Provinces for the Year Ended 1913 to 1914. Allahabad: Superintendent Government Printing, 1914-15.
Report on the Administration of the United Provinces of Agra and Oudh 1902-03 to 1916-17. Allahabad: Government Press, 1917.
Report of the Committee Appointed to Formulate a Scheme for the Separation of Judicial and Executive Functions in the United Provinces. Agra, 1947.

Report of the Muslim Public and Charitable Waqfs Committee United Provinces. Allahabad: Superintendent Printing, 1933.

Report of the Working of the Local and District Boards NWP and Oudh 1891 to 1902. Allahabad: Government Press 1902.

Stoker, T. *Final Report on the Settlement of Land Revenue in the Bulandshahr District.* Allahabad, 1891.

The Annual Administration Report of the Cawnpore Municipality 1920 to 1934. Kanpur, 1920–34.

The N. W. Provinces and Oudh Code. Calcutta: Superintendent Government Printing, 1892.

Others

A Glossary of Judicial and Revenue Terms. London: W. H. Allen, 1855.

Agnew, William Fischer. *The Law of Trusts in British India.* Calcutta: Thacker Spink and Co., 1882.

Baden-Powell, B. H. *A Manual of the Land Revenue Systems and Land Tenures of British India.* Calcutta: 1882.

Correspondence on the Subject of Education of the Muhammadan Community in British India and Their Employment in Public Service. Calcutta: Superintendent Government Printers, 1886.

Cotton, James Sutherland and Richard Burn. *Imperial Gazetteer of India* vol. 9. Oxford: 1908.

Gordon Sanderson and J. Begg. *Report on Modern Indian Architecture: Types of Modern Indian Buildings.* Allahabad, 1913.

Hunter, W. W. *Imperial Gazetteer of India*, vol. 8. London: Trubner and Co., 1881

Indian Education, A Monthly Record, vol. 4 *August 1905 to July 1906*. London: Longmans, Green & Co.

MacNaughten, William Hay. *Principles and Precedents of Moohummudan Law.* Madras: Higginbotham and Co., 1897.

Nathan, R. *Progress of Education in India: Quinquennial Review 1897-8 to 1901-02,* vol. 1. Calcutta: Government Press, 1904.

Map of the City of Delhi (Shahjahanabad), in which the Mussulmans' and the Hindus' ancient buildings have been shown; scale 12 inches per mile; copied from the map published by the Survey of India in 1873, Bashir ud-Din Ahmad Dihlavi, *Vaqi'at al-Hukumat-i Dehli*, vol. 2. Agra: Shams Machine Press, 1338/1919.

Hansard's Parliamentary Debates vol. 128 *13 June 1853-8 July 1853.* London: Cornelius Buck, 1853.

Rustomji, K. *The Law of Limitation and Adverse Possession.* Lahore: Empire Law Publishing, 1922.

The Bombay Settlement and Survey Manual, 237–9. Bombay: Government Central Press, 1914.

The Legislative Acts of 1880 of the Governor General in Council. Calcutta: Thacker Spink and Co., 1881.

Theobold, William. *Acts of the Governor General in Council from 1834 to the End of 1867*. Calcutta: Thacker, Spink and Co., 1868.

Archives and Collections Consulted

British Library General Reference Collection
Appeal Cases Heard before the Judicial Committee of the Privy Council
India Office Records and Library [IORL]
IOR/F Records of the Board of Commissioners for the Affairs of India
IOR/E East India Company General Correspondence
IOR/L/PJ/6 Public and Judicial Department
IOR/Q/13 Indian Statutory Commission
South Asia Manuscripts Collection
Punjab Archives
Ambala Agency Records
Records of the Delhi Residency
General Department
Cholia Mosque, Rangoon
Haathi Trust Digital Library
Madrassa Nurul Islam, 26 Street, Yangon
Mogul Shi'a Jama Masjid
National Documentation Center Islamabad
Punjab Public Library
Sunni Surati Jama Masjid Library Rangoon

INDEX

Page numbers in *italics* denote Figures.

Abbas, Kalbe 151
Abbasi, Zubair 208 n.51, 209 n.55
Abdali, Ahmad Shah 15
Abdul Aziz, Shah 32
Abdullah, Janab Maulana Maulvi Hafiz
    Muhammad 196 n.146
Abdul Sattar, Qari 123
Adcock, Cassie 4
adverse possession principle 201 n.55
    Lahore and 108, 120, 121, 129, 131,
        133
    significance of 200 n.42
Advocates' Association (Rangoon) 59
Agnew, William Fischer 170 n.109
Ahl-i Hadith 11, 67, 140, 171 n.7,
        173 n.50
    criticism of 34–5, 40–1
    devotion in 34
    1884 judgment on 43
    Hanafi 'ulama on 35
    JCPC on 28
    legal activism of 35–6, 39–40
    ritual choices of 33–4
    significance of 31, 33
    of Tajpur 38
Ahmad, Iqbal 150
Ahmad, Manan 171 n.8
Ahmad, Mohiuddin 173 n.45
Ahmad, Nur 114–16
Ahmad, Sayyid 33, 173 n.45
Ahmad Khan, Nawab 17
Ahmed, Hilal 9, 158
Ahmed, Qeyamuddin 171 n.7
Ahmedullah, Sheikh 38, 175 n.81
Ahmedullah of Bihar 33
Akalis 15, 142–3
Akhbar-i 'Ainah-yi Giti Numa
        (newspaper) 34

Al-Hilal (newspaper) 82
Ali, Barkat 204 n.115
Ali, Inayat 173 n.45
Ali, Mahomed 9
Ali, Omed 27, 28, 36–40, 45, 155,
        177 n.112
Ali, Syed Ameer 61, 69, 100, 125, 126
Ali, Wilayat 173 n.45
Ali, Yusuf 151, 152
alienation, of land 22
Allahabad 18, 125
Allah-hu Akbar, recitation of 30
All India Shi'a Conference (AISC) 141,
        143–4, 146, 149, 151–3
Al-Mazriqi 188 n.33
Altaf Al-Quds (Shah Wali
        Ullah) 185 n.100
amin (amen), significance of 35, 37
Amin, Nurul 44
Amritsar 150
Anderson, Michael 162 n.6, 172 n.39
Andrabi, Tahir 213 n.2
Anglo-Muhammadan law 3, 31, 37, 45,
        120, 132, 133, 162 n.6
Anjuman-i Islamia 123
Anjuman-i Islamia Lahore 148–9, 151,
        203 n.93
Anjuman-i Sadr-i Sadur 149
Anjuman-i Tamir-i Masajid 149
Ansari, Humayun 182 n.50
Appadurai, Arjun 198 nn.22–3
aqamat (congregation convening act)
        30
Ariff, Ismail 181 n.38
Arnold, David 188 n.32
Asaf ud Daula, Nawab 17, 136
Asani, Ali 163 n.13
Asar-al Sanadid (Khan) 73

Asher, Catherine 72–3
Askari, Hasan 138, 206 n.12
"Aspects of the Public" (Freitag) 8
Aurangabad mosque 71–2
    defense of perimeter of 97–104
        Muharram process conflict 99, 101–4
        1918 judgment 103
    judgment on 95
Aurangzeb (King) 29–30
authority 149
    discretionary 141–2
    of magistrates 86–94, 96, 105
awqaf 14
Azad, Abul Kalam 63
Azad, Maulana Abul Kalam 203 n.100
azan (act of calling the faithful to prayer) 30
    Safavid 102
Aziz, Arif 186 n.6

Badel-Powell, B. H. 192 nn.86–7
Badhshahi mosque (Lahore) 124, 148
Bahadur, Iqbal 140, 141
Bahadur, Lal 137, 138, 152
Bahar al-Raiq (Hanafi text) 35
Baksh, Haider 135, 137, 150, 152, 153
Baksh, Imam 117
bani. *See* benefactor (*bani*)
Bareilly 18
Bareilvi, Ahmad Raza 85, 156, 213 n.1
Barkat Ali, Malik 129, 130
Begum, Bannu 18
Begum, Bunnoo 167 n.76
Begum, Nawab Shah Jahan 73, 186 n.7
benefactor (*bani*) 3, 4, 7, 13, 14, 23, 24, 78, 114, 183 n.62
    Burma and 48, 49, 53, 54, 55, 56, 61, 62
Bengal 21
Bengal Legislative Council 208 n.51
Bengal System 183 n.67
Bhargava, Pandit Bhagwat Narayan 193 n.115
Bhopali, Sikander 33, 34
Bibi, Khatiza 178 n.11
Bihari, Qazi Muhibullah 185 n.100
Birla, Ritu 6, 41, 176 nn.95–6, 208 n.42

Blake, Stephen 187 n.16
Board of Revenue 111, 210 n.69
    land documentation of 114
    officers 3, 121
body politic 171 n.16
Bombay 21, 23, 185 n.96, 210 n.64
Boo, Hasan 49
Bose, Kali Coomar 176 n.102
Buchanan-Hamilton, Francis 168 n.84
Burma Reforms Committee 181 n.45

cadastral surveys, significance of 110
Calcutta Madrassa 31, 34
Chandra, Bipan 205 n.129
Charitable and Religious Trusts Act (1920) 143
Charitable Endowments Act (1890) 22
Chatterjee, Nandini 4, 169 nn.88, 93
Chaudhary, Latika 184 n.75
Chaudhry, Faisal 162 n.6
Chishti, Noor Ahmad 74–5
Chittagong 20
Cholia Muslim Association (Rangoon) 58
Cholias 57, 58, 180 n.33, 181 n.40
Chulia community 52
civic development, significance of 21
Civil Procedure Code section 92 (1908) 23, 151
colonial administration, significance of 87
colonial secularism 4, 41, 46, 156, 169 n.89, 176 n.103
colonial state's disavowal of responsibility, for religious institutions 19–21
"Community Building and Community Control of Muslim Endowments" (Kozlowski) 9
Comrade, The (newspaper) 82, 83
congregational prayer, leadership in
    colonial state disengagement with 40–5
    significance of 27–8
    state authorization, in Mughal India 28–31
        Tajpur mosque dispute and 36–40
    'ulama and Ahl-i Hadith and 31–6
Contractor, Muhammad Sultan 118, 201 n.57

Cordoba mosque   129
Cowasjee, B.   59, 181 n.44
Craven, Paul   192 n.91
cultural priorities, disputes of   92–4
custodians, of mosques   1–3, 11–15, 20, 22, 23, 77, 117, 121, 164 n.36, 210 n.69
  Hindu   135, 137, 141
  Kanpur mosque and   81, 85
  Mussalman Waqf Act on   143
  Rangoon Friday mosque and   47–54, 57, 61–8
  Shahidganj mosque and   113, 116
  Sikh   197 n.1
  Tajpur mosque and   28, 29, 36–9, 41, 42

Dadh Kando   90
Dadu, Yacoobji   91
Dars-i Nazami   32
darul ifta   67
Das, Bhagwan   91
Das, Jushnu   213 n.2
Dawood, Ahmed Moolla   60, 63, 68, 155, 182 n.58
Dawoodi Bohras   210 n.64
De, Rohit   5
Dehlavi, Shah Wali Ullah   32, 33, 185 n.100
Delhi   123–4, 187 n.12, 189 n.46, 202 n.85
Deobandis   67
Department of Land Records   111
deputy commissioners   110
Devi, Makhan   118
Devji, Faisal   182 n.53
devotionalism   11, 35, 130, 147, 154, 156
  magistrate's control over   86–94
  mosque perimeter control and   95, 97, 102, 103, 104, 105
Dewey, C. J.   192 n.83
Dihlavi, Bashir ud-Din Ahmad   74, 186 n.1
Dirks, Nicholas   193 n.108
district boards   21, 88, 97, 99, 100, 113, 122, 190 n.49
  reports of   195 n.135
  significance of   79–80
district commissioners   111, 114, 143

Dooply, Cassim Ajim   53
Dooply, E. H.   179 n.21
Dooply, Mohammed   181 n.44
dyarchy   212 n.90

East India Company   17–19, 21, 27
Edney, Matthew   166–7 n.68
education, in colonial India   184 n.75
Educational Syndicate of Burma   60
Eickleman, Dale   8
endowment   2, 20, 137, 156, 204 n.117. *See also* waqf
  adverse possession and   200 n.42, 201 n.55
  in Burma   48–50, 52–8, 63, 69
  Charitable   164 n.30
  custodians, authorizing repairs and renovations   164 n.36
  family   164 n.30, 164 n.37
  gift giving and   168 n.85
  history and   3, 6, 7, 9
  Kora Jahanabad and   136, 137, 139, 141–50, 154
  in Lahore   107, 108, 109, 111–14, 116–18, 120–4, 126, 128, 130, 132
  mosque perimeter control and   72, 74, 89, 100
  private act of religious and charitable benefit and   22–4
  reduction of   199 n.31
  state regulation and   12–14
  Tajpur mosque and   30, 37, 41

Falak Beg, Mirza   113
Farrukhabad   16
Fatawa Alamgiriyya (Hanafi fiqh)   29–30, 32, 35, 44, 171 nn.18–23, 185 n.100
Fatehpuri mosque (Delhi)   124, 203 n.91
fatwa   39, 44, 203 n.100
  Kanpur mosque and   82–5
Fazal, Tanweer   197 n.1, 205 n.129
Firangi Mahal (Lucknow)   32
Fleming (Rangoon deputy commissioner and magistrate)   91
Fox, Charles   60, 61
Freitag, Sandria   8, 9, 72, 156, 168 n.81

Friday mosque. *See also* Rangoon Friday mosque
   of Allahabad   18
   of Delhi, shoe seller's riot at   29
   imam of   29
   of Shahjahanabad   74
Fuzal Karim v. Haji Mowla Buksh   174 n.71, 175 nn.80–1

Gilmartin, David   124, 197 n.1, 213 n.1
Giunchi, Eliza   172 n.28
Glover, William   8, 189 n.43, 201 n.57
Gooptu, Nandini   212 n.87
Gopal, Sarvepalli   205 n.129
Government of India Act (1919)   95
Grabar, Oleg   187 n.16, 188 n.33
grants, for mosques   13
   land   18–19
Green, Nile   6, 58, 168 n.89
Guha-Thakurta, Tapati   189 n.37
Guru Granth Sahib   107

Hakim, Maulvi Abdul   144
Hamilton, W. R.   192 n.95
Hanafism   2, 28, 67, 125, 172 nn.35, 39. *See also individual entries*
   Fatawa Alamgiriyya and   29–30, 32
   on mosque   100
   Omed Ali on   37
Hasan, Mahmudul   140
Hashim, Moolla   21, 47, 49–51, 53, 55, 60, 61, 69
Hassan, Nurul   41, 44
Hastings, Warren   31
Hay, Douglas   191 n.79
Haykel, Bernard   171 n.8
Haynes, Douglas   8, 163 n.18, 168 n.85, 180 n.36
Hays, Douglas   192 n.91
Hazrat Shah Kaku shrine   113, 117
Hedaya (Hanafi text)   30
Hijri calendar (Islamic)   89
Hirschkind, Charles   173 n.50, 174 n.54
Hline, Shoay   167 n.78
Hobhouse, Arthur   45
Hosagrahar, Jyoti   186 n.2, 189 n.43, 202 n.73
Hujatullah al-Baligha   44

Hunter, W. W.   181 n.40
Husain, Hakim Nasrat   140, 141
Husain, Hidayat   145, 148, 150, 153, 209 n.60
   proposal to United Provinces   145–6
Husain, Maulvi Shah Waris   151
Husain, Murtaza   150
Husain, Saiyyid Mazhar   151
Husain, Shahid   83
Hussain, Ashiq   138, 206 n.12
Hussain, Maulana Saadat   172 n.33
Hussain, Maulvi Hakim Ahmad   34
Hussain, Nasrat   207 n.25
Hyde (Colonel)   125

Ibad, Umber Bin   213 n.5
imam   42, 171 n.23
   Ahl-i Hadith on   41
   Hanafi law on   30
   replacement of   29
   significance of   29
imambargahs   17, 99, 135, 136–8, 151, 152
Iman Wala, Nur Muhammad   15
Indian Income Tax Act (1886)   24
Indian Ratepayers' Association (Rangoon)   59, 181 n.44
Indian Trust Act (1882)   41–2, 116
Ingram, Brannon   8
Injunctions Relating to Mosques, The (Nodaihavi)   127
Iqbal, Allama Muhammad   129, 131
Iqtidar, Humeira   4, 162 n.9, 213 n.1
Ismail, M. Y.   179 n.21
Ismail, Muhammad   34
Ismail, Shah   33, 173 n.45
Ismail Ariff v. Ahmed Moolla Dawood   179 n.21, 180 n.34
Ismail Ariff v. Mahomed Ghouse   181 n.38
Ivermee, Robert   212 n.87

Jaffrelot, Christophe   171 n.8
Jahangir (Mughal)   29, 75–6
Jalal, Ayesha   207 n.34, 211 n.87, 212 n.90, 213 n.1
Jalalipura (Banaras)   36
Jinnah, Muhammad Ali   24, 130
Jones, Justin   102, 212 n.97
Jones, Reece   188 n.29

Jones, Rodney   189 n.43
Judicial Committees of the Privy Council
    (JCPC)   3, 10, 11, 46, 59, 61,
    69, 108, 129, 171 n.7, 196 n.161
  on Ahl-i Hadith prayer leader   28
  decisions of colonial judges and   4
  1891 judgment of   44, 177 n.111
  on Kora Jahanabad waqf   151
  1916 judgment of   11, 47, 61, 69
  1924 judgment of   72, 103–5
  on Shahidganj mosque   130–2
  significance of   5–6
  on waqfs   169–70 n.105
jurist   3–5, 24, 156, 157, 196 nn.146, 161
  English trust and   69
  Hanafi law and   100
  Kora Jahanabad and   135, 152–3
  Lahore and   125, 130–1
  South Asian Hanafi   172 n.35
  Tajpur mosque and   28, 29, 32, 33, 41, 43, 45

Kabir, Shah Muhammad   13
Kaflaytvi, Mohammad Abdul Hai   63–8, 157, 184 n.77, 185 nn.100–1
Kaicker, Abishek   29, 171 n.16
Kalan mosque (Delhi)   124
Kannhyalal, Rai Bahadur   75, 76, 166 n.49, 203 n.100
Kanpur mosque   71. See also magistrate
  perimeter of   78–86, 81
    dalan (washing area), fatwas, and 'ulama   81–5
karbalas   99
Karim, Fazal   38
Kasturi, Malavika   168 n.84
Katchchi Memon community   59–60
Kaur, Musammat Khem   118
Kazi Act (1880)   20
Keshani, Hussein   166 n.63
Khadim, Qari Abdul Sattar   202 n.80
Khalfoui, Mouez   172 n.35
Khan, Almas   136, 206 n.2
Khan, Amir Sher Ali   116
Khan, Aslam   118, 119
Khan, Dost Muhammad   186 n.6
Khan, Hafiz Rahmat   16
Khan, Kalb Ali   114–16
Khan, Mahabat (Peshawar)   13

Khan, Mirza Muhammad Ali   139, 140
Khan, Munshi Amir Hasan   140, 141
Khan, Naveeda   124, 158, 197 n.1, 204 n.118, 205 n.121
Khan, Nawab Zakariyya   76
Khan, Nawab Ziauddin   148
Khan, Sadiq   6
Khan, Sayyid Ahmad   73, 74, 164 n.30, 182 nn.50, 53, 210 n.68
Khan, Shafa'at Ahmad   209 n.57
Khan, Shaharyar   186 n.7
Khan, Wazir (Lahore)   13
Khan, Zain   15
Khanum, Hyatee   164 n.37
khatib   53, 63, 67
Khawaja, Asim   213 n.2
Khilafat Committee   127
Khilafat movement   182 n.50
Khoja Gujarati community   5
Khoja Ismaili identity   163 n.13
Khoja Shi'a Ismaili identity   5
Kishore, Raghav   187 n.12
Kobe Muslim society   6
Kolsky, Elizabeth   192 n.93
Kora Jahanabad   136
  and expert Muslims in court   151–3
  oversight   148–51
  heterodox associations and Muslim custodial rights at   136–42
  significance of   153–4
Kozlowski, Gregory   3, 6–7, 9, 48, 54, 69, 164 n.30, 210 n.69
Kugle, Scott   168 n.88
Kumar, Sunil   213 n.3

Laffan, Michael   171 n.8
Lahore   148. See also Shahidganj mosque (Lahore)
  Sikh rule in   15
Lahore (Latif)   75
Lahore Darbar   112
lakhiraj land   20
Lal, Kishori   101
Lal, Munna   138
land grants   18–19
land record, government control over. See Shahidganj mosque (Lahore)
Lassner, Jacob   188 n.33

Latif, Syed Muhammad   75
Law and Identity in Colonial South Asia (Sharafi)   5
Legg, Stephen   186 n.2, 187 n.12, 212 n.90
Lokhandwalla, Sh. T.   210 n.64
Lucknow   17, 32, 34, 75, 84, 149

Macaulay, Thomas   87
McChesney, R. D.   172–3 n.41
Machchli Bazaar mosque. *See* Kanpur mosque
Maddanpura (Banaras)   35, 36
Madras   6, 20, 35, 121, 150
madrassa   158, 172 n.33, 183 n.65, 184 n.87, 185 n.106
 in Burma   50, 52, 54, 56., 62–6, 68
 Tajpur mosque and   31–2, 34
Madrassa Nurul Islam   65
Madrassa Rahimiyya (Delhi)   32
magistrate   191 n.79, 192 n.91, 193 n.113
 control, over devotionalism on street   86–94
 functioning of   87–9
 and Eid sacrifice   91–2
 honorary   88, 96
 as moral authority in locale   87
 over cultural priority disputes   92–4
 political appointments of   95–7
 religious endowments and   143
 section 144 and   193 n.99
Mahmud (Justice)   35–6
Mahomed Buksh v. Sujat Ali   164 n.36
Mahomed Ismail Ariff v. Moolla Dawood and Suleiman Ismailjee   179 n.20
majlis, significance of   102, 136, 138, 139, 152
Malik, Jamal   9
Manual of Religious Feasts and Fasts   102
Manzur, Saiyed   102, 103
Markovits, Claude   181 n.40
Masail-i Thalathin (Rab)   74
Masjid Kulsum Bi   73
Masjid Shab Bhar (Lahore)   123
matam (self flagellation), significance of   102

Memons   57
Meston (Lt. Governor)   82
Metcalf, Barbara   33, 171 n.7, 175 n.91, 207 n.25, 213 n.1
Middleton, H.   203 n.85
Miller, Peter   210 nn.66–7
Mishkat Sharif (Tabrizi)   33
Mishkat ul Anwar   67
Misra, Pandit Brijnandan Prasad   193 n.114
Moolla, E. A.   179 n.21, 181 n.44
Moslem Association of Rangoon   58
Moslem World (journal)   60
mosque   171 n.23, 203 n.104. *See also individual entries*
 custodians (*see* custodians, of mosques)
 defense of   9
 demolition of   127
 1884 judgment on   42–3
 as God's land   124–31
 indenture of land for   178–9 n.19, 179 n.20
 JCPC judgment (1916) and   11
 patronage   15–17
 rights, on municipal and *nazul* land   121–4
 state regulation, in eighteenth and nineteenth centuries   12–19
 trust deed   178–9 n.19
 as unrestricted and egalitarian social space   9
 urban environs and   72–8
 Urdu text significance on   14
Mowla Baksh, Hafiz   14, 27, 28, 36–40, 42, 165 n.41, 175 n.80
Mowla Baksh, Haji   30, 174 n.71, 175 n.81
muezzin   29, 171 nn.18, 23
 Ahl-i Hadith on   41
 Hanafi law on   30
 qazi and   30
mufti, significance of   32
muhalla (neighbourhood), significance of   15, 72, 76, 117, 166 n.49, 187 n.16
Muhammadan Anglo Oriental Conference   63
Muhammad Rooposh mosque   13

Muharram 90
  disputes (1923–5) and
    magistrates 95–6
  majlis 102, 138
  procession route, along *qasbah*'s
    streets 98–9
  Shi'a–Sunni conflict over 101–4
Mul Chand, Lala 119
municipal committees, significance
    of 79–80
Murphy, Anne 198 nn.19, 23, 204 n.117
Musallim us-Subut (Bihari) 185 n.100
Muslim Educational Conference 146
*Muslim Endowments and Society in British
    India* (Kozlowski) 6, 48
Muslim Gazette, The (newspaper) 82
*Muslim Political Discourse in Postcolonial
    India* (Ahmed) 9
Muslim Private Waqf Validating Bill
    (1913) 24
*Muslims of Burma and Education, The
    (Musalmanan-i Burma aur
    Talim)* (Kaflaytvi) 63
Muslim Waqf Validating Act
    (1913) 170 n.105
Mussalman Waqf Act (1923) 143–5, 149,
    209 n.57
Mussalman Waqf Validating Act
    (1913) 130
mutawalli. *See* custodians, of mosques

Nabi, Saiyed Ali 103
Naim, C. M. 187 n.11
nazim (district administrator) 14, 21, 42
nazul (government lands) 79, 113,
    189 n.43
  rights to mosques on municipal
    and 121–4
  significance of 202 nn.82, 85
New, Than Than 189 n.47
Nizami, K. A. 182 n.53
Nodaihavi, Maulana Zafiruddin
    Purah 127–8

officer 10, 19–22, 25, 59, 90, 122, 123,
    155–8, 187 n.13, 212 n.90,
    213 n.5. *See also* magistrate; qazi
  Board of Revenue 3, 121
  Darogha Nazul 199 n.31

district 1, 2, 89, 124, 139, 143, 146,
    192 n.86
  Kora Jahanabad and 146–8, 153,
    154
  local 84, 87
  petty 1, 12
  revenue 2, 107–11, 114, 120, 121,
    124, 132, 136, 146
  settlement 116
  Tajpur mosque and 27, 31, 37, 39,
    45, 46
Osman, Newal 204 n.115

Parsi community 5
particularist Islam 7
Patail, Mahomed Esaqjee 180 n.34
patwaris (land registrars) 110, 111, 120,
    132
Pearn, B. R. 178 n.10
Persian Association 52
Pilibhit 16–18, 166 n.66, 189 n.43,
    193 n.114
Pioneer, The (newspaper) 83
political abuse, of history 205 n.129
postcolonial India 191 n.78
Powers, David 164 n.30, 170 n.105
Prasad, L. Beni 198 n.17
Prasad, Vijay 187 n.12
prayer 1–2, 7–8, 11, 14, 17, 18, 21,
    120, 155–8, 171 n.18. *See
    also* congregational prayer,
    leadership in
  in Burma 48, 52–4, 57, 67
  Kora Jahanabad and 137, 138,
    149–52
  mosque perimeter control and 77,
    81, 82, 90, 99–101
Pritchett, Francis 187 n.19
public, as arena 168 n.81
public land. *See nazul* (government lands)
public space 8–9, 13, 21, 42, 60, 156
  mosque perimeter control and 86–7,
    89, 94, 100, 102, 104
public sphere
  contemporary Islamic 8
  meaning and significance of 8–9
pukhta/pucca rights 205 n.1
Punjab 21, 66, 110, 194 n.122
  Sikh rule in 15

Punjab Archives (Lahore)   198 n.20
Punjab Laws Act and the Limitation
    Act   132
Punjab Muslim Mosques Protection
    Bill   129–30

Qanun-i Masajid   125
qasbahs (administrative centers of the
        Mughal era)   72, 98
    mosque and, relationship
        between   100
Qasimi, Ali Usman   213 n.1
qazi   14, 20, 24, 29–32, 37, 41, 61, 125,
        169 n.91, 183 n.62
    civil courts and   183 n.62
    muezzin and   30
    mufti and   32
    in Tajpur mosque   30
Qurban Beg, Mirza   113
Qureshi, Naeem   182 n.50

Rab, Maulvi Abdul   74
Rahim, M. A.   179 n.21
Rahimabadi, Abdul Aziz   33
Rahman, Raisur   98
Ram, Mewa   119
Ramizuddin (qazi of Tajpur)   30, 38
Rampur madrassa   31
Ramzan Ali mosque (Calcutta)   66
Ramzan v. the Queen Empress   39
Randeri, Mohammed Ibrahim   184 n.77
Randeria Madrassa   62, 63, 66, 68,
        183 n.65, 185 n.106
Randeris Suratis   47, 55, 57, 56, 58,
        178 n.19, 179–80 n.26
Rangoon   1, 2, 21
Rangoon Friday mosque
    diversity and disagreement in   54–7
    egalitarianism visions in management
        of   57–61
    instruction in   61–8
    magistrate functioning and   91–2
    police lines around   94
    residences around   92, 93
    significance of   47–8
    trusts, and custodians   48–54
Rangoon Municipal Committee
    (1874)   79
Rangoon Trades Association   59

rationalities of government, significance
    of   210 n.67
Registration of Societies Act (1860)   24
regulation   4, 6, 11, 22, 24, 115, 155–8
    Bengal Legislative Council
        and   208 n.51
    folk Islam and   213 n.5
    of Indian roads   192 n.95
    Kora Jahanabad and   136, 143, 144,
        147, 150, 153
    mosque perimeter control and   76,
        80, 83, 89, 92, 97, 102
    of prostitution   187 n.12
    state, of mosques   12–19
    street life and   188 n.32
    Tajpur mosque and   28, 30, 45
    of waqf, in Andhra   213 n.5
Religious and Charitable Endowments Act
    (1920)   22
religious authority, definition of   164 n.29
religious/charitable benefit, private act
    of   22–4
Religious Endowments Act (1863)   20,
        24, 148
Religious Societies Act (1880)
    (Burma)   59
Revue Du Monde Musalman
    (journal)   68
Riaz, Ali   213 n.2
Rice Traders' Association (Rangoon)   59
rioting crowd, significance of   171 n.16
Robinson, Francis   9, 72, 156, 170 n.7,
        191 n.67, 207 n.33
Rohilkhand   16
Rohtaki, Shah Ramzan   32
Rose, Nikolas   210 n.66
Roy, Tirthankar   170 n.4
Royal Commission on Public
    Services   182 n.58
Rules of Evidence, significance
    of   192 n.93
Rustomji, K.   200 n.42

Safavid azan   102
Saharanpur   103
Salamatullah, Maulvi Muhammad   83
Salam-ul Ulum (Bihari)   185 n.100
Salvatore, Armando   8
Samiullah, A. M.   194 n.120

Samvat calendar (Hindu)   89
Sanatana Dharma Sabha movement   143
Sanyal, Usha   213 n.1
Sarkar, Jadunath   166 n.49
Scott, J. Barton   8
Seal, Anil   212 n.90
Sengupta, Parna   183 n.67
sermon   8, 16, 47, 61, 63, 149
   cassette   173 n.50, 174 n.54
   Friday   2, 29, 48, 52, 53, 62, 67, 122
Shafi, Mufti Muhammad   128, 157
Shafis   43
Shah, Alison Mackenzie   73, 195 n.133
Shah, Pir   116
Shah Alamgir   123
Shahidganj mosque (Lahore)   12, *108*, *119*, 124–5, 129–30, 197 n.1
   JCPC on   130–1
   record of rights at   109–10, 112, 115–21
      Board of Revenue and   111, 114
      cadastral surveys and   110
      Hazrat Shah Kaku shrine   113, 117
      Sikhs and   112
   Sikh–Muslim conflict and   107–8
   suit of   131–3
Shahjahanpur   93
Shamsi, Abul Kalam Qasimi   172 n.33
sharafat (respectability)   65
Sharafi, Mitra   5
Sharan, Awadhendra   189 n.46
Sharar, Abdul Halim   75
shari'a   14, 30, 32, 144, 162 n.6, 185 n.100
   Lahore and   125, 128, 130
   mosque perimeter control and   84–5, 100
   significance of   4
Sharma, Shalini   197 n.6
Shaw, H. H.   102
Shi'a Mogul mosque   56, 77, 178 n.10
Shi'a nawabs of Awadh   17
Shi'as   29, 71, 84, 90, 97–9, 138, 206 n.14
   Aurangabad mosque and   97–104
   Mogul Mosque Management Scheme of   52
   of Rangoon   52
Shikoh, Mirza Sikander   18

Shiromani Gurdwara Parbandhak Committtee (SGPC)   150
shoe seller's riot (1729)   29
Shorto, Sylvia   189 n.38
Sikh Gurdwara Act (1925)   118, 204 n.115
Sikh Gurdwara Tribunal (Lahore tribunal)   118, 129, 131
Sikh rule
   in Lahore   15
   in Punjab   15
Simla Union Church   59
Sindh Mahomedan Association   127
Singh, Adya Saran   151, 152
Singh, Asa   199 n.31
Singh, Attar   118, 201 n.63
Singh, Ganda   116, 117, 119, 201 n.63
Singh, Gian   201 n.62
Singh, Hari   119, 199 n.31
Singh, Harnam   199 n.31
Singh, Hira   112
Singh, Jagga   112, 113
Singh, Jita   201 n.62
Singh, Jiwan   109, 112, 113, 116, 120, 199 n.31
Singh, Kahan   113, 117
Singh, Nikka   201 n.62
Singh, Ranjit   15, 107, 198 n.23
Sirat-i Mustaqim (Ismail)   34
Sirhindi, Shaikh Ahmad   33
Societies Registration Act (1860) (Burma)   59, 61, 181 n.47
Stephens, Julia   4, 8–9, 45, 170 n.6, 196 n.161, 210 n.67
Stoker, T.   194 nn.123, 125
Stokes, Eric   206 n.2
Sturman, Rachel   172 n.32, 210 n.67
Sunehri Masjid (Lahore)   122
Sunnis   29, 71, 90, 97
   Aurangabad mosque and   97–104
surveyors   132
   revenue   110

Tabrizi, Abd Allah   33
Tajpur mosque (Bihar)   2, 9, 11, 21, 22. *See also* congregational prayer, leadership in
   description of   14
Taj-ul Masajid   73

Takee, Muhammad 164
Tan Tai Yong 204 n.117
taqlid (following established authority in religious practice) 45
Taqwiyatul Iman 67
tasbihin (invocation of God's name during prayer) 35
Taylor, David 188 n.32
taziyadari 98, 138
taziyas 99, 138, 152
Teena Purohit 5
Terrains of Exchange (Green) 6
Thapar, Romila 205 n.129
Theobold, William 168 n.88
Troll, Christian 186 n.11, 210 n.68
trust 183 n.62, 190 n.57. *See also* waqf
  English law for 23–4
  law, colonial 6, 128
  private 169–70 n.105
  public 24, 50, 170 n.109
  significance of 49
  waqf and 7, 49–50

Uddin, Sufia 158
'ulama 3, 67, 125, 156, 157, 170 n.7, 185 n.101, 203 n.100
  and Ahl-i Hadith and 31–6
  Hanafi 28, 35
  Kanpur mosque and 82–5
  Zaman on 10
United Provinces 1, 2, 9, 12, 66, 156
  Kora Jahanabad and 139–45, 149, 151
  Legislative Council of 144
  mosque perimeter control and 71, 72, 79, 80, 88, 89, 92, 95, 97, 99, 103
United Provinces Waqf Act (1936) 151
urban environs and mosques 72–8

Van der Veer, Peter 205 n.129, 213 n.97, 213 n.1 (Ch Afterword)

Vaqi'at al-Hukumat-i-Dehli (Dihlavi) 74, 75
Variao Suratis 57
Varshney, Ashuthosh 191 n.78

Wahhab, Abdul 38
Wahhabism 37
waqf 6–7, 124. *See also* endowment; Kora Jahanabad
  adverse possession principle and 108
  boards and committees 146–8
  invalidation of 120
  JCPC on 169–70 n.105
  land 126, 128, 138
  Muslim rights, and secular governance reformulation 142–7
  private 24
  public 24
  Sufi 201 n.54
  trusts and 7, 49–50
Waqf Act (1954) 158
Waqf Act (1960) 9
Waqf Bill (1936) 146–7
"Waqf in Pakistan" (Malik) 9
Wazir, Nawab 125
Webb, Alexander Russell 60
Whitehead, Clive 184 n.75
Wilson, H. H. 202 n.82

Yahya, Muhammad 36, 45
Yegar, Moshe 180 n.33, 184 n.76
Young Men's Persian Association. *See* Persian Association
Yusuf, Nawab Muhammad 209 n.57

Zajonc, Tristan 213 n.2
Zaman, Muhammad Qasim 2, 10, 169 n.91, 213 n.1
Zamani, Mariam 76
Zaman Khan, Muhammad 99–100
Zerbadis 57
"zones of tradition" 76

www.ingramcontent.com/pod-product-compliance
Lightning Source LLC
Chambersburg PA
CBHW062141300426
44115CB00012BA/1996